Approaches to Teaching the Works of Octavia E. Butler

Approaches to Teaching the Works of Octavia E. Butler

Edited by

Tarshia L. Stanley

The Modern Language Association of America

New York 2019

85 Broad Street, Suite 500, New York, New York 10004-2434
www.mla.org

To order MLA publications, visit mla.org/books. For wholesale and international orders, see mla.org/Bookstore-Orders.

The MLA office is located on the island known as Mannahatta (Manhattan) in Lenapehoking, the homeland of the Lenape people. The MLA pays respect to the original stewards of this land and to the diverse and vibrant Native communities that continue to thrive in New York City.

Cover illustration of the paperback and electronic editions: Detail of Krista Franklin, *"Mind of My Mind,"* 2006. From the artist book *Seed (The Book of Eve) for Octavia E. Butler.*

Approaches to Teaching World Literature 160
ISSN 1059-1133

POD 2022 (second printing)

Library of Congress Cataloging-in-Publication Data

Names: Stanley, Tarshia L., editor.
Title: Approaches to teaching the works of Octavia E. Butler / edited by Tarshia L. Stanley.
Description: New York : The Modern Language Association of America, 2019.
Includes bibliographical references. Identifiers: LCCN 2019017910 (print) | LCCN 2019018364 (ebook) | ISBN 9781603294591 (cloth) | ISBN 9781603294157 (paper) | ISBN 9781603294171 (Kindle) | ISBN 9781603294164 (EPUB)
Subjects: LCSH: Butler, Octavia E.—Study and teaching. Butler, Octavia E.—Criticism and interpretation. Classification: LCC PS3552.U827 (ebook) | LCC PS3552.U827 Z54 2019 (print)
DDC 813/.54—dc23
LC record available at https://lccn.loc.gov/2019017910

CONTENTS

PART ONE: MATERIALS

Butler's Major Works with Original Publication Dates 3

Courses and Contexts 3

Interviews 4

Secondary Sources 5

Texts Taught in Conjunction with Butler's Works 6

PART TWO: APPROACHES

Introduction 9
Tarshia L. Stanley

Literary and Rhetorical Approaches

Teaching *Dawn* in an Introductory Course on Modern(ist) Literature—with a Gothic Inflection 17
John Paul Riquelme

Historicizing the Future: Teaching Historical Consciousness in Butler's Fiction 24
Matthew Mullins

Teaching Butler in a Course on Colonialism and Science Fiction 29
Aparajita Nanda

Teaching *Fledgling* as a Narrative of Love and Power 34
Lauren J. Lacey

Keeping the Science in Science Fiction: Teaching Butler in an Interdisciplinary Writing Course 40
Laurel Bollinger

"My Books Will Be Read by Millions of People!": The LaGuardia Community College Octavia E. Butler Project on *Wikipedia* 45
Ximena Gallardo C. and Ann Matsuuchi

Disciplinary Strategies and Innovations

The Politics of Living Together: Butler's Short Stories and Teaching Political Philosophy 52
Claire P. Curtis

Unchained: Using Butler to Upend How We Teach the History of Slavery 58
Amy Absher

For Adults Only: A Competency-Based Approach to Teaching Butler's *Wild Seed* 63
Deborah Wood Holton

Parable of the Sower and Antiracist Pedagogy: Reading Butler with Preservice Teachers 69
Bevin Roue and Laura Apol

Reading Whiteness in *Kindred* to Teach Transnational Pedagogy 74
Shreyashi Mukherjee

Drawing the Oankali: Imagining Race, Gender, and the Posthuman in Butler's *Dawn* 81
Edmond Y. Chang

Social Justice and Social Change

Ecocritical Ideas and Butler's "Bloodchild" and *Parable of the Sower* 90
Susan M. Bernardo

Teaching the Social Construction of Disability through the Parable series, *Lilith's Brood*, and *Seed to Harvest* 97
Sami Schalk

Clay's Ark: Teaching Butler's Vision beyond Liberal Consent 103
Beth A. McCoy

Intergroup Dialogue and Difficult Conversations: Teaching Butler at a Private, Christian, Predominantly White Institution 109
Kendra R. Parker

Butler as Feminist Philosopher: A Care-Ethics Approach to Teaching *Kindred* and *Dawn* 117
Rekik Scholler-Mekonnen

The Allegory of Shori's Cave: Teaching *Fledgling* as the Science Fiction of Racism 124
Marleen S. Barr

The Aesthetics of Afrofuturism

Teaching *Parable of the Sower* through Afrofuturism 129
Isiah Lavender III

Teaching Butler's "Bloodchild" and the Tenets of Afrofuturism 136
Kristen Lillvis

Teaching Afrofuturistic Thought Leadership in Butler's Fiction 141
Tarshia L. Stanley

Notes on Contributors 149

Survey Participants 153

Works Cited 157

Part One

MATERIALS

Butler's Major Works with Original Publication Dates

Patternist Series (all except Survivor *in* Seed to Harvest*)*

Patternmaster (1976)
Mind of My Mind (1977)
Survivor (1978)
Wild Seed (1980)
Clay's Ark (1984)

Xenogenesis Series (all in Lilith's Brood*)*

Dawn (1987)
Adulthood Rites (1988)
Imago (1989)

Earthseed Series

Parable of the Sower (1993)
Parable of the Talents (1998)

Stand-Alone Novels

Kindred (1979)
Fledgling (2005)

Short Story Collections

"Bloodchild" and Other Stories (1995)
"Bloodchild" and Other Stories (2005), includes "Amnesty" and "Book of Martha"
Unexpected Stories (2014)

Courses and Contexts

When I attempted to contextualize, for this volume, the use of Octavia E. Butler's work in the academy through a survey sent to professors, there were nearly three hundred responses. The respondents, who taught mostly undergraduate courses, said that *Kindred* was the most popular text assigned, followed closely by *Parable of the Sower*. The results were expected, as narrative and character formation mark these novels as readily accessible to students. Butler's "Bloodchild" was the most assigned short story—many respondents indicated that in their classes they used not just the titular story but also the entire collection *"Bloodchild" and Other Stories*. The only other story named specifically and consistently was "Speech Sounds."

The survey results indicate that Butler is being used quite liberally across college courses that teach African American literature, contemporary literature, women's literature, science fiction, and speculative fiction. World literature, race and ethnicity in literature, and the literature of California were also mentioned as subjects that could be explored through the work. Among specific genres to which her work is pertinent are neo–slave narratives, captivity narratives, and dystopian narratives. Butler's work is taught in composition courses, a course on the short story, and interdisciplinary courses that include women's studies, queer theory, African American history, cultural studies, and political science. Respondents found Butler useful for investigating issues around race, class, gender, sexuality, feminism, intersectionality, disability, eugenics, environmentalism, colonialism, neoliberalism, and posthumanism. The work is used to address social justice issues such as poverty, diversity, violence against women, and community-organizing practices.

Interviews

Many respondents said that Conseula Francis's book of interviews, *Conversations with Octavia Butler*, was an important and accessible source. Several of its interviews were repeatedly named as valuable for studying Butler's work: Randall Kenan's "An Interview with Octavia Butler" (27–37), Marilyn Mehaffy and AnaLouise Keating's "'Radio Imagination': Octavia Butler on the Poetics of Narrative Embodiment" (98–122), Rosalie G. Harrison's "Sci-Fi Visions: An Interview with Octavia Butler" (3–9), and Larry McCaffery and Jim McMenamin's "An Interview with Octavia E. Butler" (10–26).

Other popular interviews were Sandra Govan's "Going to See the Woman: A Visit with Octavia E. Butler" and Frances M. Beal's "Interview with Octavia Butler: Black Women and Science Fiction Genre." Respondents often cited Charlie Rose's interview with Butler on his PBS show in June 2000. John Akomfrah's film *The Last Angel of History*, which is a comprehensive look at Afrofuturism (particularly in black music), contains interviews with Samuel R. Delany and Butler. The transcript of Butler's speech on how she began writing speculative fiction given at the Media in Transition project at MIT was also heavily referenced ("Devil Girl").

Secondary Sources

The survey produced a number of secondary texts: Gregory J. Hampton's *Changing Bodies in the Fiction of Octavia Butler: Slaves, Aliens, and Vampires*, Francis's *Conversations with Octavia Butler*, Marleen S. Barr's *Afro-Future Females: Black Writers Chart Science Fiction's Newest New-Wave Trajectory*, and Sheree R. Thomas's *Dark Matter: A Century of Speculative Fiction from the African Diaspora*. I have added to the list Isiah Lavender's *Race in American Science Fiction*, De Witt Douglas Kilgore's *Astrofuturism: Science, Race, and Visions of Utopia*, Ingrid Thaler's *Black Atlantic Speculative Fictions: Octavia E. Butler, Jewelle Gomez, and Nalo Hopkinson*, André M. Carrington's *Speculative Blackness: The Future of Race in Science Fiction*, Gerry Canavan's *Octavia E. Butler*, and the special issue of *Utopian Studies* on Butler (vol. 19, no. 3, 2008).

Survey respondents further noted Thomas Hobbes's *Leviathan* (1668), Amanda Thibodeau's "Alien Bodies and a Queer Future: Sexual Revision in Octavia Butler's 'Bloodchild' and James Tiptree, Jr.'s 'With Delicate Mad Hands,'" Martha Nussbaum's *Frontiers of Justice: Disability, Nationality, Species Membership*, Susana M. Morris's "Black Girls Are from the Future: Afrofuturist Feminism in Octavia E. Butler's *Fledgling*," Pramod K. Nayar's "A New Biological Citizenship: Posthumanism in Octavia Butler's *Fledgling*," and Theri Pickens's "'You're Supposed to Be a Tall, Handsome, Fully Grown White Man': Theorizing Race, Gender, and Disability in Octavia Butler's *Fledgling*."

Instructors may also want to consider Rebecca J. Holden and Nisi Shawl's *Strange Matings: Science Fiction, Feminism, African American Voices, and Octavia E. Butler*, Ytasha L. Womack's *Afrofuturism: The World of Black Sci-Fi and Fantasy Culture*, Sandra Jackson and Julie E. Moody-Freeman's *The Black Imagination: Science Fiction, Futurism, and the Speculative*, and Walidah Imarisha and Adrienne Maree Brown's *Octavia's Brood: Science Fiction Stories from Social Justice Movements*.

Many survey respodents referred to Donna Haraway's "A Cyborg Manifesto: Science, Technology, and Socialist Feminism in the Late Twentieth Century." Instructors also recommended Philip K. Dick's novel *Do Androids Dream of Electric Sheep?*, Marisa Parham's "Saying 'YES': Textual Traumas in Octavia Butler's *Kindred*," Christine Levecq's "Power and Repetition: Philosophies of (Literary) History in Octavia E. Butler's *Kindred*," Marc Dery's "Black to the Future: Interviews with Samuel R. Delany, Greg Tate, and Tricia Rose,"

Alondra Nelson's "Introduction: Future Texts," and Andrea Hairston's "Octavia Butler—Praise Song to a Prophetic Artist." Madhu Dubey's "Folk and Urban Communities in African-American Women's Fiction: Octavia Butler's *Parable of the Sower*" was highly rated. Although it is perhaps dated, several enthusiasts were still using Darko Suvin's "On the Poetics of the Science Fiction Genre."

Texts Taught in Conjunction with Butler's Works

Many of the texts taught in conjunction with Butler's work were associated with *Kindred* and the neo–slave narrative tradition. Therefore there were multiple mentions of *Narrative of the Life of Frederick Douglass*, Harriet Jacobs's *Incidents in the Life of a Slave Girl*, and Toni Morrison's *Beloved*. Africana feminist approaches to Butler used Ama Ata Aidoo's *Changes: A Love Story* and Tsitsi Dangarembga's novel *Nervous Conditions* and her films *Everyone's Child* and *Kare Kare Zvako* (*Mother's Day*) as complements to Butler's *Wild Seed* and other selections in the Xenogenesis series. Courses or units on speculative or dystopian literature may pair Butler with Ursula K. Le Guin's *The Left Hand of Darkness*, Ishmael Reed's *Mumbo Jumbo*, Margaret Atwood's *The Handmaid's Tale*, Gloria Naylor's *Mama Day*, Walter Mosley's *Futureland*, Kazuo Ishiguro's *Never Let Me Go*, or the new collection of James Tiptree's short stories, *Her Smoke Rose Up Forever*.

Instructors looking for cognate texts when studying Butler and contemporary black speculative fiction or Afrofuturism can choose from the work of Samuel R. Delany, Tananarive Due, Nalo Hopkinson, N. K. Jemisin, Nedi Okora, and Steven Barnes, among others.

Part Two

APPROACHES

Introduction

Tarshia L. Stanley

Robert Heinlein introduced the term *speculative fiction* as a means to discuss the common threads running through the genres of science fiction and horror (Oziewicz). In recent years, the term has been adapted to denote not just science fiction and horror but also fantasy, high fantasy, and magical realism. Decades have passed since authors and critics legitimized science fiction as worthy of serious study. In 1972, Darko Suvin, one of the early scholars devoted to the study of science fiction, wrote that the genre had "particularly affected some key strata of modern society such as the college graduates, young writers, and general readers appreciative of new sets of values" ("On the Poetics" 372). Nearly fifty years later, college students are more appreciative of speculative fiction because much of their adolescent world has been shaped by the films, games, and social media commentary that were spawned directly from it. The worldview of college students today has been so affected by the concepts inherent in the speculative genre that the magnitude of that influence may at first be invisible both to them and to those who instruct them.

Because speculative texts are among the first to usher young people into literacy, they deserve more attention as another means to teach reading, writing, and thinking. This approach is particularly applicable to speculative fiction texts whose themes and subjects resonate with students who are increasingly more diverse in their experiences and outlooks. Many instructors have recognized the pliability of this genre as a tool in their interdisciplinary arsenals and have used its texts for many years, but this volume highlights the teaching of speculative fiction written by a woman of color.

In an essay from the collection *Afro-Future Females: Black Writers Chart Science Fiction's Newest New-Wave Trajectory*, De Witt Douglas Kilgore posits that an important shift is happening in African American literary criticism: social and political realism no longer set the parameters of African American contemporary literature; instead, speculative fiction is now the genre that "best captures the texture and meaning of the black experience" ("Beyond the History" 119). In other words, African American literature worthy of critique can lie outside social protest, and speculative fiction by writers of color is important. Those in classrooms who propose to teach the American or African American tradition must engage this genre because it is expanding and reshaping the interdisciplinary study of literature, sociopolitics, economics, gender, race, sexuality, and definitions of humanity itself.

Kilgore was writing about this shift in 2008, but there is actually a long and documented tradition of African American writers who employ forms of speculative fiction in their work. According to Sandra Govan, fantastic constructs were integral to Martin R. Delany's 1859 *Blake; or, The Huts of America* and to Sutton E. Griggs's 1899 *Imperium in Imperio*. Both men script black superheroes who, though they don't leap tall buildings in a single bound, act as liberators of their enslaved people ("Speculative Fiction" 686–87). Charles Chesnutt's 1899 *The Conjure Woman* is an example of fantasy and horror with instances of magical realism. In 1902–03, Pauline Hopkins's *Of One Blood* is, in the words of Deborah E. McDowell, evidence that the author was "writing in the face of perhaps the most resilient fantasy in the U.S. cultural imaginary: the fantasy of 'whiteness,' which, it could be added, was 'paranormal' in the extreme . . ." (xx). Not long before George S. Schuyler's physician crafted a machine to turn blacks into Caucasians in 1931, W. E. B. Du Bois imagined a future racially reshaped by the noxious gases of a comet in 1920s New York ("Comet"). After these initial forays into the genre, William Melvin Kelley, Douglas Turner Ward, Sam Greenlee, Toni Morrison, Ishmael Reed, Samuel R. Delany, Gloria Naylor, and Octavia E. Butler experimented with the genre in the twentieth century.

There is currently no comprehensive teaching volume dedicated to black speculative fiction, although there are articles that develop theories about that fiction, collections that frame discussion about it, and anthologies that document its practice. Perhaps the best place to begin such a discussion is with Butler, whose work allows both the framing and theorizing of black speculative fiction for the classroom.

Butler and Her Work

Octavia Estelle Butler was born in 1947 in Pasadena, California, and reared mostly by her widowed mother. Her interviews and the secondhand accounts of her life indicate that she was afflicted by an almost debilitating shyness. In an essay entitled "Birth of a Writer," she wrote, "I spent a lot of my childhood and adolescence staring at the ground. It's a wonder I didn't become a geologist" ("Positive Obsession" 127). Her abilities were often overshadowed by her fear of inadequacy:

> I believed I was ugly and stupid, clumsy and socially hopeless. I also thought that everyone would notice these faults if I drew attention to myself. I wanted to disappear. Instead I grew to be six feet tall. Boys in particular seemed to assume that I had done this growing deliberately and that I should be ridiculed for it as often as possible . . . I hid out in a big pink notebook—one that would hold a whole ream of paper. I made myself a universe in it. (128)

Her loneliness and big pink notebook seem to have encouraged her propensity for world building. Around age ten, she began her first forays into writing. But it was her close encounter with what she considered a really bad science fiction movie a few years later that had her declaring, "I can write a better story than that" ("Interview" [McCaffery and McMeramin] 13). She began sending out her stories shortly afterward, despite being discouraged by an aunt and the reality of life for an African American girl in 1960s America. When she was twenty-three she sold two stories to editors at the Clarion science fiction writers' workshop, but nothing sold for the five years after that. Then in 1976, her first novel, *Patternmaster*, was published as part of the Patternist series ("Positive Obsession" 133–34). But it was her 1979 novel, *Kindred*, that became a best seller.

Butler referred to her desire to be a working science fiction author as an obsession. It was also practically a miracle: the number of other writers of color at work in the genre in the 1970s could be counted on one hand. In 1984–85 she rose to fame when she won a Nebula, a Locus, and two Hugo awards. Her short stories "Speech Sounds" and "Bloodchild" earned her national recognition. *Clay's Ark*, the fourth in the Patternist quintet, was published in 1984. *Parable of the Sower*, perhaps her most famous novel, was nominated for a Nebula in 1994. She became the first speculative fiction writer to win the prestigious John D. and Catherine T. MacArthur Fellowship in 1995. She went on to receive the lifetime achievement award from the PEN American Center in 2000.

Butler suffered from severe writer's block after she published the *Parable of the Talents* in 1998. She meant to write a third book to round out the Parable series, but her failing health hampered the task. She published her first and only vampire novel, *Fledgling*, in 2005. Her final short stories, "Amnesty" and "The Book of Martha," appeared in 2003. She died on 24 February 2006, at the age of fifty-eight, most likely from a stroke that caused her to fall and injure her head.

In 2012, the Science Fiction and Fantasy Writers of America (SFWA) posthumously granted Butler the Solstice Award. Decided by the SFWA president in consultation with its board of directors, the Solstice is given to someone who has "a significant impact on the science fiction or fantasy landscape, and is particularly intended for those who have consistently made a major, positive difference within the speculative fiction field" ("SFWA"). The organization had previously awarded her two of its annual Nebula Awards to complement the two Hugo Awards she received from the World Science Fiction Convention. In one of her many obituaries, it was written, "Before anybody told her that black girls do not grow up to write about futuristic worlds, [the] daughter of a shoeshine man and a maid was already fashioning a place for herself in a white-dominated universe" (Stewart).

Butler's work is being used in the academy in interdisciplinary and exciting ways; it appears on syllabi in literature courses, as expected, but also in courses in history, political science, women's studies, environmental studies, economics, and ethics. Ruth Calvin's 1976–2008 bibliography of Butler's works lists almost three hundred secondary sources, a hundred of which are theses and dissertations in which Butler is the primary subject. Calvin writes, "[A] veritable cottage industry seems to have grown up around her work" (485).

In addition to marking Butler's contribution to literature, this volume introduces more instructors, and therefore more students, to the trove of pedagogical ideas and connections made possible through her work. In a time when the lines between disciplines continue to blur, studying Butler can make for dynamic exchange in the classroom, can center not only speculative fiction in general but black speculative fiction in particular in the literary canon.

Butler's body of work begins with the Patternist series, which was collected in 2007 as the volume *Seed to Harvest.* In this series, the malevolent spirit Doro creates children like himself and then monitors the results. *Patternmaster* is about the war of succession for control of the Pattern, a network of advanced human beings with psychic abilities. The Patternmaster has power over the minds and bodies of the mutes (human beings without psychic abilities) and the Clayarks, a posthuman species born as a result of an astronaut's importation of a virus on returning from a mission. As this world is further developed, Butler reveals that Mary, in *Mind of My Mind* (1977), created the Pattern. The third and final chronological book, *Survivor* (1978), is the story of the mutes who manage to escape the planet and a life of slavery. Finally, the prequel, *Wild Seed* (1980), recounts the story of the spiritman Doro and the shapeshifter Anyanwu, whose union laid the foundation for telepathic humankind and the resulting Pattern. The ensuing struggle between what is left of humanity—telepaths, mutes, and Clayarks—offers opportunities to discuss race, class, sexuality, gender, and the challenge of posthumanism.

The Xenogenesis trilogy (Guild America Books, 1989), recollected as *Lilith's Brood* (Warner, 2000), features Lilith Iyapo, one of Butler's better-known black female protagonists. Lilith is one of a few human survivors after nuclear war. The price for her life is that she must mediate between the last of humanity and their extraterrestrial Oankali rescuers. The Oankali trade in genetic material; they capture, alter, train, indoctrinate, and finally impregnate Lilith. Books 2 and 3 show how planetary displacement, community formation, and identity take center stage as this survivor and her progeny are stripped of the solely human parts of themselves.

The Earthseed collection (2000) contains the multi-award-winning *Parable of the Sower* and its Nebula Award–winning sequel, *Parable of the Talents.* A dystopian warning of socioeconomic collapse, political hypocrisy, and religious extremism, these texts provide fertile ground for analyses of the corporate nation and neoliberalism. Issues regarding environmental and social justice also abound. The ensuing economic collapse has left human beings vulnerable to famine, violence, and drug use. A hero appears who believes that they will survive only if they reframe their notions of leadership and migrate off-world. These texts compel questions about the future of life on a planet in the face of economic, social, political, and environmental degradation.

In addition to *Kindred*, Butler's other stand-alone novel is *Fledgling.* It is her homage to the late-twentieth- and early-twenty-first-century fascination with vampires, and its posthuman premise is apparent from the beginning. The protagonist, who appears to be about ten, is actually fifty-three. She is the result of genetic experiments splicing African DNA with Ina (vampire) to yield a dark-skinned blood eater immune to damage caused by sunlight.

Butler's short stories, in the collection *"Bloodchild" and Other Stories*, offer succinct but compelling ways to introduce students to subjects that range from memory and history to the investigation of the human capacity for polyamory and polysexuality.

Conceptual Frameworks

At the center of Gregory Hampton's *Changing Bodies in the Fiction of Octavia Butler* is that idea that Butler's work makes standard readings of the body impossible. For Butler the physical body cannot be housed in terminologies as limited as race and gender. "This is made possible, in part, by the genre in which [she] creates her craft" (xii). Millennial students are familiar with speculative modes of seeing and understanding, which go beyond limits, because they have come of age in an era steeped in technology and media, so Butler should appeal to them.

Keeping in mind how the study of literature has always functioned as a way into multiple avenues of critical engagement, this volume is organized in categories that are rich with curricular possibilities. It begins with traditional approaches to literature, then considers rhetoric and problem-based learning. It deals with social justice issues, the ethos of posthumanism, and the ever-evolving concept of Afrofuturism. In the process, Butler's entire body of work is engaged.

The section "Literary and Rhetorical Approaches" should prove particularly useful for those instructors who are unfamiliar with Butler's work or are new to teaching it. John Paul Riquelme uses *Dawn* and the transatlantic as organizing principles when instructing his students in modernist literature and modes of inquiry. *Dawn* allows them to question their understandings of what it means to be human when human beings lose the power and autonomy they have traditionally exerted over their own bodies and the natural world. Matthew Mullins uses *Kindred* to help students gain a historical consciousness in an American fiction course, as they construct a physical web to represent time, place, and character in the novel. With strategies for kinetic learning, they trace the influence of history and slavery on contemporary frameworks of economics, politics, and culture. Aparajita Nanda engages the texts in the Xenogenesis trilogy to open discussion about science fiction tropes as reflections of settler colonialism.

Lauren Lacey teaches *Fledgling* in a general education course on women writers. This unusual vampire novel features a vampire who has multiple genetic parents and must have many symbiotic lovers in order to survive. It is in an interdisciplinary first-year writing classroom with mostly STEM majors that Laurel Bollinger stresses the science in Butler's science fiction. She finds that students are open to works like *Parable of the Sower* and "Bloodchild" because they identify with and welcome their scientific and technological infrastructures. Ximena Gallardo C. and Ann Matsuuchi transform their students into wiki editors as they revise the entry on Octavia Butler in *Wikipedia*.

In the next section, "Disciplinary Strategies and Innovations," the contributors work in cross-disciplinary contexts or are focused on students as active leaners. Claire Curtis pairs short stories in the *"Bloodchild"* collection with *Leviathan* to encourage investigation of the Hobbesian tenet regarding human acquiescence to the idea of the commonwealth. Curtis sees the stories, particularly "Speech Sounds," as case studies for students in a political philosophy course where questions about peaceful interaction among diverse groups are at the forefront. Amy Absher uses Butler in the history classroom to discuss slavery as an inevitable master narrative. She posits that *Kindred*, *Dawn*, and *"Bloodchild" and Other Stories* disrupt notions of slavery as linear and historical and as a "crime of the past."

Deborah Wood Holton's students, adult undergraduate learners, read *Wild Seed* to enact competence-based acquisition strategies rather than content mastery alone. The alienation felt by the novel's protagonist when she travels from fifteenth-century Africa to seventeenth-century America reverberates in these students as they move through the unfamiliar world of the academy. Bevin Roue and Laura Apol use *Parable of the Sower* as a tool to acclimate preservice secondary school teachers who will be in urban classrooms. Butler's work provides them spaces to think through diversity and identity. Shreyashi Mukherjee cultivates polyvocality in her students as she brings together literature from African American, South Asian, Irish, Lebanese, and Palestinian traditions to help students articulate and code whiteness. Edmond Chang's students read *Dawn* to confront their understanding of the alien in both words and images. Drawing the extraterrestrial Ooloi allows students to confront their own understandings of difference and diversity.

According to Marleen S. Barr, in her groundbreaking 1981 collection, *Future Females: A Critical Anthology*, "it [was] time to recognize that science fiction [had] been and continues to be a leading voice in the chorus for cultural change." Science fiction "helped to make the . . . women's movement a political reality" (25). In speculative fiction, revolutionary ideas are often launched and made a reality. The section "Social Justice and Social Change" provides useful strategies for instructors employing Butler's work, particularly from justice-oriented lenses. Susan Bernardo poses questions like "What do we do when climate change causes distruption not only in resources but also social order?" and "How can leadership become environmentally responsible on an Earth that becomes more alien because it is less hospitable for us?" through *Parable of the Sower* and "Bloodchild" to introduce students to ecocriticsm. Sami Schalk challenges her students to think about the environment at the individual level, employing *Fledgling* to interrogate the culturally constructed abled body critiqued by disability studies.

Beth McCoy moves students directly into the center of heated debates when she yokes *Clay's Ark* to John Locke's *Second Treatise on Government* and reads them both in the light of campus policies on sexual consent and sexual misconduct. (In *Clay's Ark*, the alien parasite that infects humankind mutates people into hypersexed breeders without their consent.) Kendra Parker's students are asked to consider issues like rape, race, and hierarchies of power in Butler's work. Rekik Scholler-Mekonnen's students are invited to see the protagonists in *Kindred* and *Dawn* as case studies for a feminist approach to social justice. Marleen S. Barr uses *Fledgling* to interrogate race as a basis of identity.

In the section "The Aesthetics of Afrofuturism," the term *Afrofuturism*, coined by Mark Dery and developed by Alondra Nelson and Kodwo Eshun, provides a multidimensional aesthetic that collapses the division between past and future in order to interrogate the positioning of African diasporic bodies, economies, technologies, and cultures. According to Nelson, "Afrofuturism can be broadly defined as 'African American voices' with 'other stories to tell about culture, technology and things to come'" ("Introduction" 9). It is a way of thinking, interrogating, creating, and being that refutes the idea that "racial identity, and blackness in particular, is the anti-avatar of digital life. Blackness [is not] always oppositional to technologically driven chronicles of progress" (1). Afrofuturism as a lens approaches twenty-first-century social and political quandaries in ways that challenge traditional notions of leadership and power.

Speculating on the day when human beings will meet extraterrestrial life, Butler wonders what will happen: "Perhaps for a moment, only a moment, this affront will bring us together, all human, all much more alike than different. . . . Humanity, *E pluribus unum* at last, a oneness focused on and fertilized by certain knowledge of alien others. What will be born of that brief, strange and ironic union?" ("Monophobic Response" 416). Afrofuturism works towards that moment in which we recognize that we are more alike than different, that we are engaged in the same pursuit and bound by the same constraints. Isiah Lavender, who has interrogated science fiction as promulgating racial difference, contributes an essay in which his students read *Parable of the Sower* as Afrofuturists. Kristen Lillvis explores "Bloodchild" to examine the interconnectedness of African diasporic pasts, presents, and futures. Tarshia L. Stanley explores the black feminine capacity to create different models of leadership as a concrete example of Afrofuturism in action.

Additional Reading Sequences

The essays in this volume may be read in sequence or according to the texts one wishes to teach. Gallardo C. and Matsuuchi, Mullins, and Mukherjee use *Kindred* in unexpected ways. For those looking for interdisciplinary approaches to *Parable of the Sower*, Bernardo, Roue and Apol, and Lavender should be helpful. The Xenogenesis texts are discussed by Chang, Schalk, Nanda, and Parker. Novels from the Patternist series are covered in essays by Absher, Riquelme, Schalk, Parker, McCoy, and Stanley. Ideas for teaching the shapeshifter novel *Wild Seed* can be found in the work of Holton and Stanley. Bernardo, Nanda, Curtis, and Lillvis offer examples of ways to approach the collection *"Bloodchild" and Other Stories*. Stanley covers *Survivor*, the least known of Butler's works.

LITERARY AND RHETORICAL APPROACHES

Teaching *Dawn* in an Introductory Course on Modern(ist) Literature—with a Gothic Inflection

John Paul Riquelme

Overview of the Course

Readings in Modern Literature is a course in transatlantic literary modernism (English, Irish, and American) with flexible chronological and generic boundaries that enable inclusion of diverse materials, from the 1890s until well after World War II. The course questions the chronological limits, usually 1900–45, sometimes still imposed on literary modernism. I characterize modernism as part of a wider discourse of modernity that persistently raises questions in a culturally critical way about what it means to be human. Emphasizing the question of the human brings out modernism's anthropological character, against the background of Victorian and early-twentieth-century anthropology as responses to increasing and changing Western contact with non-Western peoples, including the hierarchical dimension of that contact. The significant place of cultural contact in modern literature is clear in numerous works that we read. Many science fiction narratives, among them *Dawn*, project contact across cultures and races figuratively as encounters between human beings and aliens or between human beings and posthuman beings.

The course enrolls mostly first- and second-year students majoring in arts and sciences outside the humanities who are fulfilling a graduation requirement for a humanities course from among a large number of options. The material and approach, however, are suitable for more advanced humanities students.

The format involves lecture and discussion, either as a large course, in which I lecture two or three times per week and graduate students teach discussion sections once a week, or as a smaller course without assistants that mixes lecture with discussion at every session. The lecture portion allows us to cover more texts and to attend more fully to social and intellectual contexts than would be possible with discussion only. We read short works by many authors, both poems and literary essays, some of the essays assigned in an initial two-week prelude. We also read five novels, typically the following, in this order, which is chronological: Bram Stoker's *Dracula*, James Joyce's *A Portrait of the Artist as a Young Man*, E. M. Forster's *A Passage to India*, Toni Morrison's *Sula*, and Butler's *Dawn*. In the dozen times that I have taught the course, I have changed or considered changing some readings every semester. As a consequence, I mention as possibilities below more works and authors than could manageably fit into one semester. Many options are possible between *Dracula* and *Dawn*, the course's early and closing fixed points.

My description in this essay emphasizes *Dawn*'s culminating place by focusing on resonances between it and the other readings from the long twentieth century that are not science fiction—or speculative fiction, as it is sometimes aptly called. Students read *Dawn* as part of modern literature rather than in relation only to science fiction or writings by African American authors. I frame the sequence with the claim that important examples of modernist writing, science fiction, and modern gothic overlap conceptually. The course embodies that framing vision by juxtaposing works typically thought of as modernist with slightly earlier and sometimes considerably later writings, including ones that are gothic or science fictional in character. The compatibility of the African American writings, mostly after World War II, with the earlier works indicates that they are part of late modernism or comparable to aspects of modernist writing. We read *Sula* as a late modernist text but *Dawn* as revealingly related to some modernist works, because of modernism's gothic threads, thematic concerns, and stylistic alternatives to realism. I stress that science fiction, gothic narratives, and modernist fiction all swerve from realism, though in different ways.

Modern Gothic, Modernism, and Science Fiction

As an example of the modern gothic, we read *Dracula*, a work whose multiperspectival and nonlinear open-ended narrative, nonrealistic representations, and emphasis on new technologies set it in immediate relation to modernist deviations from Victorian fiction. It emerges out of a long gothic tradition, but it also overlaps with modernism, which was nascent in the 1890s. I occasionally include Conrad's *Heart of Darkness* as another dark work on the cusp of modernism, contemporary with *Dracula*, that addresses issues of cultural contact and hierarchical thinking in a style that is not strictly realistic. *Dracula* introduces elements that return emphatically in *Dawn*, including Count Dracula's character as an alien creature—or, alternatively, as a posthuman being—and Mina Harker's heroism and androgynous turn after her intimacy with the Count, a transformation that makes her resemble Lilith Iyapo, a posthuman androgyne who is both heroic and intimate with aliens. I sometimes assign Oscar Wilde's *Salome* alongside *Dracula*, as another modern gothic work (in a different genre) concerned with hierarchies and anticipatory of modernism (in the figure of the dancer, for example) and whose central character is a strong woman, androgynous in her mimicry of male language and attitudes.

Reading a late-nineteenth-century gothic narrative early, with or without Conrad and Wilde, and ending with *Dawn* helps make visible the dark, or gothic, thread in modernism and later writing. It also allows me to characterize science fiction as developing out of earlier gothic writing after the French Revolution, starting with Mary Shelley's *Frankenstein*, a book that is chronologically inappropriate for this course but that many students know. *Frankenstein* has regularly though not universally been identified as both science fiction's originating text and an important precursor for *Dracula*, which I locate in lecture briefly between earlier gothic narratives and later science fiction.

To become familiar with key modernist writers beyond those already mentioned, students read prose by such authors as Virginia Woolf and D. H. Lawrence and poetry by Thomas Hardy, W. B. Yeats, Robert Frost, and T. S. Eliot. They also read works by slightly later authors—for example, prose by George Orwell, James Baldwin, and Alice Walker; poetry by Langston Hughes, Elizabeth Bishop, and Seamus Heaney. Just before *Dawn*, we read *Sula*, a short novel with an independent central female character, whose full name, Sula Mae Peace, echoes the name Salome, which shares the same Hebrew root with *shalom*, meaning "peace." The sequence and selection of texts make students aware that modernism emerged in generational waves that extended past World War II rather than in a briefer, homogeneous block. An initial wave began with Wilde and Stoker in the 1890s and continued through a first generation of modernists, then through a second wave of younger artists born after 1900, then through a third wave after the war. In the second and third waves, late modernism responds to new developments in human history that occur around the time of the war.

The difficulty of modernist writing creates a challenge that I address by assigning numerous short, comparatively accessible works and a few thornier modernist texts that allow students to develop a sense of modernism's permanently revolutionary aspects. The most difficult works that I include are *The Waste Land* and *A Portrait of the Artist*. I make Eliot's poem more accessible by playing in class as much of his recording as we have time for while stopping it for comment and discussion at strategic moments. This poem and *Dawn* can be put in conversation with each other in many ways. Although challenging, *A Portrait* is accessible because the central character, Stephen Dedalus, is turning into an adult, experiencing a process that all the students know well. Joyce's narrative seems on its face distant from *Dawn*, but the two works share an incisive dissolving and displacing of old categories, especially binary oppositions. In *A Portrait* the absolute contrast between flesh and spirit softens in a merger that points to a new kind of art. Like the organic ship in *Dawn*, which is not mechanical and neither plant nor animal, the new development is "Both and more" (*Dawn* 35). Like Stephen, Lilith strenuously resists relinquishing her freedom of choice in the face of well-organized, powerful forces in a narrative that is open-ended. In the conclusion of my description of the course, I turn in more detail to choice and freedom, recurring elements of the readings that are crucial in *Dawn*. I anticipate that moment here by pointing out that Lilith's closing mantra, "*Learn and run!*" (248), captures Stephen Dedalus's determination to avoid the nets that would prevent him from flying.

The Network of Connections and Issues Involving Dawn

Students encounter *Dawn* after having honed their interpretive skills and broadened their experience with modern literature across the genres. Many who normally would not read a work of science fiction discover how engaging and accomplished such narratives can be, and they recognize science fiction's continuities with modernist writing. Students frequently comment in course evaluations that *Dawn* is strange and at times disturbing but not escapist because it raises serious issues of contemporary relevance—for example, the technologically enabled possibilities for human self-destruction and for human transformation into the posthuman by genetic engineering, a technology that can be restricting and threatening or liberating. *Dawn* provides a capstone for many elements in the course's architecture of concerns: what it means to be human; the protean character of the self; the possibility of alternative gender roles and of alternative sexualities and domestic partnerships; the persistence and effects of hierarchical thinking in human culture; the at-times self-defeating, at-times affirming and transforming effects of technology; and questions about the meaning of home and the character of freedom.

Dawn exemplifies science fiction's anthropological dimension in its focus on the self-transforming, self-destructive, hierarchical, and androgynous potentials of human beings. As a technologically transformed androgyne who has survived an apocalyptic war, Lilith has become posthuman. I never taught Samuel Beckett's *Endgame* in this course, but it would be an excellent option as a postapocalyptic work by a late modernist author. Despite the fact that the play was written after World War II, when the threat of nuclear holocaust became prominent, early drafts make it clear that Beckett also had World War I in mind, because the action occurs during that war and following it (Ackerley and Gontarski 174). Its late modernist science fictional aspects point back toward the war to which earlier modernists also responded and forward to the more devastating apocalypse that Lilith survived.

Dawn's anthropological aspect is evident in Lilith's contact with the Oankali, which enables her comparative perspective on human existence. Lilith sees the aliens through human eyes and her own species thorough theirs. This moment of double vision bears comparison with the closing of Seamus Heaney's "Alphabets," in which an astronaut looks from space at his origin on earth. Lilith has the sense of her experience on the ship as "fieldwork" from which she cannot extricate herself (87). The Oankali are anthropological observers who characterize the human species as hierarchical as well as intelligent, a combination that has violent consequences (39). Regularly in the course we encounter challenges to hierarchical attitudes. Anthropological perspectives come up explicitly when we read *The Waste Land*, a work that, like *Dawn*, begins with rebirth and centrally evokes a process of emergence. Students discover the poem's debt to anthropological writing that Eliot builds into the poem's details and mentions in a headnote, referring specifically to the monumental early-twentieth-century study by James Frazer, *The Golden Bough*, on comparative mythology and religion.

The Waste Land includes science fictional and gothic elements in the sense that it raises the issue of human transformation of an apocalyptic kind involving significant technological change. When Eliot presents undead figures on their way to work in the last verse paragraph of part 1, they anticipate what later came to be called zombies. These undead evoke World War I, with its newly mechanized warfare, through the shell shock (now called post-traumatic stress disorder) and damaged limbs of the many returning ambulatory soldiers. The walking wounded inhabit London as walking dead. Part 5's apocalyptic details include bats crawling upside down on walls, suggesting that Eliot had read and been influenced by *Dracula*, a work whose title character threatens apocalyptic change and whose central female character, Mina Harker, develops into an androgyne. Central (literally) to *The Waste Land* is the androgynous Tiresias in part 3, whose presence brings uncertainties about the limits and the character of human gender identity. Yeats's Crazy Jane, in "Crazy Jane Talks with the Bishop," deserves mention here because of her appropriation of male-inflected sexual language. Androgyny is important as well in some of the short prose, specifically an excerpt from chapter 6 of Woolf's *A Room of One's Own*, where Woolf meditates on alternatives for a dominating, single-sexed identity, and Baldwin's "Here Be Dragons," in which racial integration is set in parallel with androgyny because boundaries are blurred. Along with Eliot, who was a transatlantic figure, these two modernists, one early, one late, with contrasting backgrounds on different sides of the Atlantic, challenge binary oppositions that support restrictive hierarchies of power. They do so in ways that anticipate and invite comparison with Lilith's androgyny and her other crossings of boundaries.

What I have suggested about Yeats, Eliot, Woolf, Baldwin, Beckett, Heaney, and Butler represents—with specific attention to anthropological perspectives, androgyny, hierarchies, and human self-destruction—the way the course moves through literary generations, identifying and following modernism's concerns. The frequent, memorable similarities among the texts allow us to read *Dawn* with reference to earlier moments in which cultural contact occurs, binaries and hierarchies of value and power are challenged, androgyny appears, and freedom is asserted or achieved, often by an independent-minded female character.

Sometimes the earlier moments occur explicitly as literary structure and detail, while sometimes they are suggested figuratively. *A Passage to India*, for example, focuses in its large narrative elements on the encounter between two races and cultures, one more powerful and one less so. They face the daunting challenge of building bridges to make possible a future that will replace the hierarchical relation with one that is more fluid and inclusive. Forster does not of course present the potentially cross-cultural future of the races as cross-species or posthuman in the manner of *Dawn*, but the issues of bridging, merging, and coexisting invite comparison. Cross-species perspectives do arise in *A Passage* with regard to insects (37–38). This aspect of the narrative is part of an ecological vision with implications for racial and species prejudice that appears in later modernist writing and in *Dawn*. The Oankali, for example, prohibit the killing of animals as food (90).

In Forster's narrative, Mrs. Moore and Professor Godbole accept wasps as fellow beings, while the English missionaries reach a limit in their inclusive thinking about animals and human beings when they exclude wasps. The missionaries' belief in the ontological equality of beings does not extend to stinging insects, creatures that presumably we can kill without hesitation. By contrast, in *Dawn* the Oankali are able to look in an unbiased, accepting way at something that human beings find threatening: not wasps but cancer, which they discover in Lilith. For them, cancer is potentially beneficial through genetic manipulation and trading (41). It is not to be eradicated automatically. Bishop participates in this vision by expressing a positive attitude, aesthetic in character, involving wasps in "Santarém," which is about the speaker's trip to the city in western Brazil named in the title. After she commented admiringly to a pharmacist on the wasps' nest hanging in the shop, he gave it to her, knowing that she would care for it and pass it on to others who recognize its value (as she does by writing a poem about the gift). This moment of gift exchange invites comparison with Oankali trading. The association with the pharmacy suggests that the wasps' nest, like cancer, though repulsive to some (including one of the speaker's fellow travelers), contains a healing potential that transcends conventional categories of beautiful and ugly.

Bishop's "The Fish" also participates in the ecological vision, because the speaker overcomes her culturally induced intention to kill the fish that she caught when she recognizes that it is not inferior but instead a being of dignity and beauty. The cross-species moment of recognition and acceptance does not have the racial implications of *Dawn* or *A Passage*, but it does present critically the assumed hierarchical dominance of human beings over nature, including other species, a persistent Western attitude that is arguably the pattern for hierarchies of racial dominance involving violence. An equally memorable moment of recognition and acceptance across species that involves a human being and an animal occurs in Woolf's "The Death of the Moth," in which a day moth fluttering toward death in front of Woolf while she writes turns out to be a kind of dancer who performs until it is unable to continue. In her brief narrative essay no hierarchy places the members of the two species as superior or inferior, as more or less valuable.

The dissolving of hierarchies that determine judgments, choices, and the fate of living beings in advance is bound up with issues of freedom that recur in our readings. The texts frequently expose and challenge hierarchies and restrictive systems as they present situations involving varying combinations of different species, different races, and assertive characters, sometimes male but often female. Orwell's younger self comes to recognize limits on his freedom as an agent of empire in "Shooting an Elephant," in which he kills an animal needlessly because of pressures arising from racial and imperial hierarchies. By contrast, the speaker's victory in "The Fish" is based on her choice not to kill the fish. The rabbit in Lawrence's "Adolf" refuses human attempts to domesticate him and ultimately escapes. Crazy Jane refuses the bishop's attempt to dominate her and invents, in a committed, heroic act of defiance, a distinctive, strongly declarative style of speech and thought that combines meanings and genders. Mina Harker, in *Dracula*, is also heroic and independent when she takes advantage of her androgyny and her new abilities in the wake of her intimacy with the vampire. She survives, helps track down the vampire, and protects her child, whose blood links him to the creature. In effect, she accepts what she cannot avoid and in so doing transforms what has happened to her. Choices become possible, and freedom is maximized under the circumstances, which are limiting, as human circumstances always are. In Yeats's "Leda and the Swan," Leda also faces a situation that she cannot avoid, but the poem suggests that she turns it to advantage for future human beings by apparently taking both knowledge and power from the strange, powerful creature. As black and female, Sula cannot avoid being an outsider in a white world, but by choosing the role of outsider in the black community, she becomes the glue holding the community together. Lilith Iyapo also chooses her fate in unavoidable circumstances, encountering limits and finding ways to maintain or reassert independence. Like Leda and Mina, she cannot avoid the powerful alien creature, but she can learn from it and enable a different kind of future for a posthuman community that her actions and attitudes help shape.

Historicizing the Future: Teaching Historical Consciousness in Butler's Fiction

Matthew Mullins

Why has the genre of speculative fiction been dominated historically by white, male writers? Why did so few African American writers before the late twentieth century venture into the future? In his 1994 interviews entitled "Black to the Future," Mark Dery poses these questions to Samuel Delany, Greg Tate, and Tricia Rose. Delany answers:

> [T]he historical reason we've been so impoverished in terms of future images is because, until fairly recently, as a people we were systematically forbidden any images of our past. . . . No immigrant group—neither Irish, Italians, Germans, Jews, nor Scandinavians—for all the prejudices that all of them met when they got here, and which they all had to overcome, endured such massive cultural destruction. ([*Flame Wars*] 191)

As Rose puts it, "if you're going to imagine yourself in the future, you have to imagine where you've come from" (215). The re-creation of an intentionally annihilated history has proved so integral to the African American literary tradition that a backward-looking, realistic literature has become the norm. To write speculative fiction would be to violate this norm, to hazard a fantasy of the future when the reality of the past has still not been fully confronted. Black writers who set out to explore possible futures in their fiction therefore face the contradictory demands of writing the future while navigating the expectation that they will rewrite the past.

This double bind presents both a challenge and an opportunity for teachers who want to help students appreciate and understand the work of Octavia E. Butler, one of the most important pioneers of speculative fiction in the African American literary tradition. For students to appreciate her innovation, they must be able to situate her work between the need to re-create the past and the desire to imagine the future. But before they can do that, they must be able to recognize the traditional expectations that have been placed on black writers.

In the first part of this essay, I lay the groundwork for helping teachers and students identify and interrogate the expectations that African American literature should be backward-looking in content and realistic in form. In the second part, I outline two assignments that I developed as a result of teaching Butler, which demonstrate how her fiction transcends those expectations. As a result, students and teachers will better appreciate the beauty and brilliance of her work.

Identifying and Interrogating Expectations

The expectations that direct my reading of a text and exclude other possible ways of reading tend to be invisible. Butler makes these expectations visible by using familiar story lines but situating them in an unfamiliar narrative. Whether I am teaching Butler's work in a general education course or in a dedicated unit in an upper-level elective, whether I am teaching novels like *Kindred* and *Parable of the Sower* or stories like those in *"Bloodchild" and Other Stories*, I always begin the class by asking students to consider how her work frustrates or surprises us, how that frustration or surprise makes our expectations evident, and how we arrived at those expectations, whether through passive acceptance or active consumption, in the first place.

Parable of the Sower's speculative vision of the future defies expectations that literature in the African American tradition should be focused exclusively on the past. Students should first situate the novel in a larger literary lineage, and Butler helps by writing in the voice of a young woman named Lauren Olamina, evoking slave narratives or other forms of life writing in the African American tradition with Lauren's first-person perspective and the various chapter epigraphs that resemble the kind of paratextual poems that often accompany slave narratives. *Parable* is made up of her diary entries and the series of poems she writes to express the doctrines of her new religion, Earthseed. But the familiar voice of the diary entries is immediately made strange by the date of the first installment: Saturday, July 20, 2024. The beginning of the novel combines the familiar first-person opening, "I had my recurring dream last night," the familiar poem about God and change, and the startling future date (3).

Even if some students do not expect that African American fiction should be historical and realistic, we must still help them understand how such expectations have shaped the writers and the genre. One simple way of making readers aware of their own expectations about a particular body of literature is to have them think through and name as many examples of it as possible. I'll often have students list as many works by African American writers as they can and put these up on the board. I'll have them think back over the most memorable films they've seen starring black actors. We talk about television; we talk about sports history. My goal is to get them to identify as many cultural artifacts as possible that they associate with African American art and history.

Most of the texts that students identify have something to do with slavery or its legacy. Hopefully they will come to realize that the best-known works of African American literature, film, visual art, and music are backward-looking in content. There's an excellent segment that aired on *The Daily Show* during Oscar season in 2016 criticizing the underrepresentation of people of color among Oscar nominees. Roy Wood, Jr., a correspondent, explains to Trevor Noah, the host, that the reason none of the films starring black people were nominated is that they neglected to include a very important element: slavery. "If we wanna win an Oscar, we have to make a movie about black people being oppressed," Wood exclaims. Surveying past Oscar-nominated and Oscar-winning films starring African Americans, Wood and Noah end up joking that if only filmmakers would "sprinkle that slavery" on their films, then more films focused on African American culture would win Oscars.

Parable of the Sower calls the history of oppression to mind even as it imagines what the United States will be like thirty years into the future. Butler understands the need to reclaim an erased history yet also shows that the future belongs to women and people of color as much as it belongs to the white male writers who have essentially owned the genre of speculative fiction. By setting the novel thirty years ahead and then working slowly toward a greater historical remove, she creates a future that is recognizable. The novel's "futuristic voice is predicated on the historical experience of African Americans" (Ruffin 89). This backward-looking future can help uncover the second major expectation through which we often approach African American literature: that it should be realistic.

Hortense J. Spillers has observed that certain historical and literary traditions lend themselves to realism because they are "engendered by a real world of power relations" and that, following this logic, "African-American literary development would locate its center of gravity in realism" (4). But she goes on to argue that there are many ways for artists to make history real.

Butler's *Kindred* exposes and shatters the expectations of realism that readers often bring to African American literature. The novel opens with a prologue that begins, "I lost an arm on my last trip home. My left arm" (9). The narrator, Dana, then gives us bits and pieces of the story that lead us to believe that maybe her husband, Kevin, hurt her or that maybe she's hiding some other act of violence. Either way, nothing prepares us for the first pages of chapter 1, in which she is pulled back from 1976 to the early nineteenth century. When her journey begins, she is at home and feeling light-headed. As Kevin approaches her to see what is the matter, he vanishes (13). We don't learn until the very end of the novel that her arm got stuck between past and present when a character in the nineteenth century grabbed her as she was being transported back to 1976. In this example, we are both welcomed into the story and held at a distance. Like so many of the slave narratives that begin with some version of the line "I was born," Butler opens with a first-person narrator stating, "I lost an arm. . . ."

I present the novel's more popular covers to students to show that publishers have mostly used photographic images of black women. I then ask students to analyze what kinds of expectations the covers create in their representation of slavery in contrast to how Butler, breaking the laws of the physical and literary universes, represents slavery through time travel.

Transcending Expectations

From my experience teaching novels like *Kindred* and *Parable of the Sower*, I have developed two assignments that help students appreciate Butler's ability to historicize the future. The first asks them to create what I call a timescape—that is, a visual representation of time that is not linear. The second is a reading journal modeled on Lauren Olamina's journal in *Parable of the Sower*.

In the timescape assignment, students consider the relations among past, present, and future in terms that are not mutually exclusive. Butler's work, refusing sharp distinctions of time, links past and future inextricably. Students are asked to create some form of visual representation of events from whatever Butler text we are reading. For the timescape for *Kindred*, I once had two students bring skeins of yarn to class, inspired by a quotation from Harriet Jacobs's *Incidents in the Life of a Slave Girl*: "What tangled skeins are the genealogies of slavery!" (121). They assigned everyone in the class a character, place, or time in the novel. Students who represented times and places held the loose ends of the yarn, while the students who acted as characters held the skeins. As the student leaders then walked the class through key events in the novel, the student-characters literally walked through and around the various times and places, creating a giant web of multicolored yarn. The final result was a concentration of yarn around the narrative present and the plantation house, causing one student to exclaim that this exercise illustrated how the effects of slavery go far beyond the antebellum South.

The reading journal assignment is designed to make the connection between past and future personal for students. It works especially well with *Parable* because it mimics Lauren's diary entries, but it can be assigned with many other texts. I introduce the assignment by asking students to write short summaries of their experiences reading the novel, beginning with the date and including what was happening in their lives as they sat down to read. I provide a sample journal entry from my own reading, stressing that each entry should function as a narrative with a clear story to follow. After our first class meeting on the text, I ask that instead of writing neat narrative entries as they go, they jot down a few brief notes that they will expand at a later date. I ask them to write these expanded entries in the present tense, as Lauren does, even though they're actually writing about the past. In the follow-up discussion, I ask them how they decided which brief notes to expand and also how writing about the past as if it were the present shaped their finished narratives. We finally compare their first round of entries with the second to see what the similarities and differences might tell us about how the relations among past, present, and future affect the ways we represent our experiences.

Both these assignments give students an opportunity to construct an understanding of time in which the past has a tangible connection to the future and the future can be seen as resolutely historical. Butler creates such historicized futures throughout her fiction to help us see that we cannot comprehend and analyze our present world, let alone imagine a future, if we do not have a well-developed historical consciousness. At the same time, imagining the future is vital to fully understanding the past. Without such a historical consciousness we will not question the status quo, embrace positive change, or value works of art that encourage us to do both.

Teaching Butler in a Course on Colonialism and Science Fiction

Aparajita Nanda

The importance of colonialism as a historical context for the genre of science fiction has been recognized by a number of critics (e.g., Suvin, *Metamorphoses* and "On the Poetics"; Csicsery-Ronay; and Miéville). John Rieder in *Colonialism and the Emergence of Science Fiction* states that "no informed reader can doubt that allusions to colonial history and situations are ubiquitous features of early science fiction motifs and plots. It is not a matter of asking whether but of determining precisely how and to what extent the stories engage colonialism" (3). Rieder suggests that the other of colonialism, replete with its core ambivalence, often forms the essence of science fiction narratives.

Having taught Octavia Butler's science fiction trilogy *Lilith's Brood* in undergraduate courses of African American literature at the University of California, Berkeley, I decided to make the first two books, *Dawn* and *Adulthood Rites*, the centerpiece of my senior seminar class on colonialism. Most students familiar with American history understand slavery as an extension of colonialism. Slavery is the primary focus of one of Butler's most notable (and most popularly taught) books, *Kindred*. But *Kindred* is an exception—most of her writings are in the genre of science fiction. Even as critics have read undertones of slavery in her work, she writes in her afterword to her Hugo Award–winning short story "Bloodchild," "It amazes me that some people have seen 'Bloodchild' as a story of slavery. It isn't" (*"Bloodchild"* 30). She goes on to characterize it as a love story between two different beings, even a pregnant man story. "There's one more thing I tried to do in 'Bloodchild,'" she adds:

> I tried to write a story about paying the rent—a story about an isolated colony of human beings on an inhabited, extrasolar world. At best, they would be a lifetime away from reinforcements. It wouldn't be the British Empire in space, and it wouldn't be *Star Trek*. Sooner or later, the humans would have to make some kind of accommodation with their um . . . their hosts. Chances are this would be an unusual accommodation. Who knows what we humans have that others might be willing to take in trade for a livable space on a world not our own? (31–32)

I point out to the class that Butler locates her narrative in the science fiction genre, which enables her to write about slavery or colonialism in an unfamiliar context, one free of historical baggage. Her purely speculative treatment, not beholden to the past, facilitates discussion of abstract concepts and opens up interdisciplinary approaches.

In our class discussions I emphasize that theory often tends to polarize or oversimplify, while literature, especially the novel, tends to work more on the level of contradiction and ambiguity. Butler's *Lilith's Brood* is a parable of postcolonialism that picks up concepts of colonial maltreatment and subjugation and presents us with a set of aporias found in inextricably linked discourses of power, genetics, and evolution. By revealing the limitations of these treatises and exposing the double entrendre at the heart of the colonial project, Butler disrupts the tract of postcoloniality.

For the students, Butler's form of colonialism becomes a fascinating topic for further investigation. When they read through her interviews available online and in edited versions as books (e.g., "Interview" [McCaffery and McMenamin]), they conclude that *Lilith's Brood* deconstructs the rigid binaries of oppressive, colonizing, and alien Oankali and victimized, colonized human beings, that it recognizes ambivalences in these categories by acknowledging that the Oankali are propagators of diversity and healers with an altruistic purpose and that the human beings are erratic and violent. Although the Oankali exhibit many of the traits of historical colonizers, they are not so easy to brand as oppressive, and their arguments about the benefits to the colonized cannot be dismissed as rationalizations. They do usurp the culture of the humans, and for that they may be hated despite the defensibility of their motives and actions. I agree with Thomas Foster that students have a difficult time seeing that Butler rejects "the assumption that the forms of power her aliens wield are coercive or dominating in ways familiar to us from histories of slavery or colonialism, while at the same time she does not celebrate human/alien relations as egalitarian or naively utopian" (141). When students are prompted to set aside the question of the justifications for colonization, however, they analyze the structure of colonialism in a more theoretical way, perhaps concluding that, even in the case of a bloodless coup, no colonial takeover can be justified from the standpoint of human solidarity and individual freedom.

Dawn opens in the wake of a human-led apocalypse: the human race has nearly brought about its own demise through nuclear war. The Oankali, a nomadic alien species, rescue the few surviving people but at a price: whoever opts to be saved forgoes the right to reproduce. As gene traders, the Oankali evoke Europeans in their initial explorations to establish a colonial empire (Goss and Riquelme 448). The aliens justify their control with the need to produce a hybrid species, a human-Oankali breed in which the "Human Contradiction," the Oankali term for what they see as humanity's flawed, "mismatched pair of genetic characteristics," intelligence and hierarchical reasoning, will be eliminated (Dawn 38). To implement their plan, they abduct Lilith Iyapo, an African American female, and alter her brain to make her a mother figure who will persuade the human survivors to join the Oankali fold. They claim that the new breed of constructs, rid of their violent trait, will save the human race when they return to Earth. Lilith is also the chosen progenitor of Akin, the first human-

Oankali construct. Akin first appears in *Adulthood Rites* and, like his mother, is deployed by the Oankali in the human camp.

I begin the seminar by explaining to students Edward Said's concept of the self and the other, in which the self, the Occident, is the voice of the privileged, of the unchallenged authority that defines the marginalized, voiceless other. I encourage students to respond to Butler's Oankali and human beings—whether they think the Oankali represent the self, the oppressive colonizers, and the human beings the other, the colonized victims—and to share their response with their peers. As more and more students understand the ambiguity at the heart of Butler's narrative, which refuses easy categorizations of the self and the other, we move on to discuss Homi Bhabha's concepts of hybridization, ambivalence, and mimicry. Taking his cue directly from Said's work, Bhabha deconstructs the binaries of the self and the other as interrelated constructs. Through hybridization the other defines itself in terms of the intruding, authoritative colonial self, which in turn is permanently marred by its repetitive articulation of difference from the other. The colonizer desires to create a "mimic man" in the colonized other, yet this mimic man is not a simple reflection of the colonizer. As Bhabha points out, it becomes a projection of

> double vision which in disclosing the ambivalence of colonial discourse also disrupts its authority. And it is a double vision that is a result of what he has described as the partial representation/recognition of the colonial object . . . the figures of a doubling, the part-objects of a metonymy of colonial desire which alienates the modality and normality of those dominant discourses in which they emerge as "inappropriate" colonial subjects. (88)

As my students and I relate postcolonial theory to Butler's texts, we discuss Lilith Iyapo's role as the hybridized other (a human being with an altered brain) who occupies an ambivalent position between following the Oankali agenda and saving her human wards. Does Lilith go along with the Oankalis to escape the punishment for those who dare to dissent, or, despite her victimized status, does she at some point begin to believe in the Oankali mission? The students at first see her as a type of the Bhabhian mimic man, albeit one in the making. But as they read on, they begin to consider her as a potential traitor—a traitor of both the Oankali and her human interns. Her son, the hybrid Akin, is born and bred an Oankali and learns of his human side only when he is abducted by human resistors and spends time with them in the human camp. Students identify him as a mimic man groomed by the Oankali—a finished product and not, like his mother, in the making.

A plot point that students find baffling is the abandonment by the Oankali of Akin, their virtual son, in the human camp. I draw their attention to an observation by Ruth McElroy that an "enduring feature of [colonial] surrogacy narratives [was that] men as fathers disappear[ed] as prime actors from the scene of surrogacy," leaving nation-states to "police the composition of the nation through legislative powers over women's reproduction" and the children born to them (325–26). This abandonment brings up discussions of illegitimacy and deliberate callousness on the part of colonial fathers. But students ask, If the Oankali are merely colonizers, father figures who easily betray their progeny for selfish purposes, what about their altruism, their role as benevolent saviors? It is complicated. Akin's abandonment is premeditated: the Oankali are using him as an informer who in his sojourn in the enemy camp can collect genetic information by touching the human beings with his tongue and pass it on to the Oankali. But Akin becomes a spokesperson for the human beings: taking up their cause, he asks for the restitution of their reproductive rights. Although he was brutally mistreated by his human abductors, he forms affective ties with some human beings that lead him to stand up for them. He is possibly the ideal Bhabhian mimic man, a projection of the "double vision which in disclosing the ambivalence of colonial discourse also disrupts its authority" (Bhabha 88). In a hybrid subject, divided loyalties may suggest a competition between them, but given that Akin is *a-kinsual*, his loyalties become uncertain, not subject to competitive equations, rather than divided.

Akin's situation recalls that of hybridized people who sought segregated habitats in colonized countries to find answers to the questions haunting them and who often resorted to political dissidence. Maintaining categories of citizenship that separated the colonizer from the colonized was a major goal of imperialist rule. But these categories were threatened by hybrid citizens, the product of contact zones where the European national formed sexual liaisons and affective ties with natives. There was a growing population of interracial children of European and native parentage, as well as European children who were "too versed in local knowledge" and who became virtual natives themselves (Stoler 2). Clearly, the issue was one of cultural belonging. The primary concern of the imperialist regime was how to classify this hybrid population. These citizens qualified as mimic men: they could maintain a semblance of loyalty but could also be conduits of subversion beneath that semblance. Racial vigilance, which earlier was concerned only with securing national borders and with the macropolitics of the nation, now had to contend with the micropolitics of those who inhabited the domestic domain. The management of domestic space—of parenting, of sexual morality, and of upbringing—moved from being peripheral topics of colonial interest to a central, highly political issue.

Lilith and Akin, mother and son, one by way of genetic alteration and the other by way of birth, straddle the human-Oankali divide and thereby qualify as the hybrid citizens of colonial rule. Complicit in the Oankali plan, they can betray the human beings; connected by affective ties in their lived spheres, they can foment dissension against autocratic rule. Through this mother-son duo, my students come to view the domestic, a traditionally safe space, as a site of radical disruption, a hidden source of revolutionary energy.

Lilith is introduced to us as a captive, a victim of a controlled society. The Oankali plans for organizing that society recall the creation and maintenance of rules and strictures that upheld and justified the conceit of order and well-being at the heart of colonial rule. Lilith is picked up and groomed to be a surrogate mother to the human beings; her task is to persuade them to procreate with the Oankali. Her entering the domestic space of the human survivors and educating them on Oankali teachings recalls colonial concerns regarding the bearing and rearing of children, confirming, in the words of Sidney Webb, that "the empire was rooted in the home" (qtd. in Davin 97). But the surrogate mother's refusal to abide by the tenets of colonial rule shows that control is impossible to maintain. When she rebels, the safe space of home becomes an arena of dynamic disruption.

Lilith is a nymphomaniac, sexualized to the point that her desire for the alien subadult Oankali leaves her craving sexual stimulation and satiation. Sexuality has often been used as a symbol for political domination (Said, *Orientalism* 207). Lilith overturns this notion completely as she introduces a contraband desire that rebukes Cold War domesticity and procreative sex by reveling in taboo forms of pleasure. As a powerful seductress in collusion with the Oankali, she is no mother figure (like the innocuous Eve). She becomes a center of power that, like her rabbinic namesake, destroys domestic comfort and any sacred order by creating chaos.

There are many ways in which literary texts can fictionalize history by historicizing the future. Reading *Lilith's Brood* through the lens of colonialism raises thought-provoking questions for students, and the answers are not often provided by Butler. Our discussion is open-ended, and I end my teaching with a further question: If you were subjected to the same conditions, would you side with Lilith or Akin? I want students to examine themselves, to think about the human psyche that preconditions one to enslave and colonize and how to escape a future that that repeats history. This question is especially relevant as we see China and Russia still acting as colonial empires, the United States still engaged in nation building, and religious colonialism still perpetuated in the Middle East and northern Africa.

NOTE

Some parts of this essay were taken from my essay "Power, Politics, and Domestic Desire in Octavia Butler's *Lilith's Brood*."

Teaching *Fledgling* as a Narrative of Love and Power

Lauren J. Lacey

Octavia E. Butler's *Fledgling* is a complex exploration of posthuman power relations, a revisionist vampire story, a polyamorous romance narrative, and, as my students say every time I teach it, really quite weird. Like all Butler's works, it is an unflinching elaboration of the power dynamics that play out in our world on a daily basis, which is certain to be unsettling to students and challenging for instructors. It is also an incredible opportunity to confront dominant culture and its persistent racism, sexism, and homophobia. The course in which I usually teach *Fledgling* is Women Writers, cross-listed in English and in women's and gender studies and subtitled Narratives of Love and Power. It is a lower-division general education course that explores themes of love, romance, marriage, sexuality, gender, race, class, identity, and how they interrelate in the context of women's writing. I designed it to appeal to students from throughout the small liberal arts college where I teach. *Fledgling* offers a complex treatment of subjectivity and identity that I find to be an excellent fit for such a course. Its posthuman treatments of love, power, and sexuality are different from anything else the students read in the course and are certainly a departure from the way the dominant culture treats such concepts.

On a recent syllabus for the course, I elucidate the emphasis on love and power by explaining that the class is

> about stories that tell us how things were, how they are, and how they could be. We will learn what the restrictions of early-nineteenth-century life in England meant for women through Jane Austen's witty prose, experience the frustration of wanting freedom that is unavailable to women of her time and place in Kate Chopin's novella, and wonder at the courage of Zora Neale Hurston's characters as they negotiate a world defined by racism and sexism. Throughout all these narratives, we will explore what love means, how it works, and how power structures influence it. Then, in the second half of the course, contemporary women writers will introduce us to new ways of thinking about love and power, including new understandings of sexuality, identity, and gender. Along the way, we will discuss what kinds of stories our dominant, popular culture tells about love and power all the time.

In class, I present love as a social and cultural ideal that in reality is subject to all the rules of power that structure our everyday lives. Students are encouraged to read course texts through the lens of the complex relation between love and power, and from the beginning of the semester we spend time in class discussing examples of how that relation is treated in contemporary popular culture. Common topics of discussion are recent music videos and films; popular fiction, especially young adult and romance novels; and reality television. Practicing critical skills of narrative and thematic analysis on those popular texts in the early days of the semester helps invest the students in the subject matter of the course. Butler's novel fits into the second half of the course and operates as one of the texts offering, as the syllabus says, "new ways of thinking about love and power."

Women Writers usually begins with an Austen novel. I provide literary and historical contexts to help students gain some purchase on the text, then ask them to tell me what they expect from it. The conventions of romance soon emerge, and as students learn to think about basic elements of narrative structure, they also think about the elements of a romantic narrative. Again, dominant popular cultural texts are important touchstones here for students, who consider how themes of heteronormative romance in, for example, *Persuasion* persist today. Plot, setting, character, and narration are all scrutinized for clues about how love and power operate in the text. Students are pushed to consider how the romantic narrative operates, how the idea of love seems to be defined, what kinds of power relations influence the characters in the story, if the text is critical of any of the dominant norms of the time, and if there seem to be any alternatives to those norms offered by it. This process is repeated with the texts that follow.

By the time we get to Hurston's *Their Eyes Were Watching God*, students are familiar with the process of formal and thematic analysis as well as with the focus on love and power. They tend to see Janie's relationships with Logan Killicks, Joe Starks, and Tea Cake as a kind of evolution or growth toward increasingly more equal and affectionate romantic love, but with reservations. The frame narrative that has Janie returning to her home on her own is often read by my students as a sign of her ultimate strength and resilience, because by this point in the semester the idea of a happy romantic ending has grown very suspect.

In the second half of the course, students read a selection of more contemporary texts. In addition to *Fledgling*, some of the texts I have taught in this part of the course are Margaret Atwood's *The Penelopiad*, Angela Carter's *The Passion of New Eve*, Tanith Lee's *The Silver Metal Lover*, Doris Lessing's *Love, Again*, Ali Smith's *Girl Meets Boy*, Alice Walker's *Meridian*, and Jeanette Winterson's *Written on the Body*. Of all these works, Butler's *Fledgling* most fully develops the course issues and themes, and it is the novel that students almost invariably end up writing about on the final exam because, even if they struggle with it, they have a lot to say about it. We approach the contemporary texts by thinking about how they unsettle assumptions or defamiliarize dominant narratives, particularly narratives of romantic love.

Students who have studied the models of marriage depicted in *Persuasion*, questioned in Chopin's *Awakening*, and further interrogated in *Their Eyes*

Were Watching God are encouraged to rethink assumptions about love and power through their analyses of the posthuman relationships in *Fledgling*. The object of drawing such comparisons is not to construct a problematic narrative of progress but to pay careful attention to the methods employed by women writers to examine the models of love and power in different historical and cultural contexts. *Fledgling*'s complex treatment of posthuman subjectivity furnishes students with a model for rethinking power-love dynamics in texts read throughout the semester and in current popular culture. At the same time that they are reading and discussing the contemporary narratives, they are presenting on popular culture narratives of love and power and contrasting them with the course texts. I've had many students compare *Fledgling* with Stephenie Meyer's *Twilight*, with the HBO series *True Blood* (itself based on Charlaine Harris's novels), and, on the more romance side of things, with E. L. James's *Fifty Shades of Grey*.

The very things that I value in Butler's text are, of course, what makes it difficult for so many of the students, who are taking the course in order to meet a graduation requirement and usually not because of a love of literature or an interest in gender studies. I have to find ways to help them wade into the book's challenges without drowning in them. Often we look together at the way *Fledgling* begins: "I awoke to darkness. I was hungry—starving!—and I was in pain. There was nothing in my world but hunger and pain, no other people, no other time, no other feelings" (1). Students recognize not only the first-person narration and emphasis on the narrator's confusion but also the depth of the physicality and embodiment in Butler's storytelling.

Once we have begun to talk about how Butler has us identify with a protagonist who will ultimately turn out to be so utterly different from us—so inhuman—I ask students to discuss what happens early in the narrative that makes them uncomfortable. *Fledgling*'s opening chapters, in which a character who resembles a young girl gets involved in a sexual relationship with an adult man, are unsettling to most students. Everything in the early chapters of the novel is awkward, confused, and disorienting. We spend a lot of time in class discussing what is going on, the ways in which the text causes discomfort, and the reasons why it might be important for us to be made uncomfortable.

From things that cause discomfort in the novel we move to what Shori's father, Iosif, calls "mutualistic symbiosis" (63). My students are frequently confounded by the relationships between the Ina and the human beings, the way an Ina binds seven or more human beings to himself or herself at a time, forming a kind of family, and the way the human symbionts can in turn have human families of their own. The intricacies of how these symbiont families work can lead to long class discussions, which I usually find fruitful. After all, these discussions about love and power get into issues of domination, consent, biochemistry, attraction, passion, pleasure, dependence, community, not to mention gender and sexuality. As Steven Shaviro puts it, "Butler writes of how love involves dependency, loss of autonomy, and unequal power relations; even when both sides in the relationship have given themselves over unconditionally to an Other, they are never equal in (self-)abandonment" (229). All these qualities of love are true in our lives and relationships, but they are not typically depicted in romance narratives. Susana M. Morris points out, "Through the notion of mutualism, a family system in which humans and vampires rely on each other for survival in a complex web of nonmonogamous, interracial intimate relationships, Butler challenges both the primacy of nuclear families and the dominance of repressive heteropatriachal societies" (158). There is a lot there to challenge students' conceptions.

Some students find the model of extended symbiont groups to be interesting and liberating; others focus on how human symbionts become addicted to Ina venom and can be easily manipulated and controlled by their Ina. The former group emphasizes the way community works so that no individual is isolated and how there are real and consistent efforts to get beyond jealousy; they like the acceptance and lack of judgment for different races, lifestyles, and sexualities and the genuine caring that seems to extend across most members of symbiont families. Students in the latter group are more critical of the power difference between the Ina and the human beings, the ways in which the Ina manipulate human economies and social structures for their own ends, and the biochemical control the Ina have over the human beings in their families. But whether students champion or condemn the symbiont families, or both, they see how the novel is asking them to read outside the conventional frameworks of love and power.

Reading together as described above is in fact learning to think in terms of a posthumanist worldview. As Pramod K. Nayar writes, "Shori represents an apotheosis of the posthumanist vision. This posthumanist vision calls for recognizing a 'constitutive codependency' with other forms of life and 'evolutionary history' as a history of the coevolution of species where communications and events across life forms constitute the life form" (808). Following and participating in Shori's first-person narrative of self-discovery after her amnesia and Butler's always visceral renderings of Shori's experiences give students a much stronger sense of what posthumanism is than any abstract discussion of the topic. Indeed, *posthuman* becomes a descriptive term rather than a new concept after they have been through Butler's text.

Fledgling's posthumanism can add depth to how students understand the other narratives in the course. The patriarchal figures in Austen, who control women and their choices, and Janie's husbands in Hurston's novel, who try to dominate Janie in a variety of ways, inevitably come up in class discussions. Butler's text complicates students' earlier assessments. When asked to explore something like passion versus pleasure, students quickly point out how complex Butler's treatment of the subject is in *Fledgling*. We discuss how bodily pleasure and love are tangled up with each other in the novel and make comparisons with Janie's love for Tea Cake in Hurston or the narrator's descriptions of the beloved in Winterson's *Written on the Body*. There are more difficult connections, such as history or community, which are certainly related to love and power, but less clear. We talk about historical modes of looking at love and how Butler might be revising our conceptions of it. We discuss the Ina's alternative history and the kinds of community offered by the Ina. Shari Evans argues, "With the insertion of racial difference, the history the Ina remember and the ways they bear witness to that history suggest that institutional and cultural history are potential sites of contestation" (243). In the course, history is a site of contestation throughout, as students grapple with knowledge and its production. Butler's novel pushes the issue, though, requiring students to question the degree to which any known or recorded history can be trusted.

Fledgling's narrative structure lends itself well to a second or third day of discussion that shifts focus to the Council of Judgment. The emphasis is now on Shori's status as a hybrid figure with both human and Ina DNA, and we talk about how that status is seen as either a liberation or a loss of purity for the various Ina families. My students, although they have grown up immersed in Internet technology and smartphones, are uneasy with the idea of genetically modifying the human body, yet the narrative's arguments push them to reconsider. As Shori prepares for the council, she visits Daniel Gordon, who offers insight into how the proceedings will work but also tells her why he thinks her hybridity is valuable. In discussing the attempts on her life made by those who are against the genetic alterations to her that her family did, he says, "Shori, if you had been anyone else, they would have succeeded. You not only survived twice, but you came to us with what you knew, and you led the fight to destroy most of the assassins and to question the survivors. They thought mixing human genes with ours would weaken us. You proved them very wrong" (225). Students already identify with Shori and see things from her perspective because of the first-person narrative, and here they are further urged to see her genetic alterations as strengths. Of course human readers will not like the idea that the inclusion of human DNA sullies Ina purity, and so, as we work through the arguments that are brought against Shori in the Council of Judgment, students invariably side with her and identify the Silks' claims about her genetic alterations as being adulterations as racist or speciesist.

The trial itself highlights Shori's status in the Ina community. Her memory loss becomes a reason for her adversaries to treat her as incapable of being trusted—as less than fully Ina. Theri Pickens writes, "[T]he Ina base their self-conception on whiteness and able-bodiedness so much that they fail to see how it endangers them. Their ignorance about white and abled privilege . . . opens up the space for contradiction and undermines the stability of the Ina community" (37). These are Ina like the Silks, who attack Shori's families for their work in genetically engineering human-Ina hybrids. The Silks are clearly positioned as racist, speciesist elitists who see only other pure Ina as equal and everyone else as beneath them. Shori's strength lies precisely in her hybridity, her human DNA, her dark skin, and her disability.

In the context of my course Women Writers, Butler's *Fledgling* is not just an alternative to dominant cultural narratives of love and power but also a rethinking and remaking of the ways in which students approach the concepts of love and power. The narrative takes them into situations and configurations that are deeply uncomfortable for them, unsettling their assumptions about what constitutes love, how power works, and what it means to create a life of love in a world that is inevitably bound up in relations of power.

Keeping the Science in Science Fiction: Teaching Butler in an Interdisciplinary Writing Course

Laurel Bollinger

The work of Octavia Butler is particularly well suited to courses with an interdisciplinary focus, because she herself read voraciously across many disciplines and issues. She also valued playing fair with her science, saying in a 1997 *Callaloo* interview, "I think if you're going to write something like science fiction, you do need that basic interest in science and not just a desire to write about spectacular things that you know nothing about. . . . Science fiction uses science, extrapolates from science as we know it to science as it might be to technology as it might be" ("Interview" [Rowell] 55). The care, then, with which she presents the science in her fiction requires teachers and students to approach her work in a similarly interdisciplinary fashion.

At the public, comprehensive, research-intensive, STEM-focused, regional university where I teach, I use Butler's work in a first-year interdisciplinary honors writing course. The course functions as a freshman seminar, and faculty members are permitted to select its theme. Because most of the students are in engineering or science, structuring the course around their existing interests offers me avenues to introduce humanistic approaches as well. I've used two overarching themes that fit Butler well: science fiction and science writing, where we examine the intersections of storytelling with scientific explanation in both genres; and apocalyptic narratives, which include religious, literary, and science-based end-of-the-world scenarios. Each theme gives me the full semester to pair works that speak across disciplines to one another, but the richness of Butler's writing means that even in shorter units her texts offer similar teaching potential. Many of her stories and novels might work well for interdisciplinary approaches combining science and literature, but in this essay I focus on two: the short story "Bloodchild" and the novel *Parable of the Sower.*

"Bloodchild" challenges students by confirming their initial stereotypes about science fiction—that it involves aliens and space travel—but quickly revealing itself as focused on biology, emotions, family, and ethics. In terms of integrating science with literature, it pairs nicely with basic ideas about evolution, especially those involving parasitism and symbiosis. When I teach "Bloodchild," I explain that Butler invokes the *Red Queen race*, a term used by evolutionary biologists to account for parallel evolution in linked species, where adaptations in one species affect the survival of another and so trigger reciprocal evolutionary adaptation. Biologists derive the name from Lewis Carroll's *Through the Looking-Glass,* where the Red Queen explains to Alice that to get anywhere, they must run twice as fast—their exhausting race enables them only to stay in one place (ch. 2). Species often find themselves locked in a continual race to outdo one another, and the race ends up looking not like evolutionary progress but a desperate attempt to preserve a stalemate. For instance, cheetahs and gazelles both depend on speed for survival, but evolutionary pressures keep those speeds closely aligned. In his useful book on the Red Queen race, Matt Ridley explains:

> In the world of the Red Queen, any evolutionary progress will be relative as long as your foe is animate and depends heavily on you or suffers heavily if you thrive. . . . Every creature on earth is in a Red Queen chess tournament with its parasites (or hosts), its predators (or prey), and, above all, with its mate. (*Red Queen* 19)

Ridley offers greater detail about competition between mates, particularly in mammals, where it appears that in reproduction maternal chromosomes produce the embryo body while paternal chromosomes generate the placenta. As Ridley explains, mother and fetus may struggle over resource allocation—"exactly as they later will during weaning"—but share a common genetic purpose; the paternal chromosomes are not nearly so invested in maternal welfare, and "to turn briefly anthropomorphic, the father's genes do not trust the mother's genes to make a sufficiently invasive placenta; so they do the job themselves" (*Genome* 209). If the Red Queen race occurs between parasite and host, the struggle becomes more obvious: the parasite must continuously evolve strategies to evade the host's adaptations to prevent precisely that parasitism. "Bloodchild" depends heavily on investigating these evolutionary moves and countermoves.

Because the story's focus is on an immediate dynamic in a family, we get only limited insight into the world before human beings arrived as aliens on the planet, but what we see suggests that the native Tlic were not succeeding in Red Queen terms. Whereas reproduction in mammals assumes at least détente between male and female chromosomes in the production of the fetus, the Tlic reproductive strategy is far more like parasitism. The Tlic lay eggs in a host species, and the hatched larvae eventually eat their way out—unless, as the Tlic do with humans, the mother Tlic removes the larvae to a different food source. Tlic larvae, when they hatch, release a deadly chemical into the host's body, suggesting one move in a Red Queen race, presumably generated in response to the evolutionary success of potential host animals in eliminating eggs or larvae (Butler doesn't specify whether it's done chemically or physically). As the central Tlic figure, T'Gatoi, tells Gan, the human boy she will implant, "The animals we once used began killing most of our eggs after implantation long before your ancestors arrived. . . . Because your people arrived, we are relearning what it means to be a healthy, thriving people" ("Bloodchild" 25). In evolutionary terms, the advantage to the Tlic of using human hosts lies in the fact that the two species did not evolve in competition or symbiosis with each other, meaning that where reproduction is concerned, the Tlic are ahead in the Red Queen gambit.

But the human beings function less as hosts to parasites than may initially appear, because each species benefits. As Butler describes in the afterword to "Bloodchild," the human beings have arrived on a world where "paying the rent" involves their serving as cases for the egg-laying Tlic's offspring (*"Bloodchild"* 31). Yet she clarifies that the human colonists fled a world where their survival was in question: T'Gatoi tells Gan, "[Y]our ancestors, fleeing from their homeworld, from their own kind who would have killed or enslaved them—they survived because of us" ("Bloodchild" 25). The human-Tlic dynamic therefore permits discussion of symbiosis, and students work to determine whether the human-Tlic relationship is an example of mutualism or parasitism. That the Tlic provide human beings with unfertilized eggs that improve human health and lifespan points toward mutualism.

I ask students to consider the degree to which the encounter depends on what in medical ethics is termed informed consent. Gan agrees to be implanted even though he knows all the possible negative outcomes, much as a patient agrees to a medical procedure. Reproduction is at stake for the Tlic, but from the human perspective the process resembles something like kidney donation, except that for a donor (or host, in the story) the risks are all physical, while the rewards are emotional and therefore less tangible. In the afterword to "Bloodchild," Butler acknowledges that her initial impulse was to write out her anxiety over the risk of an actual parasite—the botfly—that she anticipated encountering during a research trip to Peru (*"Bloodchild"* 30–31), but the dynamics she creates in the story are far more complex. Such analysis enhances students' understanding of the story and biology alike and permits extended conversations about the ethical responsibilities this symbiosis places on each participant.

For courses with an interdisciplinary focus, *Parable of the Sower* has an even broader array of options, and I use it to structure the major research paper for my honors first-year writing course. *Parable* functions as a cautionary tale centered on Butler's exploration of the threats facing American society in the late 1980s and early 1990s. As she describes the novel, "The idea . . . is to look at where we are now, what we are doing now, and to consider where some of our current behaviors and unattended problems might take us" ("Conversation" 337). Her research to create the world of the novel depended on her "normal behavior" of attending to both radio and print news: "[B]ecause *Parable of the Sower* and *Parable of the Talents* were largely inspired by the news . . . the news I absorbed fed right into the novel[s]" (339). These statements of intent and process give students a starting point to do their research.

When the students have read the first third of the book, or at least through chapter 9, in class I ask them to list the ways in which Butler's United States of the mid-2020s differs from our United States. (In smaller classes, we discuss it as a whole; in larger groups, I turn to a think-pair-share strategy to maximize collaborative thinking.) Students readily tease out the various threads that contribute to the dystopian world Butler envisions, which I write out on the board or otherwise capture to record in our learning management system. I want them to see the privatization of social services, the wealth gap, attitudes toward the space program and scientific research, drug use, the impact of climate change on water and food availability—in short, the details that Butler describes as resulting in "the United States becoming, slowly . . . a third world country" ("Conversation" 337). Mathew Barrett Gross and Mel Gilles's *The Last Myth* is relevant here; it has a chapter, "The Apocalypse Will Take a Little While," on what we might term slow apocalypses, where the end of the world as we know it happens gradually instead of with a single earth-changing event (123–64).

If the course is centered on apocalypse, I assign this chapter as we move to Butler, but the concept works without the book in hand. *The Last Myth* also includes a chapter (165–84 ["In Defense of a Worldview"]) on psychological research into terror management theory and worldview defense—sometimes termed mortality salience—which offers interpretive help for the refusal of Lauren's community to accept the growing crisis. Introducing terror management theory allows me to integrate another scientific approach to the discussion, although it does not directly contribute to the writing assignment described in this essay.

When we've established a clear understanding of the features of Butler's dystopian near-future world, I ask students to select one dystopian thread out of the list that they would like to research and use resources such as archived newspapers (*Proquest* has good news databases) to establish the conditions to which Butler was responding. For publishable research a scholar might prefer greater clarity on the specific sources Butler accessed—she references National Public Radio, for instance ("Conversation" 339)—but for the purposes of a first-year writing course, newspapers such as *The Washington Post* and *The New York Times* help establish the general tenor of the public conversation in the late 1980s and early 1990s, when Butler was drafting the novel. Reading archived materials, students narrow the distance between their horizon of expectation and Butler's. I then ask them to research the current state of their thread to determine if we are still on the trajectory that Butler envisioned.

For this project, I require a proposal with a brief list of resources so I can be sure that each student has found a sufficiently meaty topic. Sometimes I need to help a student consider the modern iteration of a thread more carefully. Butler's pyro, after all, is not a drug in our real world, nor does its effect—sexual arousal around the presence of fire—match well with real-world drug addictions. But the complete disregard it generates in users for the well-being of others as well as its rapid spread across the country are characteristic of several drugs, meth particularly, and may have been drawn from discussions in the press, when Butler was writing, about crack cocaine. Similarly, although the novel's privatization of the police is generally not replicated in our world, the move to private prisons (and the controversy surrounding them) does apply. Public schools have not closed down, but the attitude toward them and toward the tax burden of maintaining them resonates with the story's assertion that Lauren, although she is the daughter of college professors, cannot possibly afford college tuition. The privatization of space research seems well under way, with the recent successes of SpaceX as an example. Students have argued in favor of or against this development—in part, I suspect, because my university is heavily involved in NASA-based research. When I first began assigning this project some ten years ago, students often discounted the novel's depiction of climate change as alarmist; more recently, students point to the drought and fires in California and suggest that Butler's time line was more conservative than it might have been. This kind of research demonstrates the accuracy of Butler's predictions and shows students that science fiction can help us anticipate futures we might wish to avoid.

Looking at Butler through an interdisciplinary lens offers valuable opportunities for students to engage with the different ways in which science enters public discourse. It also enables instructors to expose students to more humanities-oriented modes of inquiry. I assign writing and engage in classroom discussions that focus on science, yet in the process I have the opportunity to address issues of race, gender, and power so critical to Butler's work and to the study of literature more broadly. I also can introduce students to science fiction centered on biology, psychology, and sociology, reminding them that science has many faces—a fact that many students find surprising and even exciting to see reflected in fiction. Such interdisciplinary work speaks to the issues that mattered to Butler and shows how science and fiction are balanced in science fiction—and how Butler excelled at that balance.

"My Books Will Be Read by Millions of People!": The LaGuardia Community College Octavia E. Butler Project on *Wikipedia*

Ximena Gallardo C. and Ann Matsuuchi

> You got to make your own worlds. You got to write yourself in. Whether you were a part of the greater society or not, you got to write yourself in. So I got to write myself in.
>
> —Octavia E. Butler

On 3 March 2014 we announced to a class of twenty-eight second-year community college students that they had twelve weeks to become experts on Octavia E. Butler's best-selling novel *Kindred* so that they could compose a research essay on it and redraft its *Wikipedia* entry. Not surprisingly, the students responded with bewilderment mixed with a slight panic. "*Wikipedia*?," a brave soul finally blurted out. "But our teachers have told us not to use *Wikipedia*!"

But in recent years academic suspicion of "the free encyclopedia that anyone can edit"[1] has metamorphosed into enthusiastic and transformative scholarly engagement.[2] *Wikipedia* projects can be found in a range of traditional, established locations: in college classrooms at Harvard, Barnard, and the University of Chicago; at the Museum of Modern Art, which has hosted the globally recognized Art+Feminism *Wikipedia* edit-a-thon for Women's History Month since 2014; and even at the National Archives and Records Administration, which has installed a *Wikipedia* Discovery Center within its walls.

Our single-class trial working on *Wikipedia*'s article for *Kindred* was so successful that it encouraged us to create the LaGuardia WikiProject Octavia E. Butler, a collaborative effort of undergraduates, Butler specialists, and volunteer *Wikipedia* editors to craft thorough, rigorously researched, well-written encyclopedic entries for Butler's fiction. Since then, two more teams of LaGuardia Community College students have collaborated in revising the *Wikipedia* articles for the novels *Fledgling* and *Wild Seed* as well as composing an authoritative biographical entry for Butler. In February 2016, a meeting of Butler scholars and Spelman College honors students contributed to the project by creating and revising the articles for the novels that compose the Patternist series—*Patternmaster*, *Mind of My Mind*, *Survivor*, *Wild Seed*, and *Clay's Ark*—during a three-hour *Wikipedia* edit-a-thon hosted by the Octavia E. Butler Society and Spelman College. Efforts continued, and a new group of LaGuardia undergraduates recently expanded the entry for *"Bloodchild" and Other Stories*, a collection of Butler's short stories and essays.

In this essay we discuss the goals, methods, and outcomes of the LaGuardia WikiProject Octavia E. Butler as it stands now, at the beginning of what we hope becomes a series of *Wikipedia* featured articles on Butler.[3] We explain why we chose to make *Wikipedia*, an environment generally dismissed by college professors and generally considered inappropriate in the college classroom, the center of our Butler pedagogy. We share what we learned from aligning the specific academic objectives of a research class on Butler to the goals of the *Wikipedia* community.

Project Goals; or, Why Wikipedia?

The overall goal we set for our students was for them to become experts on a Butler work, and that is why we fixed our sights on working in the English-language *Wikipedia*. Contributing to this online encyclopedia would require students to gain both a broad and an in-depth understanding of Butler and her work.

Editing *Wikipedia* is an outstanding instance of experiential learning, as the process requires students to shift from, as one of the edit-a-thon student participants at Spelman observed, being knowledge consumers to being knowledge creators on the Internet. Throughout, they are supported by a community of smart, caring, helpful, and sophisticated people. Editing *Wikipedia* implements and practices what we have come to refer to as twenty-first-century writing, which is Web-based, social, and collaborative, a work in perpetual progress, immediately visible and thus prompting instant feedback, and easily available and accessible. In its environment students can experience the pleasure and pain of real-world publication.

Wikipedia supplies us with a key Butler teaching moment at the beginning of the semester. As we introduce the encyclopedia's notability guidelines, we discuss the reasons for and consequences of its clear, if incidental, systemic bias: certain topics, groups, and even cultures are not yet adequately represented in its English-language version.[4] We then explain the need for WikiProjects such as ours. While a substantial number of scholars, critics, and fans would agree that Butler's work is central not just to the speculative, feminist, and African American communities but to the whole of American culture and perhaps the world, a quick browsing of archived *Wikipedia* pages reveals that before the LaGuardia WikiProject began in 2014, entries for her work were woefully underdeveloped, incorrect, and, in some cases (for instance, before the Spelman College edit-a-thon created the articles for *Mind of My Mind* and *Clay's Ark*), nonexistent.

Butler's marginal coverage in the world's most popular encyclopedia strikes a familiar chord with our students, many of whom strongly identify with her life experiences as a black, female, working-class person who attended public school and a community college. They want to rectify that deficiency, especially after they learn about her unwavering resolve to live under her own terms against enormous odds—and to make herself visible through her work. As Butler explained in a PBS interview when the journalist Charlie Rose asked her what it was about writing that was so important to her growing sense of self, "You got to make your own worlds. You got to write yourself in. Whether you were a part of the greater society or not, you got to write yourself in. So I got to write myself in." Her clear-eyed understanding of the determination it takes for those on the margins to claim a place in the human story best describes why we urge our students to become active participants in *Wikipedia*'s knowledge-sharing project: to write Butler, as well as themselves, into the greater society represented in "the free encyclopedia that anyone can edit." One of the reasons for the lack of diversity among *Wikipedia* contributors and topics is the message constantly being sent and that we sometimes repeat to ourselves as women and as people of color, "You're not an expert. You don't know enough. You are an impostor." We tell our students: Sure, much of the information on *Wikipedia* is quite appropriate and useful, but much remains undone, and much needs to be improved. If we understand who Butler was and what she was all about, we must write that in. Thus students learn that the solitary act of writing can involve a larger responsibility of collective participation.

Methods

ENG103 at LaGuardia Community College is a composition and research course whose objective is to teach students to collect, analyze, and use sources as well as to develop ideas by drafting, revising, citing, and documenting sources; by critiquing; and by editing final drafts. We kept this objective for the LaGuardia WikiProject, and the end product was the same: a thesis-based research paper. But we turned some of the individual drafting into collective editing of discrete sections of a *Wikipedia* entry on a specific Butler work. Students therefore became experts on that work in two ways: critically for the individual research essay and inventorially for the collaborative encyclopedic entry.

In practice, the course approach and the WikiProject approach generated very different observations and discussions about the texts at hand. A class conversation focused on finding provocative arguments about "The Book of Martha" for the research essay, for example, may dwell on how the writing of this story adds to the biblical canon or on the possible symbolism behind God's metamorphoses during the story. When working on the *Wikipedia* entry for the same story an hour later, a small group will engage in a long debate as to which events should or should not be included in the "Plot" section of "The Book of Martha" or what quotations best represent the key ideas in the story, while a second group will be busy encapsulating the public response to the story by aggregating and organizing the reviews of multiple critics for the article's "Reception" section. These intense negotiations on material that is normally glossed over as background information in the traditional research classroom make students aware of aspects of the story they had not previously considered.

Students also analyze a variety of contextual information normally deemed inconsequential in the research classroom. They pore over book reviews, reflecting on the importance, for instance, of the novelist Junot Diaz's declaring *Fledgling* his book of the year ("Books"); puzzle over types of literary awards (What is a Nebula Award, and who have been other recipients of it?); discuss the implications of publishing data, such as the fact that half a million copies of *Kindred* have been sold since it was first published in 1979; and consider how Butler's work is further disseminated through community events, such as the 2003 "If All of Rochester Read the Same Book" three-day program centered on *Kindred* or the adaptation of *Parable of the Sower* into an opera by the American folk-blues musician Toshi Reagon.

Most current educational projects on *Wikipedia* reproduce the format of traditional research classes: each student chooses an article whose topic the student then investigates and expands. In contrast, our classroom dynamic emulates the type of community that *Wikipedia* is and wants to be: a collection of editors creating a product through collaboration and negotiation.[5] Instructors serve as coordinators and guides (Ximena serves as editor-in-chief, while Ann provides integrated and ongoing information and digital literacy instruction) as students propose revisions, vote on the content of an entry, and contribute to it according to their academic strengths. Some students are at their best when paraphrasing from scholarly work; some, when copyediting; some, when using wiki markup to code special features of the article, such as framed quotations. As they move through groups and editing tasks, they learn about different aspects and critical viewpoints on Butler's fiction and begin developing their own arguments, which they then use to craft the research essay.

Issues

Our students have little trouble comprehending and enjoying Butler's fiction. Their struggle begins when they are required to grasp and rephrase scholarly articles for both their essays and the "Themes" section of the *Wikipedia* article. The difficulty lies partly in their language level—for a large percentage of the LaGuardia student body, English is a second language—and partly in the fact that undergraduates are not the target audience of most academic articles. Many scholars plunge into their arguments with little preamble, assuming that their readership has a clear grasp of the theory behind their analysis or of the sociohistorical circumstances surrounding Butler's authorial choices. When the protagonist of *Wild Seed*, Anyanwu, was pronounced by several academics a fictional representation of Donna Haraway's cyborg identity, a substantial portion of class time had to be spent explaining Haraway's ideas in "A Cyborg Manifesto." The interests of Butler scholars, then, tend to determine the direction of classwork, because the students' job is to understand their arguments and render them as accurately as possible for the encyclopedia.

Thus it is not strange that sections of an article end up echoing the specialized language of a scholarly text, which makes the piece hard to understand for

Wikipedia's general readership. A typical example of this issue can be found in the current version of the article for *Wild Seed*. Unable to adequately paraphrase Stacy Alaimo's argument explaining Anyanwu as a representation of cyborg identity, the group in charge of the section chose to quote heavily:

> Stacy Alaimo further argues that Butler uses the "utterly embodied" Anyanwu not just to counteract Doro's "horrific Cartesian subjectivity" but to actually transgress the dichotomy between mind and body, as Anyanwu is capable of "reading" other bodies with her own. As such, she illustrates Haraway's concept of "situated knowledge," wherein the subject (knower) does not distance itself from the object (known) and thus offers an alternative way of experiencing the world. Anyanwu's body, then, is a "liminal space" that blurs traditional divisions of the world into "nature" and "culture." ("*Wild Seed* (novel)")

Awkward if useful passages such as this one are what make the LaGuardia WikiProject Octavia E. Butler a work in progress. We hope that it will continue to be improved by future editors.

Outcomes

Perhaps the most important outcome for us is that our students gain both a broad and a deep understanding of Butler's fiction. Instead of approaching it from a single and narrow point of view—the one they have chosen or been told to argue with the support of scholarly sources—students should become acquainted with all manner of perspectives and weigh the value of each. Their *Wikipedia* entries give evidence of their mastery of the material; two outstanding examples are the article for *Kindred* and the article on Butler's life, career, and achievements.

The many practical conversations as to what is key, what should be included, what information to give about a plot (sometimes students are strongly against including spoilers), or what Butler scholars see as the text's place in culture, history, and literature obviously enrich the students' explorations in their research essays. But often students declare themselves more invested in their teamwork than in their research paper, which they consider a throwaway assignment—a means to a grade rather than a valuable artifact in itself. This high level of student engagement with the encyclopedic entry seems to be true of most *Wikipedia* projects (Roth et al.) and probably derives from the students' knowledge that their collective work will be read and referenced by many for a long time. Work on *Wikipedia* has motivated students to continue to invest in the project outside the classroom by, for example, volunteering to present on their experiences at the 2014 and 2015 meetings of Wikimedia Conference USA.[6]

Another benefit of the project is the increased visibility of and access to Butler's universe in the world's most consulted encyclopedia, which should increase global awareness of her work, especially since critical studies of her fiction are contained in the paywalled databases of academia and thus available only to a privileged minority of the population who have access. Consider the *Wikipedia* article on her novel *Kindred*. Before we began our work, the article was glaringly incomplete and had only three short online interviews as its references. By the end of the semester, it contained a detailed and accurate plot as well as an overview of eight of its major themes, background of the novel's development and publishing history, a public reaction section, and a references section containing forty-seven separate secondary sources, most of them linked to an online version of their content (fig. 1).

The article as our students left it may still be built on, but visitors to *Wikipedia* from all over the world now have a reasonably accurate and reliable starting point to learn about or begin their research on *Kindred*. At the time of this writing, the *Kindred* article is viewed 310 times a day.

LaGuardia undergraduates are keenly aware that by creating well-researched and accurate encyclopedic material on Butler's fiction and posting it to the free Web, they not only give Butler the greater exposure she deserves but also pro-

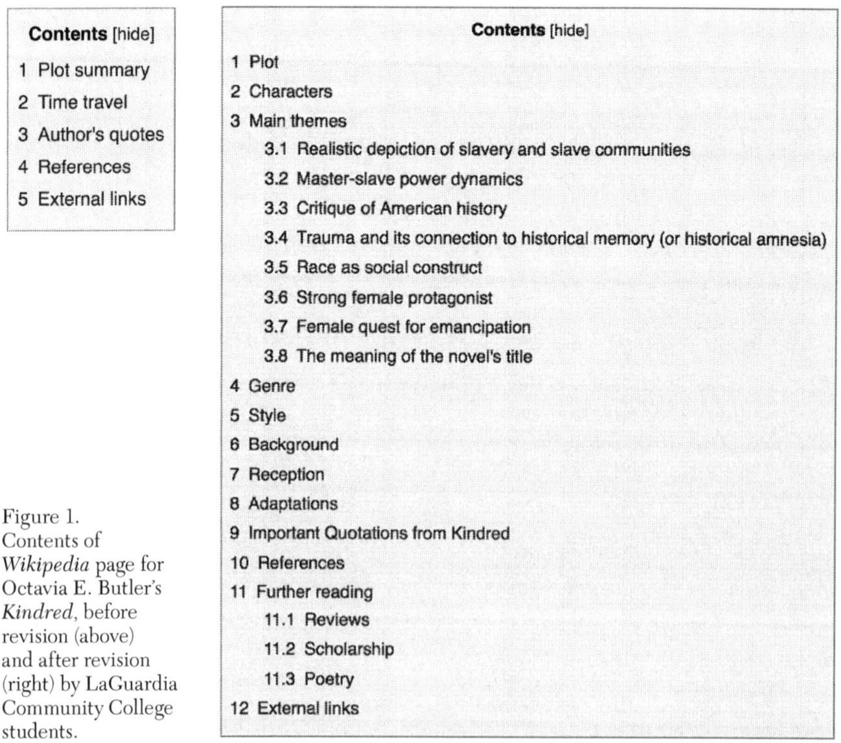

Contents [hide]

1 Plot summary
2 Time travel
3 Author's quotes
4 References
5 External links

Contents [hide]

1 Plot
2 Characters
3 Main themes
  3.1 Realistic depiction of slavery and slave communities
  3.2 Master-slave power dynamics
  3.3 Critique of American history
  3.4 Trauma and its connection to historical memory (or historical amnesia)
  3.5 Race as social construct
  3.6 Strong female protagonist
  3.7 Female quest for emancipation
  3.8 The meaning of the novel's title
4 Genre
5 Style
6 Background
7 Reception
8 Adaptations
9 Important Quotations from Kindred
10 References
11 Further reading
  11.1 Reviews
  11.2 Scholarship
  11.3 Poetry
12 External links

Figure 1. Contents of *Wikipedia* page for Octavia E. Butler's *Kindred*, before revision (above) and after revision (right) by LaGuardia Community College students.

vide an important channel of access to the scholarship on her. We suggest that it is this awareness of their responsibility in disseminating knowledge properly that motivates them to do the best work possible for the entry (while maybe putting less effort into their college papers). Students feel that the fate of Butler's work is intimately connected to their ability to present it to the world.

The Future . . . ?

The parameters of the Wikipedia Project Octavia E. Butler strike some of our colleagues as ambitious, especially because this enterprise is currently centered on a single research class for community college undergraduates. Our reply is that if those of us, students and teachers as well as fans, who understand the value of Butler's writings do not take an active role in shaping the future development of online knowledge-sharing spaces, the significance of her work, especially its challenge to hierarchical and patriarchal attitudes, will not be preserved. We therefore invite all Butler teacher-scholars and their classes to join us in the effort of creating accurate and useful content about Butler's work on the free Web.

NOTES

[1] From *Wikipedia*'s welcome message on its main page.

[2] To give an idea of the extent of educational work on *Wikipedia*, in the spring of 2018 alone, 8,340 students in 400 courses added 6.7 million words to the encyclopedia, created 703 articles, and edited 9,000 more. For more information on educational WikiProjects, visit the Wiki Education dashboard at dashboard.wikiedu.org.

[3] A *Wikipedia* featured article must fulfill *Wikipedia*'s criteria for accuracy, neutrality, completeness, and style (including the use of media) and is distinguished by professional standards in writing, presentation, and sourcing. For particulars as well as examples of featured articles, see "Wikipedia: Featured Article Criteria" (en.wikipedia.org/wiki/Wikipedia:Featured_article_criteria) and "Wikipedia: Featured Articles" (en.wikipedia.org/wiki/Wikipedia:Featured_articles).

[4] For more details on *Wikipedia*'s systemic bias, see "Wikipedia: Systemic Bias" (en.wikipedia.org/wiki/Wikipedia:Systemic_bias) and "Wikipedia: WikiProject Countering Systemic Bias" (en.wikipedia.org/wiki/Wikipedia:WikiProject_Countering_systemic_bias).

[5] For information on *Wikipedia*'s commons-based peer production model, see Cummings.

[6] For details of student participation, see "Wikifying."

The Politics of Living Together: Butler's Short Stories and Teaching Political Philosophy

Claire P. Curtis

"There was trouble aboard the Washington Boulevard bus," writes Octavia Butler in the opening of "Speech Sounds." "Rye had expected trouble sooner or later in her journey. She had put off going until loneliness and hopelessness drove her out" (89). My introductory political philosophy students are well primed to think about trouble and hopelessness after spending a week talking about Hobbes and a state of nature that is "nasty, brutish and short" (76). Butler's story of a woman in search of surviving family members in a postapocalyptic Los Angeles seems to capture the conditions of life that Hobbes describes as prepolitical. "There was no more LAPD, no more any large organization, governmental or private. There were neighborhood patrols and armed individuals. That was all" (92). But while this story seems at first glance to be a fictionalized representation of Hobbes's state of nature, which is equally fictional, on closer reading it reveals a space for both understanding and then critiquing all three classical social-contract thinkers: Hobbes, Locke, and Rousseau.

I have used works of fiction in Introduction to Political Thought for many years. Focusing solely on the abstract arguments of long-dead political philosophers often left students disoriented and disengaged. Works of fiction, however, place students in a fictional world where those abstract ideas come to life. Stories provide experimental spaces for testing hypotheses about how and why we live together. Fiction gives students the freedom to think through a "What if?" with a common set of characters living under a common set of conditions.

But it was difficult for me to find just the right works of fiction. Initially I used works contemporary to the political philosophers we were reading: Greek tragedy with Plato, Voltaire's *Candide* with the social-contract thinkers. Then I shifted to using only one novel at the end of every semester: Ursula Le Guin's *The Lathe of Heaven* provided an extended exploration of thinking about better worlds.

These choices worked, but each had its own problem. Many of the older texts were hard to read and so did not solve the problem of student disorientation. Others were too long, so that doing justice to them took too much time. Finishing the class with a novel was interesting, but it left most of the semester without the kind of experimental space that I want the works of fiction to provide.

For the last seven years I have used what I now consider to be the best option, Butler's *"Bloodchild" and Other Stories* (the second edition, which includes both "Amnesty" and "The Book of Martha"). This collection has proved ideal for several reasons. First, the short story is the right length for students to read and digest for a single class. Second, these particular stories are political in just the way that I ask students to think. If politics is, as Michael Oakeshott contended, deliberation over the conditions under which we desire to live (183–84), then these stories all engage in political deliberations under a shifting set of backgrounds. They prime students to think about how the external conditions of living, some of which can and some of which cannot be changed, affect deliberation about how to live together. Third and most important, Butler's writing, scenarios, and characters all engage students, giving them ways of connecting the larger themes of the course to their own lives.

Introduction to Political Thought is a daunting title for a 100-level political science class required of majors. Students rarely come into the class with an understanding of what the content will be. Unlike the empirical questions asked in most political science classes, in political philosophy we are asking normative questions—questions not about how things are but about how they should be arranged. Political science as a discipline understands itself mainly as describing and predicting the world, but political thought is interested in imagining the world from different perspectives. How can a group of people with disparate aims and interests live together peacefully?

To address this question, introductory political philosophy classes typically assign texts from a familiar set of historically influential political philosophers; we read Plato, Hobbes, Locke, Rousseau, Mill, Marx, and Rawls. My version of the class is structured around Plato's *Republic*, which we read over the course of the entire semester, using the themes of each book as openings for the other political philosophers to enter into the conversation. We discuss why we live together rather than apart, how living together can be made legitimate, the limits of governmental power, and the concepts of freedom, equality, justice, and obligation.

These matters are all abstract, but Butler's stories reframe them around specific scenarios and characters. What if aliens arrived who were stronger than we were but not interested in destroying us ("Amnesty")? How would this situation alter human self-understanding? What if a plague wiped out many people and our ability to communicate effectively with one another ("Speech Sounds")? Could we still learn to live together peacefully? What if an unexpected side effect of a cancer drug was to produce children who could both destroy themselves and solve many of humanity's problems ("The Evening and the Morning and the Night")? Would that change our understanding of obligation and free choice? What if human beings escaped to a faraway planet where the alien species needed organisms for gestation ("Bloodchild")? How would we balance our freedom with the need to survive? What if God came to someone and asked what change should be made to humanity ("The Book of Martha")? Would dreaming one's best life facilitate peaceful living together?

I assign these stories throughout the semester, choosing each to intersect with arguments we have already been discussing in the theoretical texts. We read "Speech Sounds" after spending two weeks on Hobbes, Locke, and Rousseau and discuss how these modern social-contract thinkers imagine the ways and reasons we live together, following Plato's discussion of the same issue in book 2 of the *Republic*. Each social-contract theorist offers a description of life in the state of nature and the motivations that that life gives us to move from the state of nature to civil society by means of a social contract. But their accounts vary. For Hobbes, there is violence in the state of nature, because we are all equal and we desire the same things—primarily we desire to survive. Our shared dislike of this violence prompts us to come together and appoint someone whose job it will be to make and enforce rules to guarantee peace. By contrast, Locke's state of nature is largely peaceful and productive, but because the bad apples of the group make living without rules time-consuming and troubling, we agree to set up a system of government based on our consent to rulers who will work to improve our community. Finally, Rousseau sees us as able to live peacefully in nature but also recognizes that life in nature is not fulfilling for human beings. So he has us move from the pastoral simplicity of nature to the mature freedom of obeying rules that we give to ourselves (with a detour through the illegitimate chains of living together without consent).

These different accounts depend on different understandings of human nature. For Hobbes and Locke we are naturally equal, free, and rational. For Hobbes, we are motivated to move from the state of nature to civil society through fear; for Locke, through a desire to accumulate and protect resources. Rousseau inverts this: we are in nature unequal and not civilly or morally free, and so we are motivated, in part, to achieve both equality (under the law) and freedom (to give ourselves the rules we must obey) by entering civil society. Though they are ordered in different ways, the concepts of rationality, freedom, and equality are essential to all three social-contract thinkers' descriptions of human beings.

Butler's story allows us to pursue an important critique of these concepts. We can begin with its seemingly Hobbesian setting: a postapocalyptic Los Angeles, three years after a virus of unknown origin has killed most of the people and left the survivors with impaired speech or reading abilities. The central character, Valerie Rye, leaves her home in Los Angeles to go to Pasadena, where her brothers once lived. The trouble on her bus ride is a fight, which is stopped with tear gas by a man named Obsidian. Rye notes that he stands back, observing, when the bus driver gestures angrily about his bus. "The least impaired people tended to this—stand back unless they were physically threatened and let those with less control scream and jump around" (93). The opening pages set a scene of impending violence that those with more control hope to avoid. One passage from the story that many students choose to discuss comes after Rye gets in the car with Obsidian and realizes that he can read. She falls into a fit of rage that makes her consider murder: "Abruptly, she hated him—deep, bitter hatred. What did literacy mean to him—a grown up man who played cops and robbers? But he was literate and she was not" (98). She does not kill him—"her rage crested and ebbed and she did nothing" (99)—but instead asks him to come home with her.

Many students reject Rye's emotional response, understanding her jealousy of Obsidian's ability to read as itself a sign of what has broken down in this society. For them the story becomes a kind of morality play: they read Butler as warning that without rational rules and the ability to effectively communicate, the Hobbesian state of nature will be violent. Here students are mirroring a common move in Western political thought, prizing rationality over emotion. But this reading turns out to be hard to sustain, and our class discussions quickly reveal how the story fails to support the idea that jealousy is the root of human instability.

First, the misreading of Butler follows from a misreading of Hobbes, that he is blaming human nature, and particularly human motivations like jealousy, for violence. In this view, it is not the the state of nature that is bad but humanity itself. But Hobbes is clear that "the desires and other passions of man are in themselves no sin" (77). Without a law that clearly states an action to be wrong, human beings cannot be held responsible for the actions that follow from their passions.

Second, if the story were merely a perpetuation of a misreading of Hobbes, then we would expect to see confirmation that jealousy is the root of human violence and a resolution that makes communication the key to solving that jealousy. The scene at the end of the story, where an unnamed man murders an unnamed woman and Rye finds the woman's two children still capable of speech, offers such a resolution. But it is Rye who speculates about the man's reasons for murdering the woman, and that speculation is not supported independently. More important, Rye decides to bring the children home, after wrestling morally about whether to do so, before she learns that the children can speak. So her own actions reject the Hobbesian reading of human nature.

More compelling as a justification for Rye's decision to accept responsibility for the young children is a Rousseauian reading, in which she decides to leave the state of nature through her decision to act in the way she knows is right. She was going to leave the children where they were—"they were old enough to scavenge. She did not need any more grief" (105)—but instead felt that "there had been enough dying" (106). Near the end of the story, she imagines a different future, one where a person like herself, a "teacher and protector" (107), could raise these children, and possibly also children unable to speak, in a world different from the hopeless one in which she has been living. Students often turn to the end of the story to make a version of Rousseau's argument that fulfilling an obligation that you recognize as your own is needed to live peacefully with others. Rye, in this reading, is freed from the chains of living with the man across the street, who "had made it clear that he wanted Rye to become his third woman" (96), simply by resolving to live her life differently.

This hopeful reading of "Speech Sounds" seems to be in the spirit of the social-contract thinkers, who all believe that human beings make decisions to change the circumstances under which they live, thereby creating a system of legitimate governance. But it ignores the persistent dread that the conditions of the story create. I ask my students what they assume will happen in the next ten days, ten weeks, or ten years after the end of the story.

One cannot fail to see that life after the end of the story will be influenced by the degrees of impairment suffered by the people living in postapocalyptic Los Angeles. Martha Nussbaum criticizes the social-contract thinkers for claiming that it is advantageous to everyone in the state of nature, because everyone is equal, to enter into the social contract, which establishes rules to prevent violence and protect property. But what if everyone is not equal? In theory, mutual advantage depends on human equality, but more likely it is decided by those who come to the table to make the contract, so the advantage will not be for everyone.

To whom would the contract not be advantageous? Consider the conditions Butler has created: a virus that has affected people differently, killing some, depriving some of speech (Obsidian) and some of literacy (Rye) and some of both. Rye notes that people are not impaired to the same degree and observes how the less impaired stand back and how the more impaired perceive this as "an attitude of superiority." "Such 'superiority' was frequently punished by beatings, even by death" (93). In her world there are children, a group that she initially rejects as having "no future" (101), and presumably there are the elderly (although absent from the text of the story), those who have had accidents or were injured in fights or came down with other illnesses that would be prevalent in a world like that of the story: cholera, typhus, infection.

A contract for peace would seem to be beneficial to all those who have fewer abilities than Rye and Obsidian. But why would those at the table agree to a contract for those whose impairments would cause them to gain more than they could contribute? "If people are making a cooperative arrangement for mutual advantage," then mutual advantage would demand that each party sees a potential gain to be made from the other party and would avoid "those who will demand unusual and expensive attention . . ." (Nussbaum 104). Hobbes, Locke, and Rousseau have no place in their theory for those who are not equal. Butler's story makes clear both the fact that the state of nature includes wide varieties of people and that the possibility of any agreement to live together peacefully will have to address everyone.

"Speech Sounds" reveals the folly of imagining that we live under only one theory of human motivation or one understanding of justice and obligation. The story at first presents what seems to be a Hobbesian world of violence. But it also reveals Lockean motivations for personal betterment in the absence of any system of rules—for example, the bus driver who uses pictures of goods he will accept in exchange for a ride on his bus (94). It suggests Rousseauean motivations to live one's life as a person willing to accept obligations, as when Rye accepts responsibility for raising the two young children. But the story can be read as going beyond these readings to put forward a disability studies criticism of the social contract itself.

No single understanding of either the state of nature or the human desire to create community can make sense of this story. Instead, students have to sift through the differing theories and then read the story to find moments of parallelism and moments of divergence. They then have to decide for themselves whether this narrative of moving from the state of nature through consent to civil society—a narrative that has been particularly influential in the political tradition of the United States—is in fact useful for answering the question of how human beings can live peacefully together. Butler's story encourages students to mix and match ideas about human motivations and to be skeptical about the arguments of the social-contract tradition.

Unchained: Using Butler to Upend How We Teach the History of Slavery

Amy Absher

One day, I prompted class discussion by asking the students to consider, in pairs, the following question:

> Maya Angelou, in *A Song Flung Up to Heaven*, asked, "How did it happen that we could nurse a nation of strangers, be maids to multitudes of people who scorned us, and still walk with some majesty and stand with a degree of pride?" How might Octavia Butler, given her writing style and presentation of the African American experience, have rephrased this question?

To answer it, the students needed to think like Butler.

I was teaching a humanities course on slavery. One of my goals was to have the students link and compare the past with the present. Butler's use of time travel and alien abduction, in her novels *Kindred* and *Dawn* as well as in her short story collection *"Blood Child,"* provided the basis for the class to imagine those connections. In asking the students to consider Butler's work, I was asking them to challenge their previously held beliefs concerning slavery.

One student suggested that Butler would not have asked, "How did it happen that we could nurse a nation of strangers . . . ?," because she was concerned more with the present and the future than with the past. He argued that in *Kindred* she always brings the conflict back to the present. Other students disagreed, pointing out that, by asking largely the same question but changing the *us* and *we* pronouns to *I* and *me*, Butler was always trying to force readers into her stories so that they could experience the situations and conflicts firsthand. Still other students said that she would have asked not a "how" question but a "why" question, because everyone knew how people became enslaved; what was needed was an explanation of what enabled the enslaved to live lives of dignity. The last group felt that her question would have been about the past, present, and future.

As a science fiction and fantasy author, Butler spent her career giving voice to the enslaved by recovering their experience and conveying it to readers through the lens of imagined and symbolic worlds. My class was an undergraduate humanities seminar, of twenty students from various majors, that took up the history of American slavery, usually called chattel slavery, and juxtaposed it with the various forms of modern slavery—debt peonage, sex trafficking, and the enslavement of refugees, for example. Had it not been for the presence of Butler's work, the syllabus would have been a standard history or international affairs course. With Butler, we could move beyond the historical.

According to conventional scholarly wisdom, marching in a straight line from past to present makes the past appear flawed and the present enlightened. Moving thematically instead of chronologically allows us to compare more and challenge the Western custom of seeing cause and effect as linear, but then we lose the sense of change over time. Butler invites us to treat time as flexible so that topics and eras touch one another, which undermines our linear view of history and in particular our deeply held beliefs about slavery. With her, we became time travelers who contemplated what was, what is, and what we hoped would never be.

I realize I am proposing an unconventional and problematic pedagogy. After all, isn't the study of history all about chronology and evolution? When we study history, aren't we bound by concepts of change over time and by causality? Normally I would agree, but with the study of slavery we are seeking to dislodge white superiority and the dominance of Western concepts, which are the traditions that gave us the linear study of history. The study of slavery requires a different approach, one that will seem ahistorical to some, messy to others. In fact this course was difficult and took a great deal of planning.

Teaching the Class

Discussion and writing were the primary tools in the course for arriving at understanding. Class time moved between the students' writing discussion questions and their working in groups of two or three to answer a question. One involved the quotation from Angelou (211), with which this essay began; another asked students to consider this:

> In African American literature, and African American history for that matter, there are things, ideas, and people that are so obvious, and yet somehow they are treated as though they were invisible. Think about the primary character in *Invisible Man* surrounding himself with lightbulbs so that he will be seen [Ellison 13]. Other examples you might be familiar with are the hauntings at the center of *Beloved* and even violent acts like rape in *I Know Why the Caged Bird Sings* and *The Color Purple*. If we have to, we could name this literary device "the hypervisibility of the invisible." Given what you have read in *Kindred*, how and why does Octavia Butler draw on this authors' tool?

There were many ideas put forth that day in class, but the idea that had the most staying power throughout the remainder of the semester was that the hypervisible invisible were the slaves themselves: the slaves were so obvious that people stopped seeing or acknowledging them. We reached this insight only by combining literature with history.

We took our comparative approach further by moving among history, literature, and current events. The students found that discussing the literature gave them the vocabulary to describe the worst atrocities in history and that their literary analysis gave them ideas about current events that went beyond pity.

A humanities education concerns more than being able to read critically. We want the students to discuss the larger questions: What does it mean to be human? Is there free will? How do we arrive at truth? Such questions can be comforting in that they provide distance between the students and the difficult topics they study. But students should not leave class at the end of the semester feeling that oppression is far away and has no bearing on their lives. They should understand that they are not safe.

Students Challenging the Conventional Narrative

When we teach students the analytical skills to critique and challenge accepted knowledge, we first ask them to consider what they know. At the start of the semester, I asked my students to brainstorm their knowledge and ideas about slavery. They explained they were taught that states' rights, not slavery, was the reason for the American Civil War. They were aware of human trafficking, a kind of slavery today, but did not realize that it was a problem in Cleveland, where they were living and going to school. They were unfamiliar with debt peonage and the other forms of involuntary servitude. They thought that slavery might apply to their own lives, because they felt the burden of school debt and saw their lives after college as the servitude of working to pay off that debt.

As our class progressed, we encountered various forms of slavery from chattel slavery to the experience of labor in a time of genocide. We asked what slavery was and if there was a difference between old and new slavery. My students concluded that slavery was difficult to define, because it took many forms.

One student thought that the similarities between different forms of slavery required that we understand slavery not as a line or continuum from slavery to freedom but as a wheel: "when the wheel is turned, elements of old slavery [lead to those of] new slavery . . . [and] elements of new slavery [point to those of] old slavery." The student understood that at its core slavery is an "economic system under which people are treated as property." This reason for oppression unifies our understanding of slavery, yet the wheel still turns, because economic and legal systems change. This understanding of slavery is very different from the history he learned in school. His notion of a wheel meant that American slavery did not end with the Civil War. The student concluded Butler had helped him realize that there are no straight lines.

Another student described Butler's presentation of the master-owner as the "trope of the parasite, the host, and the symbiont." She argued that this trope figured "prominently in Butler's science fiction, much of which is fundamentally engaged with survival and adaptation of otherness in both the physical and personal spheres." What the master-owner wanted was to survive and reproduce. Because survival depended on creating hybridity, the student decided that it was a mistake to see Butler's work as being about slavery. It was actually about survival. One group exploited, and another group made the choice between resistance, death, and being exploited. "In this context, infection and contagion must be navigated and coped with, as must hierarchies and violent drives," the student wrote. But my student was not sympathizing with the slaveholder-parasite. Rather, she was trying to understand the choice that Dana, the protagonist from *Kindred*, and Lilith, the protagonist from *Dawn*, made when they submitted to the master-owner. If we were to see Dana and Lilith through the lens of slavery, they would become overseers facilitating rape and genocide. The student acknowledged that this was troubling but observed that Butler's work is complex and should be appreciated for its containing many perspectives.

Another student came away with a different perspective on slavery. He felt *Kindred* asked this crucial question: "See how easily slaves are made?" "Butler forces the reader to look at American slavery," he argued, because she "creates the hypervisibility in her novel" by highlighting "the everyday lives of the slaves and contrasting them with a modern-day perspective." Therefore we are forced "to see what would not otherwise be observable." "When society expects certain ideals and they are followed without any hesitation," this student wrote, "the masters become slaves to their own ways." His classmates agreed, feeling that we all are slaves to our bodies' desire to exist and survive.

Butler develops the invisibility of her slave characters, the student further noted, by using the passive voice. In *Dawn*, the passive voice reveals the aliens' attempt to create invisibility, in this case regarding the original human DNA, in order to erase all traces of humanity from the survivors. Lilith appears to choose to help the aliens. But the student believes that she has no real choice: survival on Earth is impossible because of the devastation of atomic warfare.

Even more troubling to my students than the question of identity in slavery was the constant reappearance, some might say hypervisibility, of rape in Butler's writing. The students were struggling through a semester when campus sexual assaults were in the news and their own campus community was meeting to define *consent*. Rape in "Bloodchild" and *Dawn* therefore took on extra emphasis. Can there be true consent in an asymmetrical relationship? If one consents to intercourse to save another from rape, is that consensual sex? Does a person always have free will?

One student chose to write her final paper on this section of the class reading and discussion. As she explained it, "The survival of the main character in each of Butler's three tales *Dawn*, 'Bloodchild,' and *Kindred* is contingent on the symbiotic relationship between the two races of beings." Scholars share this point of view, but the student diverged from them by refusing to see the characters as defined by the terms *rapist* and *victim* or *parasite* and *host*. She argued against seeing the characters as tropes in any way: "Seeing the stories as slave narratives makes it too easy for readers to dismiss the victimized characters as having no power, when in reality Butler shows that they have the ultimate choice: to survive or to sabotage life for the whole system." The student reasoned that the works were not about slavery because the characters were always permitted a choice. Her classmates disagreed, asserting that in relationships of inequality there can be no consent. This student countered by pointing out that our culture's definition of *consent* should not be considered a universal principle.

This student recognized that *Dawn* came at the end of a twenty-year period of writing that began with *Kindred*, a time in which Butler was thinking about "interdependence, choice, and what it means to be human." *Dawn* represented the author's empathy with the isolation of Lilith, who wakes up and finds herself held by aliens who plan to genetically trade with humanity to create a new species. The student suggested that readers "discard their preconceptions and dig deeper into the workings of interracial [and interspecies] interdependence."

When I assigned *Dawn*, I had the students read the first ninety pages and stop at the moment Lilith is attracted to another human being. The students, certain that the story was about slavery, likened it to what they had read concerning Mauritania in Kevin Bales's *Disposable People* (80–120). This approach, where I present the students with what they think is slavery by starting them with *Kindred* and then upset their understanding by moving them on to "Bloodchild" and *Dawn*, might be called "the turn of the screw" method of teaching, which can be learned from Butler's writing: at first things seem predictable, but read on, and you will be surprised.

The students all understood, from their reading, how a human being can be turned into a slave. They saw that slavery persists because people throughout the system feel unable to break free from the exploitation or from the power it confers. Those involved in slavery stop thinking for themselves and accept that they cannot change the world. For many students in the class, this realization was unsettling.

The day I asked them to transform the Angelou quote into a Butler question, almost all drew on Butler's essay "Furor Scribendi" and argued that resistance was the reason African Americans survived history and were still able to walk with pride. Resistance is not just how to survive slavery but how to end it as well.

Reading Butler helped my students find these new, creative, and deeper understandings of slavery. It was as if her work had freed them from conventional thinking. I imagine the class as a sheet of paper. On one edge are the words "American Slavery"; on the opposite edge, "Modern Slavery." If the paper lies flat on a desk, one can only draw a straight line between the two. Our discussion would be linear and free of complexities. But if we add Butler, the sheet of paper is no longer flat: she allows us to pick up the paper and bend it so that the two edges touch.

For Adults Only: A Competency-Based Approach to Teaching Butler's *Wild Seed*

Deborah Wood Holton

For over thirty years, I have taught adult learners at DePaul University's School for New Learning (SNL). Founded in 1972, SNL is one of the oldest schools of its kind, a student-centered, interdisciplinary college dedicated to educating, at both the graduate and undergraduate levels, underserved adult learners who are at least twenty-four years of age. The college offers several undergraduate programs, including one that is competency-based. The Council for Adult and Experiential Learning, "a national nonprofit that works at all levels within the higher education, public and private sectors to make it easier for people to get the education and training they need" ("Linking"), distinguishes between competency-based and traditional postsecondary education programs, noting that

> Competency Based Education . . . awards credits based on whether students can prove they have mastered competencies—the skills, abilities, and knowledge—required in an area of study. Students can work at their own pace, and the school will certify what they know and what they are able to do. If the student already has the knowledge, he or she can move on to the next set of materials. . . . [With] documented competencies, employers will know that the employee they plan to hire is career-ready and has the skills and knowledge necessary to perform well in his or her new position. (*All* 4–5)

At SNL, students in the undergraduate competency-based program must demonstrate their knowledge and skills across three areas: lifelong learning, liberal learning, and the focus area to achieve their liberal arts degree. Unlike traditional postsecondary students, they do not select from a menu of courses that compose a major. Instead, with the support of an academic committee similar in design to what one typically has in a graduate program, they each create and implement an individualized plan that incorporates a diversity of life and work experiences, expertise, interests, knowledge, and skills to make meaning and add value to their education. The theoretical approaches of experiential and adult learning formulated by John Dewey and David A. Kolb, among others, are central to SNL's conceptual framework that guides every aspect of work with students in and outside the classroom (Ryan 2–3). Furthermore, SNL's assessment principles are grounded in adult-learning best practices, which acknowledge that

> Learning is iterative and deepened when directed toward goals.
>
> Assessment is conceptually separable from instruction—it focuses on outcome rather than input.
>
> Learning occurs from interaction with and among a wide variety of knowledge sources, [including] the experience of others and one's self. . . .
>
> [And that] self-assessment is a significant link between external assessment, learning, and development. ("Assessing")

Effective course design will incorporate these and additional college assessment directives to maximize learner success. The question for faculty becomes, In what competencies will my content knowledge and expertise fit?, rather than, Which topic do I want to teach? Those who teach to competency are not only content experts; they are also learning facilitators who use their knowledge and expertise to engage students in the delivery, management, and assessment of learning from multiple perspectives in compliance with each of the competencies the course offers.

My advanced seminar, African American Fiction: Octavia E. Butler's *Wild Seed*, operates on these principles. Although my course draws on my scholarly and creative interests in the arts and humanities in general, and African American cultural history in particular, it also reflects my grounding in adult and experiential learning practices. Both vantage points helped me create spaces that encouraged self-reflection, self-assessment, inquiry, and creativity in the service of my students' competency development.

Wild Seed is an evocative and compelling origin-love story about two immortals, the progenitors of the Patternist lineage for which Butler's Patternist series is named (*Seed*). Set against the backdrops of the Atlantic slave trade, Middle Passage, and American slavery, the novel chronicles the meeting and 150-year relationship between Doro, an entity that must consume souls to live, and Anyanwu, a shapeshifter with gifts of strength and healing. I selected this book because it is, in its entirety, as dense and lush as the African terrain Butler describes as the novel opens. *Wild Seed* is not only a model of speculative fiction, with its complex characters, exemplary dialogue, provocative scenes, and thematic interweaving of religion, history, race and gender, eugenics, and folklore, but also an extraordinary opportunity for competency-based learning.

I met Butler in 1985, at the Black Woman Writer and the Diaspora conference at Michigan State University in East Lansing (see Butler, "Interview" [Rowell] 65). Our conversation left such an impression on me that I began reading her work with more attention. Aspiring to write creatively, I found courage in her writing journey and knew that my students could as well. These threads of interest wove together into a course idea for an advanced elective seminar that would promote student competencies through an engagement with the novel. I also wanted to see if I could spark students' interest in Butler and her work by letting them spend what I envisioned as "oasis time" with *Wild Seed*

(Paul). My course design, then, had to feature activities, assignments, and learning strategies that led to competency outcomes and at the same time exposed students to the pleasures of intrinsic inquiry as they gained new knowledge.

Students who enroll in the advanced elective seminars have completed prerequisite courses in critical thinking and research methods. In those courses, "students explore the value and practice of being an integrating thinker in today's increasingly complex world. . . . [They] demonstrate [their] competency by considering one phenomenon, problem or event through the lenses of at least two different approaches to creating and expressing knowledge" ("Competencies").

In my seminar, students explain and interpret a theme or issue in Butler's novel by identifying a problem to create new knowledge through the lens of creative writing and African American cultural history. But in creating the seminar, I had to assume that students, by virtue of their diverse learning plans, would not be familiar with science fiction, Butler, Butler's work, or the African American experience. Also, because students often take advanced electives as they near the end of their residency, those in my seminar might also be enrolled in other courses that would require considerable research, reading, and writing. Finally, I had to consider the additional responsibilities that adult learners often have that could tug on their pocketbooks and time.

My seminar had to capture the interest of students and add value to their lives. The assignments had to be iterative so that they had the opportunity to develop their integrative learning skills. With an awareness that students may need support in articulating what they knew and could do, I drew from Melissa Peet's "Integrative Knowledge Portfolio Process" (17–25).

Below are the two competency statements (E1 and E2) for the course with their associated learning outcomes (LOs).

E1. Can explain a topic of interest generated from direct engagement with a fictional text from at least two academic disciplines within the liberal learning categories.

- LO1. Can identify a research topic derived from direct engagement with a primary fictional text.
- LO2. Can use integrative knowledge principles to investigate the chosen topic from two academic disciplines within the liberal learning categories.
- LO3. Can evaluate the two major academic disciplines regarding their limitations and potentials as they apply to the primary text.

E2. Can apply knowledge from two or more academic disciplines in the liberal learning categories to the interpretation of a fictional text and synthesize one's findings for an audience.

- LO1. Can investigate an author's ideas and perspectives on her or his work as they apply to one's research topic.
- LO2. Can compare scholarship about one's topic relative to each chosen academic discipline.

LO3. Can analyze, drawing from LO1 and LO2, the author's use of knowledge from one or more academic disciplines in the creation of a fictional world.

LO4. Can present to an audience a synthesis of one's research that includes a discussion of the value of integrative knowledge and its application to actual situations.

In addition to Butler's text, I recommended learning resources such as Conseula Francis's *Conversations with Octavia Butler* and Deborah Gray White's *Ar'n't I a Woman? Female Slaves in the Plantation South*. I also placed on reserve a range of scholarly articles about both integrative learning and Butler.

After aligning the learning outcomes to class activities and assignments, I designed the class schedule and created lesson plans that included scaffolding to support students in their iterative processes. For the duration of the course, I used *PowerPoint* and other teaching strategies to support visual learners, organize and reinforce ideas, and highlight scheduled activities. I gave brief lectures on history to illustrate how Butler's text provides details that students may miss in their first reading and on creative writing with emphasis on science and speculative fiction. In the remaining weeks, the students and I analyzed together featured readings so that they could better appreciate how scholars draw from their disciplinary perspectives and illuminate pathways for the creation of new knowledge.

To create a safe space for the free flow of ideas and the sharing of frustrations that invariably arose and to strengthen our learning community, I rearranged the room in the seminar-style circle to make the point that, although I might be at the helm, I was a learner too. I introduced Brenda J. Allen's "Working Assumptions for Class Interaction," which we discussed at length during the second session. As the course developed, I supplemented and modified assignments where needed in response to and in collaboration with the students.

By the end of the course, students produced assessable evidence in support of their demonstration of competency with Butler-related content. They had read *Wild Seed*—without my prompting— numerous times. They read and analyzed scholarly articles and compared Butler interviews outside of class in search of insights into their research interests. They engaged in learning strategies, such as mind mapping, freewriting, and in-class multimedia activities, and they developed an electronic portfolio. They wrote eight learning-journal entries and two essays, led one discussion reflecting their ongoing research, presented through *PowerPoint* or other visual means a synthesis of their learning, and reflected on their competency development and achievement through an exercise I created to mine their knowledge.

I taught *Wild Seed* for the first time during the 2016 spring quarter. We met once a week, three hours per session. Among the eight adult learners enrolled, only one knew of Butler and her work. Most were taking other courses along with my seminar. For some, given their schedule and spring graduation target, mine was the only advanced elective seminar available to them. That first night, after the usual introductions and syllabus review, I invited them to read the text aloud. They were hesitant at first, but we soon found our rhythm as we took turns reading the opening chapter. Drawing on my acting skills, which I often employ in other courses to nuance and amplify textures in the author's language, characterization, and sensory details, I closed the exercise by reading from "With concealed excitement . . ." to "Is this enough?" (*Wild Seed* 15–16). By the time I finished, *Wild Seed* had germinated in their imaginations. One grinned and said that she needed a cigarette even though she didn't smoke. Another announced that it was time for him to go home because he had more *Wild Seed* reading to do. We finished the class with a group activity in which the students speculated on what they thought would happen next. They left excited to find out.

Student responses that first session exceeded my expectations. Concerned that students would find their first encounter with science fiction a challenge instead of a reward, I had included a caveat in my syllabus to forewarn them:

> Be advised: Octavia E. Butler's *Wild Seed* speculates on events that are rooted in history. It does so in ways that are provocative, adult, and disturbing in places. It addresses moral themes that question societal norms and expectations. You are encouraged to "suspend your disbelief and judgment," so that you may investigate the fictional world the author has created as well as the themes and issues she presents in it. (Gardner 38)

Their first task, then, was to read for enjoyment with an open mind. Students returned eager to talk about Doro and Anyanwu and to ask about the things they did not understand. We explored Butler's terrain systematically and mindfully, making observations and noting potential topics along the way. I brought in maps, books, and audio folktales. We visited Web sites and went on a virtual field trip. We talked candidly about racism, domestic violence, color consciousness, apartheid. All the while, we looped back to integrative learning and its role in the workplace, home, and family, and I stressed that having multiple vantage points contributed to problem-solving and creativity.

As the weeks progressed, the students not only declined their session-break time, which they usually covet in a three-hour evening class, but also lingered after class, wanting instead to continue their discussions about Doro and Anyanwu and Butler. They shared their research and probed for ways to further their inquiries. Here is the midpoint reflection of my student Ashley Ray, who adds to her evidence of competency when she writes:

> Though slavery only ended in the century before, and though the residual effects of slavery have still not abated, many twentieth-century readers had already been desensitized to the horrors of slavery, and were intentionally taught to ignore its impact on the Americas. By presenting a story

> of slavery that included supernatural elements, Butler was able to show the damaging effects of transgenerational trauma in a way that would not cause readers to arrest their empathy. She also used chattel slavery as a backdrop but not as the exact circumstances of the protagonist to accomplish two things at once: to provide a continuous whisper in the reader's ear about what happened during slavery in the Americas, while keeping the reader at a safe distance from their social conditioning to close their heart to the historical truth of slavery. By writing about slavery in science fiction, Butler makes the topic of slavery accessible to those who have been socially conditioned to avoid it at all costs.

By the end of the course, students expressed excitement about reading more of Butler's work and about continuing their research. Their culminating presentations dealt with investigations in religion and its role in reconciliation, domestic violence, mythology, leadership styles, healing at the cellular level, the roots of apartheid, violence against women, psychology, and mothers in oppressive settings. They discussed at length how they were already applying their integrative learning skills to their work situations. They expressed confidence in their ability to take the time to view a problem or issue from multiple angles, just as they had done together through active and iterative engagement with Butler's *Wild Seed*.

During the last class, one student remarked that thanks to her learning in the course she could never again read a novel as she used to; now she would search for insights into the human condition hidden in its pages. All the students agreed. For them, my seminar proved to be more than another academic hoop to jump through as they neared graduation. It was an invitation for adult learners to expand their learning boundaries, to flex their inquiry muscles so that they could embrace the unknown as they continued their journey in the creation of new knowledge.

Parable of the Sower and Antiracist Pedagogy: Reading Butler with Preservice Teachers

Bevin Roue and Laura Apol

When it comes to the teaching of literature, the fiction of Octavia Butler is widely and regularly lauded for its thoughtful examination of issues of race. But less attention has been paid by educators to the skillful ways she contextualizes her messages about race by placing them in the complex web of present-day social issues. In *Parable of the Sower*, she depicts a future of economic slavery and racial violence but grounds this dystopia in recognizable contemporary political ideologies that create and uphold racial oppression. As a result, a careful examination of the explicit and implicit power structures in *Parable of the Sower* can support antiracist pedagogy across a variety of educational contexts.

Parable of the Sower *as a Dystopian Novel: Neoliberalism, Contemporary Slavery, and Racial Oppression*

While framing her dystopia in apocalyptic terms—the brutality of a drought-parched land, roving bands of displaced people, and even cannibalism—Butler includes in the setting for her novel a functioning government with a clear neoliberal agenda. By connecting corporate and political ideologies to explicit racial oppression and violence, she provides unmistakable commentary on the relations among economics, neoliberal politics, and racial injustice. These intersections are most visible in her description of President Donner's government, which has policies that lead directly to slavery and racial oppression: gutted social safety nets, dismantled government programs, and financial incentives provided to white-owned and white-operated businesses but not to the workers, who are predominantly people of color. Business and safety policies are deregulated and reregulated to favor corporations and force people of color, like the character Emery, into slavery. In her account of the role of corporate institutions (specifically the corporate towns and slave factories), Butler makes a direct link between neoliberal economics and racism: that corporate towns like Olander are mostly white is the result of racially motivated business strategies, and in the slave factories, the slave drivers are white, the slaves are not.

Parable of the Sower connects an imagined, horrifying future to ideologies today, thus allowing students to contemplate, through literature, the relationship between current politico-economic agendas and racial violence as well as to speculate about the future outcomes of those agendas. Using speculative fiction to challenge conversations around white privilege, economics, and racial oppression allows students to explore issues of contemporary relevance.

Parable of the Sower in a Teacher-Education Classroom

Because it is so effective in using present-day economic and political ideologies to foreground issues of race, we chose *Parable of the Sower* to use in our teaching. The novel allows us to engage our students in discussions of ideas that are important to them both as students and as teachers in training but are often avoided because they are discomforting.

We teach Butler's novel primarily to elementary education majors in an advanced children's and young adult literature course located in a college of education. They tend to view literature as a tool to advance other curricular goals, like reading, science, and social studies. Our goal is different: we emphasize literary theory and interpretation rather than pedagogical techniques. We want our students to view literature as literature, not merely as a text to be taught. Instead of requiring them to design lesson plans, we ask them to provide their own interpretation of a text and then reflect on the process.

The course in which we use Butler's work is titled Issues of Diversity in Children's and Young Adult Literature. It is organized around issues rather than compartmentalized units of various marginalized or underrepresented groups. We delve instead into white privilege, systemic racism, and social inequities, examining portrayals of these issues as they come up in literature and the ramifications of these portrayals for schools and schooling.

Like much of the United States teaching force, our students are overwhelmingly white, middle-class, and female, and they are entering a context of schools and schooling that is now numerically dominated by children of color. Many of them want to understand the lived experiences of their students but have grown up in an education system that promoted and valued difference-blind or colorblind stances toward race. The already complicated work of antiracist education is made exponentially more difficult when students believe that they don't see race and that they shouldn't talk about it.

Being white teacher-educators, we are reading Butler's text from a privileged perspective and have more in common with the white residents of the corporate towns in *Parable of the Sower* than we do with the characters of color like Lauren or Emery. Our job is therefore to challenge not only our predominantly white students but also ourselves to move out of comfort zones and resist easy readings that focus on dystopia but ignore the troubling issues of race.

We want our students, as future teachers, to engage with the genre of black speculative fiction in ways that foreground the hard work these texts do in the interest of social change. Most school classrooms and many teacher-education programs relegate speculative literature by and about black and brown experiences to the periphery of the curriculum or exclude them completely. When texts about nonwhite experience are included, they most often focus on historical narratives or contemporary accounts. As important as slave narratives and civil rights stories are, when we bring Butler into our literature class, we want these future teachers to see that black writers work across a full range of genres, creating texts that do not always fit with teachers' and administrators' expectations for pedagogically relevant, multicultural literature. We hope that they will incorporate that range into their own future classrooms and recognize that Butler's speculative fiction speaks to issues of race with a clarity and power not apparent in many school and teacher-education curricula.

Teaching Parable of the Sower

Most of our students are unfamiliar with speculative literature, assuming that realistic and historical fiction are the genres most useful for their future classrooms. Those who have read dystopian literature usually know only popular young adult series, such as The Hunger Games and Divergent—in other words, a polished Hollywood version of dystopia. Butler's novel, however, presents a critical dystopia in which black voices and black experiences are central. We open the class with a brief discussion on racism and sexism in speculative literature, pointing to examples such as the social media fallout regarding the depiction of black characters in *The Hunger Games* and the whitewashing of the film *The Last Airbender*. This discussion frames the work of Butler in current cultural media events and provides a segue into her more speculative texts, like *Kindred* and *Dawn*, where she pushes the genre of fantasy and science fiction into new realms regarding race and gender.

We turn to *Parable of the Sower*, beginning with activities that involve small-group discussion of issues that run through the novel, providing focus questions to help support students' conversations. Some focus questions are:

> How does the concept of slavery evolve through the course of the book?
> What principles do you see in how business, corporations, and government operate in the novel?
> What pattern do you notice in the interaction among corporations, government policies, and slavery?
> What is the author asking readers to consider about these issues and principles?

Students are then asked to reread excerpts from the novel that illustrate or demonstrate the ideas underlying these questions. The excerpts focus on the role of President Donner (27), the depiction of small businesses (17–18), the makeup of the corporate town of Olivar (118–22), the experiences of the former slave Emery (287–88), and the slave factories located on the Canadian border (323–24). After this rereading, students are invited to freewrite their thoughts and to share their thinking in their group.

We do this extensive scaffolding because *Parable of the Sower* is a fairly lengthy read, almost a hundred pages longer than *Kindred*, and in content and style one of the more challenging books assigned in our course. Doing focused readings, spending time discussing in small groups, and writing in response to early understandings of the issues help students feel more confident and allow them to try out their ideas in an environment less threatening than that of a whole-class conversation.

The whole-class discussions are challenging but allow us instructors to hear, support, and develop student thinking in a way that ensures the benefit of learning from and with one another. The field of education has an extensive record of research on the difficulty of facilitating discussions on race, particularly antiblack racism, with white students. Because *Parable of the Sower* deals directly with race and because the setting is not dissimilar from that of the contemporary United States regarding climate change and government policies, many challenges, resistances, and epiphanies occur during the discussions.

One of the most persistent issues we encounter is silence. Many of our students avoid talking about race entirely. The reasons for their silence are complex: inexperience, discomfort or uncertainty, outright hostility to the subject. Silence can be a coping mechanism or an avoidance strategy—sometimes both. Putting students in small groups helps to some degree: our students feel more comfortable discussing race that way than in a teacher-led, whole-class discussion. When the conversation is open-ended, students can pass over aspects of race or instances of racism and go to an issue they find more comfortable or familiar—for example, poverty. Asking them to ground their conversations in moments from the text that we see as discussion-worthy enriches their engagement with complex, difficult ideas.

Students also often use coded language to divert the conversation from race: euphemisms such as "inner-city" or "urban," veiled references to "some people" or "some communities." Our response to coded language requires careful attention to students' intent. This is one reason why we introduce *Parable of the Sower* late in the semester. After a few months together, we have had time to foster a classroom community and develop a professional relationship with students. We gain insight into their ways of engaging and disengaging with sensitive material. For example, our students have sometimes made the connection between Butler's dystopian United States and cities like Detroit or Flint, which have large black populations devastated by corporate and government policies. But they often prefer to talk about high-poverty areas rather than black communities, making invisible the role that race plays in these crises. We believe it is pedagogically irresponsible to let them focus on poverty without recognizing the toll that government funding initiatives (like Flint's emergency management) or corporate outsourcing (like General Motors' layoffs) take specifically on communities of color. When students use coded language, we push for clarification, believing that to avoid the topic of antiblack racism does a disservice to them and to their future students.

A third situation we encounter in whole-class discussion occurs when white students draw parallels between the novel's representation of racial oppression and their own personal struggles. A middle-class white student, for example, might claim that she can relate to the poor people in Lauren's group because her own family did not have much money when she was younger. There may be points of connection, but we find in general that our students rely too much on relatability as a reading strategy. It ignores the role that race plays in Butler's story. *Parable of the Sower* is not relatable to most of the students in our class. We must get students to think in terms of social systems and the injustice of neoliberal policies. Their personal responses to the text should be validated, but so should the content and intent of the text itself. To avoid the easy personal response, we push students during the discussion to reflect on their reading strategies. If they say that they connect to Lauren because they grew up poor, we ask how that background knowledge shapes their understanding of the book, then ask how Lauren's experience differs from theirs. We encourage them to consider what aspects of the novel they might miss when they approach it only through their own experience.

Despite these challenges, our discussions around *Parable of the Sower* are consistently rewarding. It is exciting when students make connections between Butler's vision of the future and their own understanding of contemporary issues. In addition to contemplating conditions in struggling cities, our students also grapple with matters like modern racial segregation and their own experiences learning what it means to be white—topics one student called "real-life issues." *Parable of the Sower* gives students an arena in which to think about the relations among neoliberal policies, contemporary slavery, white privilege, and racial oppression not only in literature but also in the world around them. Butler creates a dystopia but uses as its basis the world our students live in but rarely recognize: a place in which corporate and political ideologies privilege whiteness, enact antiblack oppression, inflict poverty, and re-create systemic slavery.

As preservice teachers, our students need to recognize the interconnected strands that affect their professional field—political battles over school funding, school discipline, high-stakes testing, corporate influence in education policy—and that play out more widely in politics, economics, and culture. The speculative elements of *Parable of the Sower* help us facilitate complex and sometimes unsettling discussions about contemporary race and racism and to encourage antiracist pedagogy both in our classes and in the classrooms our students will one day create.

Reading Whiteness in *Kindred* to Teach Transnational Pedagogy

Shreyashi Mukherjee

How do we teach students the complexities of resistance without replicating the binaries that inform othering events—xenophobia, civil war, and genocide—which are present-day global realities? In response to this need, I would propose the teaching of race, gender, and nation through a course entitled Reading Transnationalism: Agency and Resistance in Contemporary Women's Fiction. Offered as a senior seminar to English majors or to graduate students, this course incorporates the following novels taken from African American, South Asian, Lebanese, and Palestinian literatures respectively: Danzy Senna's *Caucasia*, Taslima Nasrin's *Shame*, Amrita Pritam's *Skeleton*, Kamila Shamsie's *Burnt Shadows*, Etel Adnan's *Sitt Marie Rose*, and Liana Badr's *The Eye of the Mirror.* Negotiating diverse histories and political and social institutions, this course invites readers into unfamiliar territories. It moves beyond area studies and brings together texts as varied as Octavia Butler's *Kindred* and Briege Duffaud's *A Wreath upon the Dead,* which are otherwise taught separately as American literature, black literature, women's literature, and Irish women's literature. This particular textual pairing helps students rearticulate whiteness as an invisible hegemony—an ideology and a social reality. Such a comparative reading as I suggest with this pairing, and others that this course generates, can broaden student worldviews and foster polyvocality.

Kindred *and* A Wreath upon the Dead

Kindred presents students with whiteness as a power structure and ideology. First, students can be asked to consider Dana's dealings with Rufus. Though Dana saves Rufus more than once and gives evidence of her humanity, Rufus cannot overcome his indoctrination in whiteness and makes repeated attempts to read her as a subordinated subject. He feels threatened by her independence and accuses her of acting white. His disconcertion is evident in his interpretation of her defiance as an attempt at whiteness; he rages, "You think you're white! . . . You don't know your place any better than a wild animal" (164). He unconsciously postulates whiteness and blackness as different places or social locations. Through his treatment of Dana, students can understand whiteness as a hegemonic construct that permits the privilege of determining blackness as servility, which separates whiteness and blackness from biology.

The black slave Alice makes evident whiteness as a "'white' frame of reference" (Keating, "Investigating" 427). For students, she is a complex figure because she does not neatly fall into the idea of sisterhood through which we often read black women's interactions with each other. She misreads Dana's relationship with Kevin as a betrayal of race loyalties; this misreading is suggested in her naming Dana a "*White-nigger*" (160). Scarred physically and psychologically by slavery and unaware of the liberatory possibilities that Dana encountered through the civil rights movement, Alice has a worldview composed of binary identities—white and black, power and powerlessness—that whiteness promotes to facilitate slavery. But Dana demonstrates before students a different identarian consciousness. She can think of connecting with white characters such as Rufus and Kevin, though the plot subjects her to a "'white' frame of reference" through her family history.

The ability to shift gears between different strategies makes Dana an example of "oppositional consciousness" (Sandoval 10). She can represent to students the possibility of subverting a dominant society while being subject to its norms. Her convincing Alice to surrender to Rufus's lust in order to survive can show students the power of historical oppression. That Dana eventually kills Rufus suggests that her character "weav[es] 'between and among' oppositional ideologies"—such as resistance as survival and resistance as active opposition—as circumstances demand (14). She can ally with Kevin, who as a white man in the culture of slavery must accept its supremacist narratives, but also undermines those narratives by helping slaves escape. These characters force student discussions to move beyond the reductive binary of the "good non-'whites' and the 'bad whites'" (Keating, "Interrogating" 909) and help students understand whiteness as a power structure forcing blacks and whites alike to perpetuate the white racist dominion. But through the examples of Dana and Kevin, the novel makes evident to students that it is possible to subvert whiteness and resist racism.

Duffaud's novel describes English settler colonialism in Northern Ireland as white-on-white oppression with racist undertones; her Maureen, like Dana, apprises students about the need to confront hidden discourses of whiteness to bring about change. The English racialization of the Irish is evident in the liberal reformer Charles Kingsley's historic description of the Catholic Irish as "the human chimpanzees" whose white skin causes anxiety to the colonizer desirous of identifying a racial binary (white-human versus black-animal) with skin color: "[T]o see white chimpanzees is dreadful; if they were black, one would not feel it so much, but their skins, except where tanned by exposure, are as white as ours" (308). Maureen uncovers this English blackening of the Irish in her anticolonial rewriting of Kingsley's trope. A Catholic Irish person born in Claghan, Northern Ireland, she remembers that starvation compelled her friend to perform as a white "monke[y]" and accept the food an English tourist threw at them (12). Her explication that whiteness hides the class oppression underlying English imperialism shows students that whiteness "colonizes the definition of other norms" (Dyer 128).

Reflecting on one's location in a power hierarchy is a necessary step to bridging divides. Maureen identifies her Catholic Irish identity as open-ended, being both marginalized and oppressive—a valuable point for those students who occupy multiple power locations with regard to caste, class, gender, race, ethnic, and national identity but are taught in public discourses to ignore this differential layering. An episode from the novel that contests monolithic narratives of identity has Maureen living in a French chateau and watching television images of starvation in Ethiopia; she sees "a toothless shawled woman huddled in dramatic close-up against a windy rock, holding a dead baby" (119). This commonplace experience of being a voyeur to human suffering can lead to a discussion on whether to accept social-global inequalities as a fait accompli or do something about them. Maureen's awareness of the privileges of her white metropolitan identity, privileges denied the poor Ethiopian woman, begins Maureen's journey toward antiracist consciousness. Maureen demonstrates to students the need to be observant to "a thousand famines, a million inhumanities" operating worldwide (122).

Other Pairings, Fictional and Nonfictional

In addition to *Wreath,* other textual readings included in the course pair well with *Kindred.* Danzy Senna's *Caucasia* can build on *Kindred's* treatment of race as a social construct. In *Caucasia,* the mixed-race, light-skinned Bridie seeks to be black but is excluded from the black community and forced to pass as white, thereby disassociating race from skin color. Novels such as *Eye, Sitt Marie Rose, Shame, Skeleton,* and *Burnt Shadows* do not engage with race. They do, however, examine exclusionary discourses based on other identarian markers—ethnicity, gender, nationality, and religion—investigating how these social constructs are utilized to create and reinforce marginality. As *Kindred* does with slavery, these narratives negotiate contested histories and violent events that are part of communal memory and communal identity: the Lebanese civil war, religious riots in the Indian subcontinent, the Indian Partition, and the Hiroshima and Nagasaki genocides, respectively. When juxtaposed with *Kindred,* they allow students to consider transnationally how the past is a palimpsest for the present and how numerous are the faces of othering and resistance.

An important theme that connects these novels with *Kindred* is the effort to find rapprochement with the other. *Kindred* presents a pragmatic discussion of engaging with the racial other—the stereotypes we encounter and the assumptions we make when we bridge divides. Though Dana acknowledges that Kevin is traumatized by witnessing slavery firsthand, it is significant that Butler indicates at least two episodes when Dana finds that her white husband reminds her of Weylin. Kevin's accent makes Kevin "sound a little like Rufus and Tom Weylin" (190). This resemblance between Dana's husband and the slave owners, slight at first, grows in the novel; Dana "see[s] things" in Kevin that "remin[d] . . . [her] of Weylin" (195). In another instance, her cousin misreads Dana's bruises from antebellum Maryland as Kevin's "work" (116)—a postbellum enactment of "white men preying on black women" (119), which the prologue indicates is an established assumption. The police jail Kevin for hurting Dana, though Rufus caused her injury. Since the plot does not portray Kevin as a brutal man, this misreading of the facts suggests the pain and trauma bequeathed by slavery and racism. Discussion of such assumptions can bring into the classroom the difficulty of talking about race beyond binaries; it is a process burdened by reluctance, anxiety, blame, and historical guilt. Here students can be reminded about bell hooks's observation that "[s]tereotypes black folks maintain about white folks are not the only representations of whiteness in black imagination. They emerge primarily as responses to white stereotypes of blackness" (341).

The view of hooks that marginalized subjects often project identarian binaries in response to domination fits other works read in the course, works that, like *Kindred,* acquaint us with the necessity of understanding the other but, unlike *Kindred*, are unable to narrate reconciliation. Badr's *Eye* protests Palestinian deaths in the Lebanese civil war and offers an instance of Palestinian-Lebanese friendship, but the friendship ends in betrayal. In Adnan's *Sitt Marie Rose,* the Christian female protagonist crosses cultural and religious boundaries to help Palestinian refugees, but her humane actions make her the other to her community and cost her her life. In *Shame*, Nasrin criticizes religious fundamentalism but sees violence as an infectious disease: a Bangladeshi Hindu boy responds to the pain of his sister's kidnapping and death in a religious riot by raping a Muslim prostitute. *Skeleton* offers a more enabling picture: the female protagonist is a Hindu girl who allies with her Muslim kidnapper-husband to save other women. These narratives, together with *Kindred,* can foster discussions on the complexities of identity formation under and despite oppression. They can suggest to students that for oppressed subjects survival is often the hidden script of resistance.

Reluctant to narrate the true cause of her injuries—her forced travel into history—Dana realizes that "there was no honest explanation . . . [she] could give them—none they would believe" (9). If she told "the truth," she'd be "locked up—in a mental hospital" (11). So her journey becomes a "grim fantasy" (qtd. in Crossley 269). Students can be asked whether she fears disbelief and punishment solely because of the uncanny nature of her experience or whether her time travel unearths a repressed narrative, the contemporary legacy of slavery embodied in white America's kinship with black America. Dana's disinclination to speak is similar to that of Duffaud's Maureen and Badr's unnamed narrator. These authorial figures, apprehensive about protesting exclusionary politics, have a real-life parallel in Tasalima Nasarina living under fatwa. Through these characters and this person, students should understand the danger of challenging racist and sexist institutions and practices.

The following broad questions can be worked into discussions on individual texts throughout the semester:

What stereotypes and hegemonic discourses do the authors included in the course challenge or reinforce in their discussions of the other?

What representations emerge when marginalized groups rewrite their depictions in dominant discourses, as Butler and Badr do with slavery and exile, respectively, and as Adnan, Nasarina, and Pritam do when they rewrite history as women?

What formal strategies do the authors use to criticize institutional persecution and envision change?

These questions can be particularized with respect to *Kindred*:

Dana encounters Rufus as a white child and kills him in self-defense at the end of the novel. How does he become her enemy? What roles do plantation slavery and racism play in his growth into an oppressive figure? How would you apply Richard Dyer's discussion of whiteness to Rufus and Dana's relationship in the novel?

Why does Alice call Dana "*White-nigger*"? Is Alice supporting Rufus's view that Dana thinks she is white? What kind of assumptions do Alice and Rufus make about their respective racial others?

Kevin observes, "This could be a great time to live in . . . go West and . . . see how much of the Old West mythology is true," to which Dana responds, "West. . . . That's where they're doing it to the Indians instead of the blacks!" (97). How does Kevin's ignoring of Native American subjugation suggest his indoctrination in whiteness?

What do you make of Dana's fusing Rufus and Kevin after she returns from antebellum Maryland? Is their perceived similarity a manifestation of her traumatic experiences in slavery? Or is the novel indicating through these parallels that Kevin's racial and gender identities make him susceptible to "cultural patterns of dominance" (Crossley 276)? Discuss with reference to Kevin and Rufus as white men in the novel.

Reading a "book of excerpts from the recollections of concentration camp survivors" prompts Dana to make the following observation: "Germans had been trying to do in only a few years what the Americans had worked at for nearly two hundred" (117). How does this view connect with the novel's rewriting of Old West mythology?

Dana narrates, "I turned on the radio . . . tuned in . . . a story about the war in Lebanon." Then, the "news switched to a story about South Africa—blacks rioting . . . and dying wholesale . . . over the policies of the white supremacist government" (196). In a novel on race, why does Butler mention the Lebanese civil war and apartheid?

Dana and Kevin are writers who cannot write their experiences of antebellum slavery. Dana "tried to write about what had happened, made about six attempts . . . and threw them all away" (116). Why do both have difficulty in writing about slavery?

Dana loses her arm at the end of the novel. Why are we informed of this loss in the prologue? Do you think *Kindred* is a cautionary tale about the perils of negotiating the past? Why or why not?

Nonfiction included in a course like this one supports the ideas about race put forward in fiction. AnaLouise Keating, through her own experiences, introduces students to ideas of memory, voice, language, and representation. She collapses the private and the social and models for students the difficult but necessary process of discussing race without othering. Students can be introduced to Keating after they read Michael Omi and Howard Winant's discussion of race as a social discourse and Dyer's discussion of whiteness as power-hierarchy. These texts help students confront their biases about race; they also provide them with critical lenses and vocabulary for understanding and speaking about race as a construction and an ongoing vehicle for oppression.

Other Assignments: A Brief Discussion

The assignments are designed to help students understand that emancipation from oppressive narratives such as race cannot be gained from any one space and that coalition building involves political juxtapositions as well as differences. To this end, students can be asked to scrutinize the relations among various marginalized communities—such as that between African Americans and the Irish in America and in Ireland. Students might complete short reports and presentations on early Irish republican interactions with antislavery abolition movements and consider the value of Frederick Douglass's sojourn in Ireland. This comparative pedagogy might be continued in written assignments where students choose a single text for a short paper and then expand it by including another text for a longer paper, finding connections and divergences between themes, forms, histories, and viewpoints.

I value creative writing assignments because storytelling forces students to imagine alternatives to the hegemonic structures they have inherited. For example, a discussion on minor characters in *Kindred*—such as Dana's uncle and Kevin's sister—can be followed by an assignment in which students write short narratives that flesh out these characters. They can be provided guidelines that ask them to consider specific issues, such as the role of whiteness in creating insular ideas of authentic blackness and white purity. When students who predominantly function as readers in classrooms turn into storytellers, they can construct an enabling meaning of their own lives and move away from simplistic understandings of social systems inherent in attributing whiteness as practice to white physiology.

This course introduces students to a transnational study of oppression and resistance to it. *Kindred* and other women-authored narratives—taken from black

American, Northern Irish, Middle Eastern, and South Asian canons—interrogate the invisible discourses that fuel othering. Students are encouraged to think about traversing epistemological and ontological binaries (and boundaries) that inform discourses of race, gender, and nation. Through assignments and nonfictional readings (e.g., those regarding whiteness and critical race theory), they are asked to engage with ideas of voice and representation and prompted to think about the complex, difficult, and often traumatic process of enacting change. Teaching is an act of faith, and the hope is that in this course students will come to the understanding that we all share a world and have the responsibility to make it better.

Drawing the Oankali: Imagining Race, Gender, and the Posthuman in Butler's *Dawn*

Edmond Y. Chang

In the call for submissions to *Dark Matter II: Reading the Bones*, Sheree Thomas writes that science fiction and fantasy, particularly by writers of color, "have always offered readers bold, extraordinary ways by which to examine society. The results have often been visionary, with writers acting as unflinching voyeurs who deliver engaging, sometimes scathing critiques of our traditions, values, nightmares, and dreams." Octavia Butler's Xenogenesis trilogy—*Dawn, Adulthood Rites,* and *Imago*—imagines a postapocalyptic Earth where humanity has been saved by the Oankali, an alien race with the ability to trade and manipulate genetic material. Butler, whose work is consciously interdisciplinary, intersectional, and pedagogical, unflinchingly engages questions of race, gender, sexuality, class, power, technology, and the environment. The transformation of human beings by the Oankali and the miscegenation of both species challenge what it means to be human and alien and even what it means to be posthuman. Based on my courses that focus on Butler's *Dawn*, the first novel in the trilogy, published in 1987, this essay takes up the theoretical and pedagogical questions raised by the Oankali. It focuses in particular on a drawing assignment called "Imagining the Oankali," where students are asked to draw, represent, or create their idea of the aliens as a way to make visible how the novels dramatize different identities, embodiments, and intersections.

Dawn begins in media res with the annihilation of most of the life on planet Earth following a global nuclear war. It is the extinction-level destruction that draws the attention of the Oankali, an alien race of gene traders that travel the galaxy in search of life forms with which to exchange genetic characteristics, information, and experience. The Oankali save the remaining human beings, placing them in suspended animation aboard their giant living ships, and set to work to heal and restore the planet. Hundreds of years later, the novel's primary character, Lilith Iyapo, an African American woman, is awakened, trained, and slowly integrated into the Oankali plans to return humanity to Earth. Lilith, evocative of the biblical first but defiant wife of Adam, is told by Jdahya, the first alien she gets to know, "Your Earth is still your Earth, but between the efforts of your people to destroy it and ours to restore it, it has changed" (33–34). It is eventually revealed to Lilith (and to the others when they are awakened later) that the mutual survival of both humanity and Oankali is predicated on the intermingling of the species. Human-Oankali hybrid offspring will be the future. Jdahya continues, "We'll put you in areas that are clean of radioactivity and history. You will become something other than you were" (32). Both humanity and the Oankali have left the species with little choice, and Lilith must come to terms with the ambivalence of the circumstances that are simultaneously salvation and slavery, evolutionary and exploitative, transformation and cooptation. Over the course of the novel, she realizes that she and the humans she leads must give into these changes in order to survive. They must accept, endure, even come to enjoy radically new understandings of race, species, gender, sex, desire, sexuality, and ultimately family.

This assignment was inspired by my friend and fellow instructor Sue Shon, who also taught *Dawn* at the University of Washington and who prompted me to think about, describe, and draw what I thought the Oankali looked like. I remember musing over adjectives and key words like *strange, alien, humanoid, bipedal, tentacled, eel-like, uncanny, unearthly, skin, soft, cilia, monster, monstrous, grotesque, gray, gross, fleshy, shimmying, shaggy, stinging.* Shortly thereafter, I made a drawing of the Oankali. Therefore, I put Butler's words to work in a remediated way. I typed up the entire passage where Lilith meets Jdahya for the first time (13–14). I printed the text out as long lines, carefully cut apart the lines with ruler and blade, and laid, layered, bent, and glued the lines into a rough, humanoid contour. My Oankali is a mixture of pencil, text, collage, figure, texture, and positive and negative spaces. The ideas of hybridity, form, and ambiguity between the human beings and Oankali in the novel interested me. I wanted to evoke something like Tolkien's Ents, not quite human, a walking tree, given the Oankalis' affinity for plants, with branches and language and roots. I wanted to capture the difficulty and possibilities of trying to describe, to capture in words, a totally alien being, utterly without stable terrestrial referents. In the passage, Lilith's need to gender Jdahya reveals the normative desire to anthropomorphize, to humanize, to render familiar that which is unknown.

Since my informal conversation with Shon in 2012, she and Megan Hyde, an artist, went on to collect and curate an exhibition of similarly inspired drawings. The show, *Xenology: Drawing in Response to Octavia Butler's* Dawn, debuted two years later as part of Wild Seed, the second annual interactive community birthday celebration of Butler in Seattle, Washington. In the companion exhibition book, Hyde and Shon explain:

> The *Xenology* drawing project began as a playful exchange between us, two Octavia Butler fans, each curious how the other envisioned the alien species called "Oankali" in Butler's *Xenogenesis* trilogy. Independently we both drew what we thought the Oankali looked like. We found the results exciting and consequently opened the exchange to over twenty friends and family, artists and nonartists alike, from all over the world.

I was honored that my Oankali drawing was included in the exhibition (fig. 1).

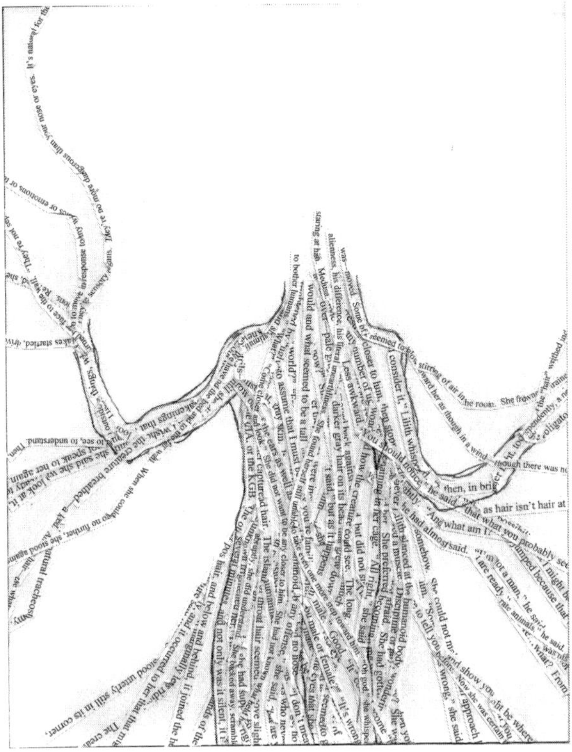

Figure 1. Edmond Y. Chang, Oankali drawing, 2012, pencil and collage on paper.

Imagining the Oankali: The Assignment

It was in the spirit of these provocations and inspirations that I created the "Imagining the Oankali" assignment in classes that included *Dawn* on their syllabi. I used it at the University of Washington and at Drew University, in courses like Mediating Identities: Technologies of the Self, Posthuman Narratives, Introduction to Queer Theory, and Dark Matters: African American Science Fiction, between 2012 and the present. The assignment prompt read:

> For this exercise, draw or create a one-page visual representation (8.5" × 11") of what you imagine Octavia Butler's *Dawn's* "Oankali" to look like, be like, act like, live like. How do you represent or convey something conveyed only through words, inferences, and expectations? Consider the initial descriptions of Jdahya. You can use digital tools, hand draw, or use mixed media, but keep it flat. Be creative and think critically. Given that one of the central tensions in *Dawn* is a decentering of the "human," consider what it means to try to represent something alien, monstrous, different, nonhuman, posthuman, or even inhuman.

The assignment is an invitation, a multimodal exercise that provides students an opportunity to practice, process, and produce a different kind of analysis, expression, and learning. It allows for what Peggy Van Meter and Joanna Garner call "learner-generated drawing," which is "a strategic process . . . learner-generated drawing is goal-directed, serves to organize knowledge, and when matched to the task, improves learning. As such, learner-generated drawing is similar to other strategies such as summarization, self-questioning, or prior knowledge activation" (287). Van Meter and Garner believe that drawing as part of classroom pedagogy improves observational processes, acquisition of content-area knowledge, and text comprehension; facilitates the writing process; and improves student affect.

The Oankali as imagined, drawn, and understood by a handful of my students are shared in this essay with their permission. These Oankali are what Hyde and Shon termed a "xenology," an exploration of alien strangers, "an intense, interrogating study of what becomes perceived, categorized, and known as 'the foreign'" (1). The pieces and responses to them have been curated from across different courses and institutions and reflect a generative curiosity and willingness not only to satisfy the assignment itself but also to articulate the value of Butler's writings, the power of science fiction, and the questions and fraught answers posed by the Oankali. Each drawer-learner was asked to respond to three questions:

> What inspired you to create your drawing? What did you hope to convey or focus on? In other words, why this form?
>
> How was the drawing exercise useful? How did it help you read, understand, analyze the Oankali? the novel?
>
> Why was reading *Dawn* important to you? In other words, if you had to recommend the novel to read (or to teach), what would you say?

Imagining Race

Some of the drawings and responses articulate ways that *Dawn* and the Oankali confront questions of race and racism through the metaphor of an alien species. Like a lot of science fiction, *Dawn* pays little attention to terrestrial race, though the novel does mark different human beings as belonging to pre-Oankali divisions of race and ethnicity. For example, Lilith's race is signaled by comparisons between her skin color and that of the other human beings she meets. At the beginning of the novel, a child named Sharad is put into Lilith's cell; Sharad is described as "a small boy with long, straight black hair and smoky-brown skin, paler than her own" (10). Race and ethnicity are conveyed also by the names and surnames of the novel's characters: Lilith's last name, Iyapo, is Nigerian, meaning "many hard situations"; Fukumoto is a Japanese man who chose to live out his life among the Oankali aboard their spacecraft; Joseph Li-Chin Shing is a Hong Kong–born Canadian man whom Lilith becomes romantically involved with.

But in the face of the greater threat of the aliens, a trope common to the genre, the human beings ignore or overcome their differences of race, nation, and language in order to survive. Racial anxieties vanish in the presence of the Oankali, the fear of forced miscegenation with aliens who are invaders, colonizers, and oppressors. Anxieties about race also become mapped onto women's bodies, motherhood, and the reconfigurations of space, domesticity, and the nuclear family. Aparajita Nanda notes, "Racial vigilance, which earlier was concerned only with securing national borders and with the macropolitics of the nation, now had to contend with the micropolitics of the domestic domain of individual citizens and their family lives" (774). Some of the drawings attend to these issues and in particular acknowledge that the novel was written by an African American woman writer.

Ted Lee, a student in my Mediating Identities course at the University of Washington, wrote in response to their drawing (see fig. 2):

> Speculative fiction like *Dawn* has a powerful potential because it allows us to imagine things outside of what we often define as "reality." *Dawn* tackles subjects like multiple genders outside of the man/woman binary, the nature of humanity, and the concept of aliens and "otherness" in ways that allow productive discussion about these otherwise very difficult topics. Butler's *Dawn* is especially valuable as its main protagonist is a black woman, a representation that is rare in literary fiction read within a university setting, allowing students who belong to marginalized groups to feel comfortable in contributing to the classroom conversation.

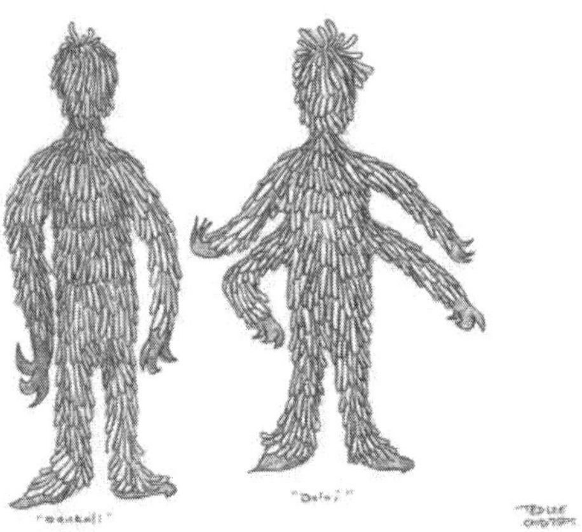

Figure 2. Ted Lee, 2012, pencil on paper.

Imagining Gender and Sexuality

The Oankali, as Lilith and the awakened human beings discover, have three genders: male, female, and ooloi, which is not precisely neuter. All three genders are needed in order to form a family and have children. The Oankali genetically modify the human beings to conform to their own sexual functions and means of procreation. For example, Lilith's need to gender Jdahya as male, as a he, reveals the problem of biological and cultural constructions of sex, gender, and bodies. Lilith herself is regularly misgendered in the novel by the other human beings because her Oankali-engineered enhancements have made her stronger, an able fighter, capable of manipulating alien technology, and thereby too masculine, not a woman and ultimately not human. Nancy Jesser argues, "Butler's fictions offer us a good place to . . . explore her relationship to biological narratives of gender difference even as her plots contest the socially constituted boundaries of racial difference. Difference matters in Butler, but racial difference matters differently than sexual difference" (38). Some of the drawings focus on the concerns with sex and gender, especially through the visualization of the ooloi. It is difficult to imagine the mixing of human and alien blood and bodies. The drawings feature what it means to be different and to think about the fear of and violence against difference.

According to McKenzie Chapman, who took my Introduction to Queer Theory course at Drew University (see fig. 3):

Figure 3. McKenzie Chapman, drawing of Jdahya, 2015.

> I drew Jdahya with the rough form of a man since he was described as such, including a head, neck, two arms and two legs extending from a torso. What Lilith thought was hair were actually many tentacles covering his body, and they seemed to cover everything. I drew the tentacles all over Jdahya, trying to shade the areas described as darker as a deeper gray. Because Jdahya was tasked with greeting Lilith and informing her of an alien race and the decimation of earth, it would make sense that his form was humanoid. The Oankali wanted to introduce Lilith to aliens with someone who was at least a recognizable shape. . . . *Dawn* was important to me because I had never read a science fiction book written by and starring a woman of color before. Octavia Butler's different life experiences made for a completely unique read in the white-male-dominated genre of science fiction. She wrote about gender and sexuality in ways that I had never considered, and that could definitely make people uncomfortable.

Imagining the Posthuman

The drawings and responses grapple with what it means to be human, not human, and posthuman. According to Cary Wolfe, posthumanism

> names a historical moment in which the decentering of the human by its imbrication in technical, medical, informatics, and economic networks is increasingly impossible to ignore, a historical development that points toward the necessity of new theoretical paradigms (but also thrusts them on us). (xv–xvi)

Dawn and Butler's other works ambivalently engage these paradigm shifts. The definitions of what it means to be human and, eventually, posthuman get bound up with Butler's negotiations of race and gender and the bioengineered body. Naomi Jacobs writes, "[T]he posthuman body need no longer be confined to one gender, one sexuality, one race, one subjectivity" (94).

Also from my Mediating Identities course, Bryan Hall wrote (see fig. 4):

> The exercise was useful in that it forced us to pull out our mental picture of the Oankali and put it to paper. Enabling us to ask why we chose to draw certain elements. What I remember specifically from this exercise was the fascination with why the Oankali were so humanoid. Being masters of their own form and genome, why would they choose a bipedal humanoid form? I don't think this question would have come about so strongly had it not been for the drawings.

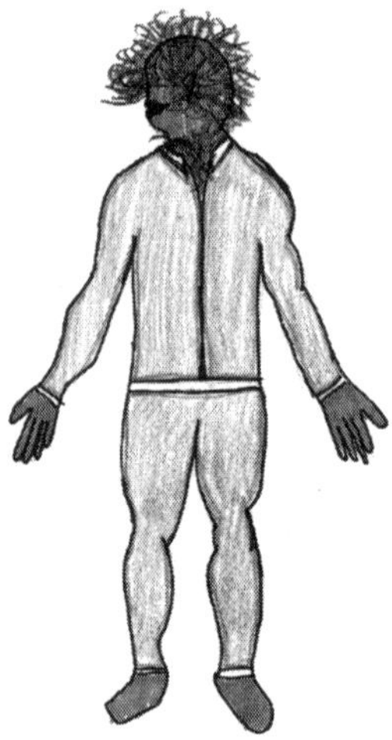

Figure 4. Bryan Hall, 2012, colored pencil and marker on paper.

Imagining Possibilities

All the images and reflections on race, gender, sexuality, alienness, posthumanity, and science fiction more generally overlap and represent the intersections, resonances, and oppositions of these terms and embodiments. In the words of Hyde and Shon, drawing

> functions as a tool for visualizing elusive, unknown forms beyond human comprehension. At the most basic level, *Xenology* works as an exploration in translation and interpretation from words to images. The project questions how drawing as a medium represents what has been portrayed via language as a radical difference. (1)

What the students imagine, what the students encounter in the text, and what the students reflect on and respond to may not always be easy, tidy, or necessarily hopeful. *Dawn* and Butler's other worlds are always dystopian and utopian, perhaps *ambitopian*. They function as what Mary Louise Pratt calls the "arts of the contact zone," the social spaces where "cultures meet, clash, and grapple with each other, often in contexts of highly asymmetrical relations of power, such as colonialism, slavery, or their aftermaths" (34). Though the relations of power narrated by *Dawn* and visualized by the students' drawings are fictional, Butler's stories and worlds do not shy away from exploring these difficult questions and posing difficult answers.

It is these acts of imagining new, different, radical possibilities that are at the heart of reading *Dawn*, teaching Butler, and making drawings of aliens. "Imagining the Oankali" is simple in its invitation but surprisingly complicated, nuanced, and challenging in its execution. The exercise demands of the students to be drawer-learners, to be creative in ways that are often outside their comfort zones. It is not a test, a book report, or a paper—the more traditional activities of a literature course—but it shows what students understand from their reading and allows them to transform that understanding into an artifact that is unusual but can be analyzed. In my courses, I stress the critical value of the drawing in and of itself, but the assignment could be paired with more formal methods, like writing and reflection. Most important about "Imagining the Oankali" is that the students are told and assured that the assignment is high-risk but low-stakes. They are graded on their ability not to draw but to derive inspiration and insight from the novel, graded not on how artistic their drawings are but on how well their drawings spur conversations among image, text, and their fellow students. In an interview, Butler said, "I mean, science fiction is supposed to be about exploring new ideas and possibilities" (Potts and Butler 322). Reading, writing, and pedagogy should do the same.

SOCIAL JUSTICE AND SOCIAL CHANGE

Ecocritical Ideas and Butler's "Bloodchild" and *Parable of the Sower*

Susan M. Bernardo

In the junior-level, discussion-oriented science fiction course I teach, Aliens, Cyborgs, and Time Travel in Literature and Film, I include Butler's *Parable of the Sower* in the section "Ethics and Environment." I also include "Bloodchild" but have typically engaged with that text in the section "Aliens and Monsters." The sections of the course act more as ways to begin conversations about texts than to limit the ways we approach them. Our class discussions typically consider multiple approaches to the texts and films we are studying. One approach, ecocriticism, is especially helpful in a study of these two Butler texts, since a major tenet of ecocritcism is "that human culture is connected to the physical world, affecting it and affected by it" (Glotfelty xix).

Because both *Parable* and "Bloodchild" feature youthful protagonists, these texts draw students in but then complicate their responses. The ecocritical elements of both narratives highlight the idea that humans must negotiate challenging environments because of species-wide choices that have disrupted the ecosystem. The texts provoke questions such as, What do we do when climate change disrupts not only our natural resources but also the social order? How can leadership become environmentally aware and responsible on an Earth that is less hospitable for us or on another planet where resources are not under human control? The symbiotic relationship in "Bloodchild" represents the interconnectedness of people and world that occurred back on Earth as it explores the pressures that arise from living in an alien environment.

Gan's and Lauren's experiences center around family relationships that undergo environmental strains that force each character to make choices. Lauren must learn how to survive while exploring and sharing her Earthseed beliefs, and Gan must come to terms with establishing a relationship with T'Gatoi and the Tlic reproductive cycle. Each also helps create physical and emotional conditions that influence those around them. Both, living under constraints, take action and narrate. Lauren at first appears to have more choice in her situation than Gan has in his, but we see that he too exercises his will within the environmental-biological limits he faces.

Species Negotiations in "Bloodchild"

Students most often respond to "Bloodchild" as a horror tale because of the insectoid bodies of the Tlics. Gan's description of T'Gatoi's movements makes the alien physically vivid for them:

> T'Gatoi whipped her three meters of body off her couch, toward the door, and out at full speed. She had bones—ribs, a long spine, a skull, four sets of limbs per segment. But when she moved that way, twisting, hurling herself into controlled falls, landing running, she seemed to be not only boneless but aquatic—something swimming through the air as though it were water. I loved watching her move. (9)

Students do not share Gan's appreciation of T'Gatoi's movements. However, when I ask them to contrast Butler's tale with the film *Aliens*, which also focuses on reproduction in a hostile environment and features gruesome aliens, they see that Butler presents a possible symbiosis or interdependence rather than the monstrous and inevitable destruction of a human host that the film shows.

We also work with Michael Swanwicks' story "Slow Life," which focuses on the coming together of a scientist-astronaut named Lizzie and an entity who inhabits the extrasolar world that she and her colleagues explore. The native and Lizzie are fundamentally unlike each other but manage to communicate telepathically, and the being helps rescue her. The interspecies contact disturbs the entity, since, as it says, "Multiplicity. Motion. Lies. You showed us a universe infinitely larger than the one we had known." The entity also reveals that the notion of individuality that Lizzie brings to it is like death to its sense of being and wholeness (175, 178). The native exists physically in the story through images that a probe acquires. The narrator describes the images of the native as "[b]eautiful in the way that the great European cathedrals were, and yet at the same time undeniably organic" (172). The outlook for humanity at the end of the story is not bright: the being is sure that human beings will destroy themselves, but the idea that the two of them can communicate at all gives the tale a positive tone. The relationship between the Tlic and human beings in Butler's stories is more developed than in "Slow Life," since it is not about first contact, but students have more difficulty accepting interdependence in Butler's story than they do in Swanwick's, primarily because of the insectoid form of the Tlic.

In discussing interdependence, Sarah Outterson cautions readers to approach Butler's work with the emphasis on "what we have to learn in order to survive" (451). As Brigitte Scheer-Schäzler frames the situation, Butler focuses on "the cost of life under the most precarious circumstance" (315). Jim Miller offers the view that "the ideal for Butler seems to be a society which respects individual differences, but not at the expense of the greater good, of society as a whole" (347)—or, we might add, of the species as a whole. That the interrelationship between Terrans and the Tlic goes back generations helps the reader understand that the arrangement works to keep both species alive and even flourishing. Gan describes T'Gatoi as being on the margins between Tlic and Terran: "T'Gatoi was hounded on the outside [outside the Terran Preserve]. Her people wanted more of us made available . . . we were necessities, status symbols, and an independent people. She oversaw the joining of families, putting an end to . . . breaking up Terran families . . ." (5). T'Gatoi is actually related to Gan, since "[s]he had been taken from my father's flesh when he was my age" (29). Gan's mother, Lien, and T'Gatoi have known each other a long time, and T'Gatoi was the one who introduced Lien to Gan's father. The link between the species for Gan's family is personal as well as biological, since he spends lots of time living with T'Gatoi and she visits the Terran family often, bringing them sterile Tlic eggs that help prolong human health and life.

Despite these links, the relationship appears unequal, as students are quick to point out, because T'Gatoi has political power and Terrans do not; however, Gan renegotiates their bond when he insists on keeping the rifle in the house. He says, "If we're not your animals, if these are adult things, accept the risk. There is risk, Gatoi, in dealing with a partner" (26). He asserts his ability to choose his personhood and redefines himself in both biological and emotional ways. Gan's coming of age includes this key interspecies relationship; thus he needs to figure out how to work in the environment his ancestors journeyed to when they fled Earth. The uneasiness that marks the tone of the story, however, sets readers up to expect a different ending. Gan briefly considers alternate outcomes when he threatens to shoot himself with the rifle and when he initially tells T'Gatoi to go to his sister, Xuan Hoa, to implant her eggs. He knows that Hoa desires to bear the Tlic young (25), but he understands both that he would be sacrificing her because of his own fear and that he has had a long relationship with T'Gatoi. He realizes that he wants to "keep you [T'Gatoi] for myself." On her side, T'Gatoi reaffirms their link when she says, "I couldn't believe I had made such a mistake in you" and "I chose you, I believed you had grown to choose me" (28). His insistence on spreading knowledge of the birthing process among human beings makes him a voice for his species and a bridge between the two, just as T'Gatoi acts as a bulwark that prioritizes the safety and fair treatment of human beings. It is unclear, however, that human knowledge of the process will achieve what Gan thinks it will—a decrease in human fear and a subsequent willingness to partner with the Tlic.

Both species mean to survive, but avoiding speciesism becomes a difficult task. By this point in the course students have read Philip K. Dick's *Do Androids Dream of Electric Sheep?*, and we have discussed Sherryl Vint's article on speciesism in that text. Her view is that Dick's protagonist, Deckard, sees nonhuman animals as objects and status symbols, thus undermining the idea the novel articulates about the importance and humanizing affect of having links with animals. This commodification of animals causes alienation of human beings from what Vint calls their "species being," and until that objectification ceases, there is little hope for recovering humanity and human relationships with the environment and animals (124–25). Vint also quotes Peter Singer's definition of speciesism: "a prejudice or attitude of bias toward the interest of members of one's own species and against those of other species" (114). By the end of "Bloodchild" the reader sees T'Gatoi and Gan as representatives of an ongoing process of cross-species adaptation. As Amanda Thibodeau puts it, Gan holds "both T'Gatoi and himself responsible" (273). The class can reach these conclusions about the story through discussion of concepts such as speciesism and environments and by reading attentively. That students retain their distaste for the Tlic, however, illustrates how ingrained our species perspective can be.

Adapting to Survive and Thrive in Parable of the Sower

Like Gan and his family, who live on a planet far from Earth and thus must adjust, Lauren and her family experience a series of adaptations caused by their shifting environment. Despite this similarity, students are far more receptive to Lauren's situation and contexts than they are to Gan's. The unraveling of groups, from the community of Robledo to Lauren's family, presents an opportunity for the protagonist to re-create her place in the world, though the opportunity comes at a terrible cost. The environment in the novel puts extreme pressure on people. The world in which Lauren lives, a place of almost no advanced technology, seems odd to students, but her resourcefulness and the key role knowledge plays in the book are easier for them to grasp.

The protagonists understand the pressures their worlds exert both on themselves and their communities. Lauren prepares for a time when her community will no longer be able act as a bulwark against a crumbling social order. She sees that desperation can lead to increasing violence and moral decay. With her grab-and-go pack and its inventory of supplies from clothes to seeds and books, she works her way to a worldview that she names Earthseed. Her response to a devolving world is to think about ways to reestablish humanity elsewhere—off-world. Early in the novel her admiration for the astronaut who died and wanted to have her remains left on Mars (21) signals to readers that she respects risk-taking and has a broad view of possible environments for people to occupy.

Whereas her family represents nostalgia for a world that cannot be restored, her journey away from Robledo after drug-mad people destroy it shows us that she "intend[s] to survive" (58). In creating a new group after the destruction of Robledo, Lauren understands the way a community can work even if its physical location is uncertain. After six years of drought and a sharp decrease in the standard of living, human society unravels in Lauren's southern California home. The notion of home or connection to place consequently suffers. As Madhu Dubey puts it, "Butler's representation of Robledo forcefully repudiates notions of place-bound community, and the journey section of the novel reaches for a more complex way of imagining community that is not coextensive with place . . ." (115). If community is no longer tied to place, then it becomes centered on the people in the group and their willingness to stay together and form a unit. Community in this way is a type of symbiosis—interdependence leads to the possibility of fuller, more peaceful lives.

They face a paradox, however: for the group to grow, they must accept new people, but to remain safe, "they must be suspicious and fight against their values [of acceptance]" (Baccolini 25). Lauren's hyperempathy creates a similar tension between compassion and self-preservation. While her condition makes her more compassionate, it also makes her more lethal when faced with a physical threat. This tension adds to the pressure that she, Harry, and Zahra feel. The novel "demonstrates powerfully the nexus between environmental degradation and social in/justice" (Mayer 190). Unlike "Bloodchild," it does not make us look at a link between human beings and another species, but it does stress the importance of human diversity and remains anthropocentric.

This, however, does not mean that the natural world plays a minor role in the book. Lauren's focus on understanding the world she walks into when she leaves Robledo keeps the reader focused on the question of resources. Her idea that Earthseed will flourish among the stars both creates a far-reaching goal and acknowledges that humanity has indeed exhausted the environment that Earth offered. "The novel's focus on human responsibility and action indicates that its didactic concern is not primarily with the ecosphere but with the human" (Rieder 83). The issue for students then becomes more nuanced than simply how the environment works in the book; it shifts to the complicated relationship between social order/disorder, leadership, and natural resources.

Lauren's position as narrator and writer of Earthseed verses shows readers many ways to negotiate these relationships. An example from the novel of the dynamic among community, safety, and resources that works well in class discussion is the scene at the water station when Lauren and Harry help Travis, Natividad, and their baby, who have been targeted by a group of human marauders, whom Lauren refers to as "two-legged coyotes" (202). Just before this incident, she had told Harry and Zahra, "We're a pack, the three of us, and all those other people out there aren't in it. If we're a good pack, and we work together, we have a chance. You can be sure we're not the only pack out here" (182). She admits that the baby "attracted my attention, my sympathy" (202). The water station passes for an organized, civilized business setting. As Melanie Marotta points out, people require "a symbiotic relationship between technology and nature" in order to survive (39), and this water station, an oasis both literally and figuratively, provides that. Inside the station there are goods for sale, but as Lauren says, "People going in have money. People coming out have water, which is as good as money" (201). Lauren, and anyone else who wants to survive, must manage the risk that comes with the available resource. The problem is how to go beyond the basics of survival to create something more like a society and less like an animal pack. As one of Lauren's Earthseed verses says, "There is no end / To what a living world / Will demand of you" (137).

The idea in *Parable of the Sower* that a natural resource can be the source of conflict connects with the class's conversations about another novel, Frank Herbert's *Dune*. Students read Herbert's novel in sections alongside their reading of Butler. By the time we get to the second half of her novel, we are far enough into Herbert's to see the influence that the spice from Arrakis has on civilization and the importance of the control of the supply of water. The need for the wise use of commodities resonates through the two texts.

Lauren writes, "All that you touch, / You Change. / All that you Change, / Changes you" (79). On Arrakis, Paul changes as he encounters the Fremen and spice and expands his being, but he also knowingly causes shifts in power structures and even reaches the point where he can destroy the spice. As he says, complete control over something must include the power to destroy it (Herbert 476). Lauren would agree: she understands civilization as "a means of combining the intelligence of many to achieve ongoing group adaptation. . . . Civilization, like intelligence, may serve well, serve adequately, or fail to serve its adaptive function. When civilization fails to serve, it must disintegrate unless it is acted upon by unifying internal or external forces" (101). Students often think of Lauren as capable and constructive, but part of her belief system includes an acknowledgment of the destruction that adaptation and struggle can entail. The biological model that her language alludes to emphasizes the need for diversity. Students often cite these Earthseed verses of hers:

> Embrace diversity.
> Unite—
> Or be divided,
> robbed,
> ruled,
> killed
> By those who see you as prey.
> Embrace diversity
> or be destroyed. (196)

It is possible to read this statement as a demand for the acceptance and tolerance of the other, but the destruction part of the verse points to the commonplace of biology that a species that is not diverse will not survive.

Encounters between people and their environments are central to Butler's "Bloodchild" and *Parable of the Sower*. In both texts, the ideas of combination, ingenuity, and symbiosis underpin the dynamic between people and nonhuman others and between people and nature. How Butler's protagonists manage their situations and how their relationship to others and to natural resources play out reveal patterns of social adaptation combined with their individual wills. Both Lauren and Gan become leaders who help reshape the views of their societies in the face of both personal and species-wide challenges.

Teaching the Social Construction of Disability through the Parable series, *Lilith's Brood*, and *Seed to Harvest*

Sami Schalk

Disability studies is an interdisciplinary field of study that attempts to understand how societies define, label, value, and treat differences in bodyminds and behaviors.[1] It is quite useful in teaching the work of Octavia E. Butler, and Butler's work is valuable in teaching key concepts in disability studies. The field explores how the concept of disability has varied by time, place, and culture, and Butler creates entirely new and different times, places, and cultures in which disability and ability take on shapes and meanings different from those in the real world. Often students want to know how the identity of the author relates to the content of the texts. I have found it helpful, therefore, to inform them that Butler indeed had the learning disability dyslexia. She also did extensive research on disability and disease.

Because disability studies is newer than the fields of race, gender, and sexuality studies, it has been influenced by them in many ways. One example of that influence is the use of the term *social construction*—the idea that knowledge of the world is learned through society's implicit and explicit messages. In this essay I discuss the social construction of disability and how I introduce and then complicate this concept in my classes. I examine how Butler's Parable series, *Lilith's Brood*, and *Seed to Harvest* can provide concrete yet imaginative avenues for students to understand the social construction of disability in complex and nuanced ways.

Societies create the meanings and boundaries of the term *disability* through physical and attitudinal environments. These environments reflect a society's ideology of ability, which Tobin Siebers defines as "the baseline by which humanness is determined, setting the measure of body and mind that gives or denies human status to an individual person" (8). I discuss with my students some concrete examples of the social construction of disability. One is how a building with stairs creates disability for a wheelchair user, whereas a building with ramps and elevators does not. That is, in an accessible space, a wheelchair user can move about just as easily as a non–wheelchair user even if they move in different ways. The problem resides not in the bodymind of the wheelchair user but in the construction of the environment.

It is often an easy first step for students to recognize how physical spaces are created in ways that exclude recognizably disabled bodyminds. I ask them to think further about how other elements of the physical environment demonstrate what kinds of bodyminds are expected and welcomed in a particular space. A simple exploration of one's campus reveals the ideology of ability, in terms of how far a student is expected to walk between classes, the presence or lack of Braille on signs, and how many elevators and wheelchair-accessible restrooms are available in each building. I particularly like pointing out seemingly benign and mundane things in the classroom, such as our desks: What do they reveal about the sort of bodyminds that students are supposed to have? In many classrooms on my campus the desks are small, stiff, uncomfortable, and designed for right-handed people. Students realize that these desks might make being in a classroom difficult not only for people with certain disabilities but also for left-handed students, pregnant students, and students of above-average size or height. I often have a few students tell how the design of a desk makes it hard for them to write, focus, or feel comfortable. Attention to the physical environment is a useful and concrete way to begin discussions of the social construction of disability, but my goal is to get students to understand the nuances and complexities of how disability is constructed through attitudes, behaviors, laws, expectations, and other societal norms as well.

In chapter 2 of *The Rejected Body,* Susan Wendell defines the social construction of disability as both the "subtle cultural factors that determine standards of normality and exclude those who do not meet them from full participation in their societies" and the ways in which "social conditions . . . straightforwardly create illnesses, injuries, and poor physical functioning" (36). In the worlds that Butler creates, both disability and ableism (discrimination against people with disabilities and preferred treatment for people without disabilities) exist, but these worlds have expectations, norms, and possibilities for bodyminds that are very different from those in the world we inhabit. Through the physical and attitudinal environments of Butler's fictional worlds in the Parable series, *Lilith's Brood*, and *Seed to Harvest*, students can begin to see how disability is socially constructed and apply this understanding to the real world.

In the Parable series, the main character, Lauren Olamina, has a disability called hyperempathy, which causes her to share the pain and pleasure of those around her. Given the dystopian setting of the story, she shares much more pain than pleasure. As Lauren writes, "I'm supposed to share pain *and* pleasure, but there isn't much pleasure around these days" (*Parable of the Sower* 12). In a more utopian, violence-free context with the exact same bodymind, Lauren would perhaps be considered privileged to be able to share the pleasure of those around her. In her world, however, she must hide her hyperempathy because it can be used against her to make her incapacitated by the pain of others. As the series shows repeatedly, people with hyperempathy, especially children, are targeted by company-town bosses and kidnappers because sharers are considered easier to control than nonsharers. Even though some people in the novels think of sharers as having special powers, every sharer knows that hyperempathy in this particular physical and attitudinal environment makes their lives particularly difficult and vulnerable to abuse. In terms of the social construction of disability, the Parable series demonstrates how social contexts impact bodyminds differently, influencing how people can exist in the world, for example, with or without pain. By thinking about how much Lauren's society influences her physical experience of hyperempathy, we can see how her disability is socially constructed—determined by the interaction of bodyminds and physical and attitudinal environments rather than by inherent qualities of bodyminds alone. The difference between Lauren's hyperempathy in a dystopian context and hyperempathy in a utopian context might be paralleled for students to the earlier-discussed example of a wheelchair user in a building without ramps or elevators and a wheelchair user in a building with ramps and elevators.

Lauren's disability is both new and congenital. Hyperempathy results from one's parents' taking Paracetco, a pharmaceutical treatment for Alzheimer's that was abused by people wanting to increase their focus and concentration. This aspect of the disability in the series provides an interesting spin on Wendell's argument that society can directly create illness and injury. Wendell primarily discusses the material construction of disability through war, poverty, and the lack of access of basic resources such as food, water, and medical care. In Butler's dystopian near future, however, disability is also accidentally created by modern medicine. The Parable series, therefore, encourages readers to not merely place this straightforward form of the social construction of disability outside the United States and the Global North; they should consider also how even valued and positive aspects of modern life may be changing our bodyminds in ways that are disabling. To connect this to the real world, I have talked to students about the use of asbestos insulation and lead paint in the early and mid–twentieth century, materials that were thought to be technological improvements until their dangerous and disabling effects were discovered. Students may also be interested in the history of the drug Thalidomide, a sedative-like product used by some women to combat morning sickness that caused limb impairments in many infants, primarily in Europe.

In Butler's *Lilith's Brood*, an alien species called the Oankali saves what is left of humankind after a nuclear war. The Oankali are, as they call it, traders, but what they trade is genetic material, mixing the best of themselves with the best of other species to continue to evolve. The Oankali plan to interbreed with human beings, carefully selecting genetic material from both species to create a new, better one. This alien species is attracted to the dangerous yet alluring combination in human beings of intelligence and hierarchy as well as several other genetic aspects, especially cancer. Early in the series, the character Lilith learns that the Oankali have treated her cancerous cells to prevent them from growing. They are excited by what they refer to as her "talent for cancer," believing that they can manipulate genes to control and focus cancer's rapid generation of cells (*Dawn* 22). When adjusted by the Oankali in their careful reproductive blending, cancer becomes the ability to heal quickly and even regenerate limbs in the bodies of human-Oankali children, known as constructs.

This talent, which our world considers dangerous and disabling, becomes an incredible ability in a new, alien world. The nonrealist context of *Lilith's Brood* allows readers to see how bodyminds can be interpreted and treated differently in different environments. Since *Lilith's Brood* is set in a distant future, students might consider how technology, from something as simple as eyeglasses to something as complex as a robotic prosthetic limb, has changed what disability means in our own time.

Lilith's Brood also demonstrates how culture shapes perceptions and definitions of disability. Throughout the series, the Oankali use strikingly patronizing and ableist language when discussing human beings. After studying human genetics and culture, they are certain that humanity will destroy itself without having its genetic flaw of combined intelligence and hierarchical thinking corrected. As a result, the only human beings permitted to have children are those who agree to live with the Oankali and bear constructs. Human beings who refuse the trade, referred to as resisters, are sterilized and permitted to live on their own until they all die out. Akin, the first male construct to be born to a human mother, questions this practice. He asserts that human beings should be allowed to reproduce on their own, just as the Oankali have a sect, called the Akjai, who do not mate with human beings. Akin reflects:

> Who among the Oankali was speaking for the interests of resister Humans? Who had seriously considered that it might not be enough to let Humans choose either union with the Oankali or sterile lives free of the Oankali? Trade-village Humans said it, but they were so flawed, so genetically contradictory that they were often not listened to. . . . He did not have their flaw. . . . He was Oankali enough to be listened to by other Oankali and Human enough know that resister Humans were being treated with cruelty and condescension. (404)

Akin understands and agrees, to some extent, with the Oankali's belief in humanity's inherent disability, yet he questions the ableist response of sterilizing resisters. With this example, students could compare the ideology of ability and the social norms of the Oankali with those of human beings. To the Oankali, human beings are disabled, even though the human beings do not think of themselves that way. This comparison allows students to consider how different attitudinal environments create vastly different perspectives on bodyminds and behaviors, constructing disability in the process.

In *Mind of My Mind*, the protagonist, Mary, creates the Pattern, a psychic web of individuals with various telepathic abilities who become connected to her and one another. In the real world, telepathic abilities are considered to be either fictional or rare, but in Butler's Patternist series it eventually becomes the case that only those who are telepathic have power, wealth, and status in society. Nontelepathic people live as "conscripted servants" or slaves, influenced, controlled, or owned by the Patternists to varying degrees (*Seed* 394). Referred to as mutes, nontelepathic people are disparaged and looked down on because they do not meet the threshold of ability necessary to be understood as full, valued subjects in this newly constructed society centered around the Pattern. While characters in *Mind of My Mind* explicitly connect the treatment of mutes to racism, this treatment can also be read as a form of ableism, because people without certain bodymind abilities considered basic or fundamental to humanity in their society are deemed inferior or broken rather than merely different. Reading the treatment of mutes in the series as ableism can open up space for students to think critically about how ableism functions in similar and different ways in the real world.

In the third book in the Patternist series, *Clay's Ark*, people who have been affected by a microscopic extraterrestrial parasite are attempting to build a new life for themselves and their children outside the confines of the rest of society so as to not create an epidemic. Infected human beings become stronger and have enhanced senses, yet they also appear emaciated and sweaty, and their skin is gray. Children of infected human beings have similarly enhanced senses but are even further outside the norms of humanity, with smaller bodies and the ability to move quickly on all fours. Noninfected human beings in the book refer to these children as animals and monsters. Once again, the perception and judgment of nonrealist bodyminds in the text requires a shifting of expectations by characters as well as readers. By drawing parallels between bodymind norms in the fiction of *Seed to Harvest* and bodymind norms in the real world, instructors can help students begin to question the disability-ability divide in contemporary society. In the text, discussions of who is and who is not human are based upon issues of ability and appearance. One might ask, therefore: What abilities or aspects of bodyminds do we consider essential and why? Why are certain differences valued or considered insignificant while other differences are considered reasons for pejorative treatment? By answering these questions in the context of the novels as well as in the real world, students will see how ideologies of ability and social constructions of disability undergird so much of whom we view as fully human, deserving of fundamental human rights, and worthy of respect and humane treatment.

The many representations of different bodyminds in fantastic settings in the work of Butler can be used to teach about the social construction of disability not only in the physical environment but also in the attitudinal environment—the ideology of ability that shapes a society's baseline for which bodyminds and behaviors are considered normal, acceptable, and valuable and which are not. By reading Butler's nonrealist work, students are prevented from easily applying their realist expectations and understandings of what is and is not a disability. Butler mixes ability and disability purposefully in her texts to make us question the boundaries of these categories and reveal their socially constructed nature. I encourage any disability studies classroom discussion of Butler's work to focus not only on the mere existence of different kinds of bodyminds but also on her fictional societies' different valuations and expectations of bodyminds, behaviors, and abilities. This kind of discussion, when carefully connected to real-world issues, can help students develop a more nuanced and complex understanding of the social construction of disability in order to identify it and deconstruct it in their own everyday lives.

NOTE

[1] In disability studies, the term *bodyminds* is used to refer to "the imbrication (not just the combination) of the entities usually called 'body' and 'mind'" in order to remind us of the inseparability and interconnectedness of ourselves as human beings (Price 270).

Clay's Ark: Teaching Butler's Vision beyond Liberal Consent

Beth A. McCoy

Octavia Butler's work helps students think critically about liberal consent, a legal concept understood ideally, according to Saidiya Hartman, as "a voluntary agreement" that is "unimpinged by relations of power and dominance" and "free from constraint or compulsion" (111). Emerging from federal and state law as well as the best practices of organizations against sexual assault, the sexual misconduct policy governing the college where I teach defines *affirmative consent* as a "knowing, voluntary and mutual decision among all participants to engage in sexual activity" without intimidation or coercion ("Definition"). Discussing the misconduct policy in the classroom allows students to consider how respecting consent is indispensable for protection against many kinds of harm. And it alerts them to how Butler novels, such as *Mind of my Mind* and *Parable of the Talents*, attend to the nonconsensual sexual and psychological violence committed by state and nonstate individuals and groups. But reading the policy also prepares students for something that many find surprising and distressing: Butler's fiction problematizes consent as well. *Clay's Ark* illuminates consent's historical entanglement in the decidedly nonconsensual force that produces the supposedly autonomous liberal subject. When Blake Maslin—a white man, father, and physician—disavows consent's troubled history and sparks a pandemic, Butler teaches a lesson that can feel almost unbearable: faith in liberal consent can stage or restage the very violence that it is understood to prevent.

Butler's work often engages classical liberalism, but because not all students have taken political philosophy, I assign John Locke's *Second Treatise of Government* (1689) to demonstrate how consent enforced by and through the law emerges from nonconsent's violence. According to Locke, native peoples wasted abundant land and waged war against "industrious and rational" Englishmen (21). Such wasteful belligerence rendered the indigenous akin to the earth itself: a feminized natural resource ripe for the "disproportionate and unequal possession" and distribution that hardworking, rational men had allegedly "agreed to" through what Locke calls "a tacit and voluntary consent" (29). In this way, indigenous peoples—including black Africans, in whose bondage Locke was invested—serve nonconsensually as the liberal state's basis. Locke thus imagines liberalism as a scenario wherein, as Wendy Brown puts it, "one group surrenders selfhood so that another group can have it" (161). That surrender is accomplished through a consent that, according to Brown, signifies "the presence of power, arrangements, and actions that one does not oneself create but to which one submits" (162–63). Put another way, nonconsent begets the consent that becomes "the standard of right and wrong" enshrined in the United States "established, settled, known law" (Locke 66) and eventually college policies. Though students eagerly talk about how Lockean thought informs their everyday lives (e.g., they feel they own the parking spaces they have waited for), they refuse to consider how such thought informs consent. Their refusal isn't surprising. Pressured themselves to become "industrious and rational" liberal and neoliberal subjects who make good, healthy, individual choices, they find it hard to accept that what they rely on as a methodology for preventing violence emerged from and as structural violence.

Unfolding in the twenty-first-century California desert, *Clay's Ark* immediately confronts students with the logical outcomes of this allegedly consensual "disproportionate and unequal possession." A "vast rich-poor gap" has deepened: the "corporate" United States government ignores "human rights, the elderly, the ecology," and "throwaway children" to favor the resource-hoarding rich, who see themselves as attacked nonconsensually by those economically ghettoized "sewers and cesspools" (588, 570). Returning to this already violent world, Eli Doyle, a black scientist, crashes the Clay's Ark spaceship and brings with him an extraterrestrial symbiont that has flipped the Lockean colonial script and obliterated liberalism's illusions about pure human autonomy. Possessing Eli with an unstoppable "compulsion" to spread it (489), the organism renders suicide impossible. When he sabotages the ship, the organism makes him survive to infect a ranch family without their consent or knowledge. Even though the organism forces him to do this, he feels "responsible" (608), an irrational response that functions as a classic Butler trap. Indeed, students take the bait. Noting the canny textual detail that infecting someone "feels sexual" (499), they judge Eli according to the college sexual misconduct policy's terms and hold him responsible for performing a nonconsensual act that, as they put it, he simply should not have done. Confronted with the organism's distinctly illiberal reality, students across identities and political perspectives declare that Eli starts the novel's violence. To them, he is a bad liberal-neoliberal subject, a criminal who has simply failed to make the good choices they are sure that they would make in his position.

Butler complicates such judgment as Eli, Meda, and other infected people work hard to face and shape this new world's limits and possibilities. Determining to spread the organism to only a few at a time, they forge a society based not on consent but on sparing "billions of uninfected people" from a pandemic (516). They don't cloak their actions in the legalities of guilt and innocence; instead, they soberly avow both the violence that they do and the violence that they did but no longer do. In other words, they confront the gains and losses of the alien symbiosis even though it's sometimes hard to tell the gains from the losses. For instance, when the organism dissolves patriarchal monogamy and prompts a "harem" (529) system, which Eli admits he enjoys, the community infects additional men and crafts a complex, thoughtful, gender-equitable system wherein, unlike the privileged "walled-in types," "people at least give a piss about each other" (578, 580). Scent rather than sight or law binds people together, and so this symbiosis spells the end of visual and political regimes, in which many are considered unworthy of love and personhood. The organism compels heterosex and reproduction, which are perhaps alien mandates; eases women's fertility, labor, and childbirth; and ignores the incest taboo. Killing most of Meda's family, it liberates her from the pleasureless isolation required by daughterly obligation. It ends rape and redeems the rapist Ingraham ("Take away the gang and give him something better and he turns into a person" [526]). It sunders Steven Kaneshiro from his family and his violin, an "amputation" (533) that may or may not be balanced by news that in an infected person severed fingers can regenerate. The community members exult in their organism-heightened speed, precision, senses, and strength, but their infected skin crawls with the longing for a faraway sun's red glow.

Writing about *Kindred*, Christine Levecq asserts that such complex ambivalence leaves Butler's readers "neither hopeless nor without scars" (550), but in *Clay's Ark*, students see the scars only, which is curious, because the organism confers benefits that many of them say they long for: caring families, an end to sexual violence. It distributes those benefits to all people, not just a few. Students protest that even if there are benefits (they are skeptical), those benefits result through Eli's original nonconsensual act and are thus suspect, even obscene, no matter whom they help and no matter how equitable the distribution. Under pressure, the students reach the very conclusion they had avoided when reading Locke's vision of consent that emerges from nonconsent. In other words, when confronted with the Clay's Ark community, they conclude that a society founded on nonconsent is absolutely illegitimate and unworthy of consideration.

Where the students' trajectory lays the groundwork for an important learning moment, Blake Maslin's philosophical stance leads to catastrophe. Readers meet Blake on a family trip with his twin sixteen-year-old daughters: Rane, who has a personality resembling his, and Keira, who is dying of a leukemia that twenty-first-century medicine has failed to cure. Thus far, the father has "managed to shield" the teenagers from the country's "sewers and cesspools" (570). He is driven in part by grief: a "sewer slug" murdered his wife, Jorah, the black social activist and reformer who convinced him to "[put] in time at one of the cesspool hospitals," work he likened "to trying to empty the Pacific with a spoon" (588). After Jorah's death, however, he manifests what Hartman terms "white anxiety about impending *dissolution and engulfment*" (206) and lives according to what Jean-Jacques Rousseau criticized as Lockean liberal philosophy's central tenet: "Perish if you will; I am safe and sound" (37).

Sidelined by a desert storm, the family is kidnapped by Eli and Ingraham and taken to the ranch to be infected. Identifying with the white father regardless of their own racial identities, students conclude (again) that violence begins with Eli, yet Butler quickly reminds her readers that, as Frank Wilderson III might put it, violence "precedes and exceeds" him (76). When Eli first sees the older white man traveling with two young black women, he misreads the scene as sexual and racial predation. The snap reading is offensive, but it indicates that Eli, by his race, recognizes the ghosts of nonconsent. Blake, however, does not.

At the ranch, Blake sees how the organism distributes gains and losses far more equally than liberalism has, but he feels that this equity is an injustice, an unnatural state in which, as he terms it, "people like us" are forced without their consent to experience loss where they should experience only gain (502). To quote the former Chicago mayor Harold Washington (Rivlin), Blake finds this "fairer than fair" situation intolerable. Determining to go back to what the philosopher Charles Mills terms "white" or (dryly) "'just' liberalism" (1382), Blake decides to "escape and go to a hospital; that was all" (363).

Here, it's useful to assign Dorothy Roberts's *Killing the Black Body* and Harriet Washington's *Medical Apartheid* to illuminate the history flowing through Blake's disastrous plan. Even though students might know about the infamous Tuskegee Syphilis Study, nonconsensual medical experiments performed on incarcerated persons, or how Mississippi doctors sterilized Mrs. Fannie Lou Hamer without her knowledge or consent, they interpret these episodes as isolated bumps on an otherwise just road. Roberts and Washington show that such violence has instead been widespread, frequent, and systemic; moreover, they show how it was deployed to solve what white supremacy and antiblackness constructed as black criminality and hypersexuality. According to classical liberal thought, such DuBoisian problems disrupted liberalism's natural consensual order and nonconsensually violated white (and upper-class black) autonomy. Because students sometimes question whether Butler intended us to read *Clay's Ark* in this grim light, I point to her voracious research and to the fact that as she began to write and publish the Patternmaster series in the 1970s, systematic nonconsensual medical violence against black people and nonblack people of color "received a high profile" (Athey 7). Butler may have been particularly aware of *Madrigal v. Quilligan* (1978), a federal suit filed by Mexican American women sterilized without informed consent in Los Angeles County Hospital, just ten miles from her Pasadena birthplace.[1]

As a doctor confronted with an organism that violates his consent, Blake tries to take shelter both in and against liberalism's history of medical nonconsent. As a person already struggling to live in symbiosis with that organism, Meda accuses Blake of being complicit in the nonconsent. After she infects him, she permits the physician to examine her flesh with his medical kit, which finds that the symbiont is "unidentifiable" and "incomprehensible" (193). Butler thus establishes that his hospital plan is delusional: if medical technology can't stop Keira's leukemia, what can it do with an organism it can neither identify nor understand? Blake pressures Meda to leave with him and get help, but what he really wants is the surrender of Meda's symbiotic selfhood so that he can recover his own selfhood. Meda alludes to medical nonconsent when she responds angrily that his plan will end up incarcerating her family, especially the children whom the uninfected perceive as older than other children.[2] Blake insists that "nobody would take" the children, but Meda cuts him off: "They'd take them. They'd treat them like *things*. If they killed them—accidentally or deliberately, it would be just one of their *problems* solved. . . . So if you're afraid of an epidemic, Doctor, don't even think about leaving us" (500; my emphasis). Meda has no knowledge or personhood that the doctor, like Justice Taney, feels bound to respect. Using his worthless medical kit to drug Meda while she sleeps, he gives the lie to his assertion that nobody would incarcerate or experiment on her family, illustrates his drive to purchase his autonomy through the nonconsent of others, and begins his escape with Keira and Rane.

This escape produces the very violence that the doctor claims to want to prevent. Leaving behind the only people who can help them through the compulsion's now-blossoming symptoms, Blake drives his family right into a sewer, where they are kidnapped again, this time by one of the nomadic car families that the Lockean state has cast off as human waste. Driven increasingly by the organism, the Maslins witness, endure, and participate in spectacular violence: dismemberment, gang rape, and murder. Rane is decapitated, her head thrown out a door. Using his new symbiotic powers, Blake escapes again, only to be run over by a truck. The compulsion keeps him alive long enough to infect the driver, who unwittingly goes on to start the pandemic. It is the organism that makes Blake spread the disease, but it's his faith in classical liberalism's nonconsensual consent that brings him to the crossroads. Later, news of a globe engulfed in disease, terror, and flames reaches the ranch: the infected going through their terrifying symptoms without support, thought, or knowledge. Whereas the Clay's Ark community had managed the organism's spread by building a society, the newly infected are out of control. The ranch was an island before, but now it is even more isolated, a quiet space for grieving and reflection on the possibility that Blake's philosophically informed actions cut short.

In a course on Butler's fiction, I teach *Clay's Ark* last, because its quiet allows students, stunned by the novel's violent climactic cascade, realize that Blake's thoughts, words, and deeds mirror the discursive violence they've performed all semester. When they read *Fledgling*, "Bloodchild," and the trilogy of *Lilith's Brood*, the class criminalized Tlic, Oankali, and Ina for failing to hew to liberal frameworks of consent. For instance, when learning that *Fledgling*'s Shori will perish if she cannot bite, feed on, and enter into symbiosis with human beings, students repeatedly forgot that textual fact and declared instead that because she bit without consent, she just should not eat. Blake's folly now prompts them to return to this declaration with some shame, for they now realize that they had decided that Shori should just die. Some swept their hands sideways, as if emptying Shori's life into a garbage can; others used subordinate clauses like "Even though there are problems with consent, Shori still should not have bitten." With the clarity and maturity that the extended encounter with Butler's work cultivates, they confront the Blakean liberal compulsion that has been in operation in them: "people like us" (502) should determine and enforce the protocols, even if it means that others die.[3] They admit that they had to perform such violence over and over again until it accumulated enough for them to realize it, much as Blake didn't understand what he'd been doing until he actually started the pandemic.

Is *Clay's Ark* no more than a cautionary tale about how not to behave? Does the novel unfairly indict Blake and Blake-like readers by minimizing human terror in the face of crumbling illusions about consent and autonomy? These critiques could be mounted, I'd suggest, were it not for Butler's careful portrayal of Keira. By the end of the novel, Rane and Blake have died, but Keira lives, infected but healthy (the organism cures her leukemia), grieving but full of possibility (she is pregnant). She lives, Butler suggests, because, unlike Blake and Rane, she has nothing to escape back to. She has a future to reach for. At the ranch, Blake worries about what infection will do to Keira's chemotherapy-compromised immune system. His concern, of course, is not misplaced (Eli worries similarly), but, once again, it's a bit disingenuous, providing cover as it does for his phobic response to the emotional, intellectual, and sexual "understanding" (468) burgeoning between Keira and Eli. To be sure, Keira is (troublingly) two years below California's long-standing age-of-consent legal threshold of eighteen, but Blake's real problem appears to lie with the fact of her *becoming.* Indeed, Butler represents her as a mature, desiring black woman, a person for whom the existing medical and political order offers nothing, an individual who never consented to cancer and whom the law says cannot consent. All of these things prompt Keira to see possibility where her father and sister say absolutely none exists. Indeed, where they objectify infected adults as "stick people—menacing, utterly terrifying in their difference and their intensity" (509) and the children as "[t]hings" (572) that are bred, Keira perceives complex, vulnerable *persons.* Recognizing this, Blake protests that Eli doesn't know what Keira "needs," but Meda shreds his medical and affective paternalism; in the "instant before [Blake] could lie," Meda states that *he knows* that *Keira* knows what she needs (484). What Keira *needs*, of course, is a future, something that classical liberal law, consent, methodology, or reform (given Jorah's final motherly lesson) can never provide. She knows that she desires Eli as he does her, fully recognizing gain and loss, risk and benefit, known and unknown. As the organism is already endemic in cows and soil, she knows she may already be infected. And so she who has nothing to lose, she whom consent cannot protect, she who cannot *even* consent—*she* reaches for possibility by taking takes Eli's hands. So she takes Eli's hands and demands that we all consider what could have been.

NOTES

[1] For more on *Madrigal v. Quilligan*, see Gutiérrez.

[2] Many people have long known that black children, unlike white children, are not allowed innocence and instead are cast early and nonconsensually into the older realm of "quarrelsome and contentious" nonpersons (Locke 21).

[3] For more on a related yet different classroom response, this time to the Xenogenesis trilogy, see Foster.

Intergroup Dialogue and Difficult Conversations: Teaching Butler at a Private, Christian, Predominantly White Institution

Kendra R. Parker

My course Which Bodies Matter? Victims and Victors and Villains, Oh My!, a first-year seminar, was designed using intergroup dialogue as a pedagogical framework. It incorporates Octavia E. Butler's "Bloodchild," *Dawn*, and *Fledgling* to demonstrate the value of Butler's fiction not only for bridging gaps between literature and social praxis but also for facilitating conversations surrounding consent.

Proponents of intergroup dialogue have long maintained that dialogue is a learner-centered approach that fosters greater student understanding (Lea et al.; O'Neill and McMahon). Developed at the University of Michigan, Ann Arbor, in the 1980s (Zúñiga et al. 2), intergroup dialogue is best understood as a facilitated, face-to-face encounter that aims to foster innovative levels of understanding between two or more identity groups (Zúñiga and Nagda). In 2009, researchers described *dialogue* as a "collaborative communication process that engages students in self-other exchanges that illuminate intellectual and experiential similarities and differences" (Nagda et al. 4). As the demand for diversity, inclusion, and multiculturalism in higher education increases, intergroup dialogue has become a staple pedagogical tool because it "encourages students with different identities to get to know each other" while also promoting an "understanding of one's racial-ethnic, gender and other social identities as well as understanding those of others" (Nagda and Gurin 43). Using intergroup dialogue, I encouraged my students to grapple with issues like racism, consent, and rape through "Bloodchild," *Dawn*, and *Fledgling* without my having to establish a literary or historical context for Butler's fiction. By presenting them with an author who confronts such social realities in a fictional way and then engaging them in dialogue-based learning by prompting them with questions about consent, race, rape, power, and agency, I facilitated a series of conversations in which they bridged the gap between fiction and reality and made lasting connections between contemporary, real-world events and Butler's texts.

At Hope College, the first-year seminar is a required, fall-semester-only course for all incoming students. For my course, I consulted *Difficult Conversations: How to Discuss What Matters Most*, in which Douglas Stone, Bruce Patton, and Sheila Heen provide information on how to successfully facilitate and engage in difficult conversations. I offered students three guidelines for speaking with clarity and power: realize that truth is not universal, offer context for your opinions, and dwell in a space that is receptive to questions and invites open-ended conversation. I referred to these guidelines for peer-to-peer dialogue as virtues of dialogue. For Butler's work to have a relevant, practical, and personal effect on students attending a private, Christian, liberal arts college, these virtues of dialogue are indispensable. They allowed students to develop clear communication skills, helped them foster healthy relationships with one another, and opened up a space for them to discuss consent.

Many students at the school had little experience engaging in thoughtful conversation about diverse cultures, so I created four phases to help them move beyond resorting to silence or stereotypical opinions in the classroom. The four phases—camaraderie building, preparing to read Butler, reading Butler, and after reading Butler—originated in part from Biren (Ratnesh) A. Nagda and Patricia Gurin's four stages of intergroup dialogue: group beginnings, exploring commonalities and differences of experience, exploring and dialoguing about hot topics, and alliance building and social action. My phases, like Nagda and Gurin's, were never completely self-contained: each developed throughout the semester. I articulate them here but never made them explicit to my students, just as I did not reveal to them that intergroup dialogue was my pedagogical method.

Phase 1: Camaraderie Building

The goal of phase 1 is to create a space for engagement, to foster community building, and to encourage healthy relationships. First-year seminar students must attend a session the Saturday before classes begin; it is held during orientation and move-in weekend. To start, I give each student an index card with five wide-ranging questions. Students must seek and find answers without asking their parents or me. They may turn to the person next to them or tentatively cross the room and introduce themselves to other students. Gradually they interact with one another, move out of their comfort zones, begin collaborating. Camaraderie building continues with a *Twitter* scavenger hunt I devised to help students familiarize themselves with the campus and to alert them to certain campus services. I ask them to take selfies at specific locations and post them on *Twitter* using #LearningHope by the end of the first week of classes. The final task in establishing camaraderie is a name quiz: students must recognize the faces and know the names of all their classmates.

These three experiences—the seek and find, the *Twitter* scavenger hunt, and the name quiz—provide benchmarks for the students to build camaraderie. The seek and find has them become vulnerable and turn to others for answers and clarity. The scavenger hunt fosters community for two reasons: first, not all have *Twitter* accounts, so they take usies (an usie is a group selfie); second, many do not want to get lost on campus, so finding different venues with a partner gives them confidence and also helps them get to know each other. Some students have already become fast friends, so it is natural for them to do the scavenger hunt together. The name quiz encourages the recognition of another person's humanity, an acknowledgment of utmost importance when difficult conversations are to come. I make it a point to know all my students' names by the end of the first class period—that effort on my part builds camaraderie between the students and me.

Phase 2: Preparing to Read Butler: Exploring Gender, Race, and Stereotypes

Phase 2 introduces students to the subject matter of Butler's fiction before they read it. It occurs during the first four weeks of the semester. In a unit called "Gender, Race, and Stereotypes," they read Robert Bogdan's "The Social Construction of Freaks," interrogate gender representations in Disney's *Mulan*, respond to Jennifer Siebel Newsom's 2011 TEDx Talk, discuss Marlon Riggs's *Ethnic Notions*, and converse about #BlackLivesMatter and #iftheygunnedmedown. The purpose is to help them navigate different lived experiences and begin conversations about how their experiences relate to the varied social systems that construct the experiences of others.

To facilitate conversations on difference in general and on gender, sexuality, and race specifically, I present students with a "Systems of Oppression" handout I put together on the basis of Rita Hardiman, Bailey W. Jackson, and Pat Griffin's "Conceptual Foundations" (see appendix 1). I ask students to interpret, in groups of four, this information in their own words and then use it to reflect on their first four weeks in the course. They must make "I" statements to articulate their emotional response or their intellectual perspective and support their claims with some text. After spending time in small groups asking questions and paraphrasing one another's statements for clarity, they come together as a class circle to have a larger conversation about the topic.[1] At the end of the class circle, I direct them to the questions on the left side of the handout, which are designed to prompt their thinking about the material that will appear in the next unit. By now they should be examining their assumptions about difference, gender, race, and representation.

Phase 3: Reading Butler

I designed phase 3 to make students intellectually and emotionally uncomfortable. They are to apply the dialogue skills they acquired to express themselves and process unfamiliar information. At the end of week 4, they are assigned "Bloodchild" in preparation for the unit called "Agency, Power, Survival, and Consent." They must also read Elyce Rae Helford's "'Would You Really Rather Die Than Bear My Young?'" for context, watch both *The Hunger Games* and *The Hunger Games: Catching Fire*, and, finally, read *Dawn*.

In our opening discussion of "Bloodchild," students share their discomfort with the material. I ask them what made them uncomfortable and why and have them use "I" statements in their responses. In a class circle, we consider kinship bonds, incest, race, and enslavement in "Bloodchild." I present them with the tasks of defining consent and thinking about its presence or absence in Butler's story. They do this by working in small groups. The following week, they discuss the films *The Hunger Games* and *The Hunger Games: Catching Fire* as a way to talk about power and agency. Then they revisit "Bloodchild" and the "Systems of Oppression" handout to see how power and agency can compromise a person's ability to consent. They conclude that the protagonist in "Bloodchild" must acquiesce because of the threat of his sister's impregnation.

Phase 4: After Reading Butler: Real-World Application

Like Nagda and Gurin's fourth stage, where students apply their new understanding of dialogue, inequality, and identity to social justice pursuits (69), in my fourth phase the students can make explicit connections between Butler's texts and daily concerns in the United States: they talk about how consent, power, and coercion can affect not only their lives but also the lives of others, such as Jahi McMath (she was pronounced dead in California but treated as alive in New Jersey), Brittany Maynard (she chose physician-assisted suicide), and Marlise Muñoz (she was declared brain-dead but kept on a ventilator).[2]

Students read *Dawn* and participate in a virtual classroom session, which includes a prep that asks them to read certain news articles, create a discussion board thread, discuss how consent informs a particular case, and indicate how the case reminds them of *Dawn* or "Bloodchild" (see appendix 2). In this session, we use a chat-room setting to explore their thoughts. They then read a peer-reviewed article about *Dawn* and explain how it has given them another perspective on the novel, and they comment on the posts of their peers. These online interactions engage students who might not otherwise speak in class; they also give students more time to articulate their feelings than they would have in class.

For our in-class discussion of *Fledgling*, students participate in a speed dialoguing activity. I print out three sources from the Internet; separate the class into four groups (see appendix 3); give three one article each, an article about the convergences of power, agency, consent, or race; and ask the fourth group to discuss consent, inebriation, and addiction in *Fledgling* specifically. The questions to address are whether or not characters give consent and whether or not the protagonist's actions are taken in self-defense or as a way to assert agency. After seven minutes, I yell, "Switch!," and the groups switch articles. The process is repeated until the class is over. Speed dialogue helps students approach different issues—the rape of men by women, binge drinking, campus sexual assault—with a keen eye. Further dialogue emerges, and the students leave with more questions than answers.

The semester culminates with a final reflection essay. One student, Kaelyn, articulated how the secular, speculative course content created a space for her to define her spiritual, moral self on her own terms:

> . . . I wouldn't say I've been exposed to a diverse array of opinions. For several years I've been anticipating Hope's "atmosphere of search and confrontation that will liberate the mind." To me, being in a school filled with unique viewpoints and strong opinions is freedom. . . . During my First Year Seminar, my class discussed many controversial topics. Though at times the confrontation was alarming, it allowed me to explore the opposite opinion and, as Hope College explains it, "define moral values and make moral judgments."[3]

Kaelyn's experience was not atypical: many of my students share her background, many are unfamiliar with Butler's work, and, like Kaelyn, many are reluctant to express their views out of fear of being labeled judgmental or closed-minded.

Kaelyn's reflection and anonymous student evaluations showed me that implementing intergroup dialogue and assigning Butler's fiction were effective in getting students to participate in difficult conversations in and outside the classroom.

Kaelyn made a deeply personal connection to Butler's fiction:

> One part to my First Year Seminar thoroughly stuck with me. My class read a book called *Fledgling* by Octavia Butler. . . . Like Shori, I don't completely know who I am. . . . Like Shori, I'm not worried. I am exactly who I am meant to be and though I may not be enlightened to it yet, there is a need in this world that only I can fill and I'm going to fill it.

Her identification with Shori, a black female vampire, though Kaelyn is a young white woman, was one of the reasons I have continued to incorporate Butler's work in at least one course every semester. Butler's universality encourages critical engagement with intersections of race, gender, power, and sexuality; her fiction allows bridges to be built, relationships to be formed, and dialogues to emerge, making the Earthseed mantra "All that you touch, You Change. All that you Change, Changes you" (*Parable of the Sower* 3) resonate on a college campus, a Christian campus—Hope's campus.

NOTES

[1]A class circle is the physical arrangement of desks or chairs that makes all students equally visible, so that they can easily look at one another when engaging in difficult conversations.

[2] My students read about Maynard's case in class, and I reference McMath and Muñoz to provide context and to complicate conversations.

[3] Kaelyn is quoting from a statement about Hope College's philosophy of education ("Philosophy").

APPENDIX 1:
Systems of Oppression

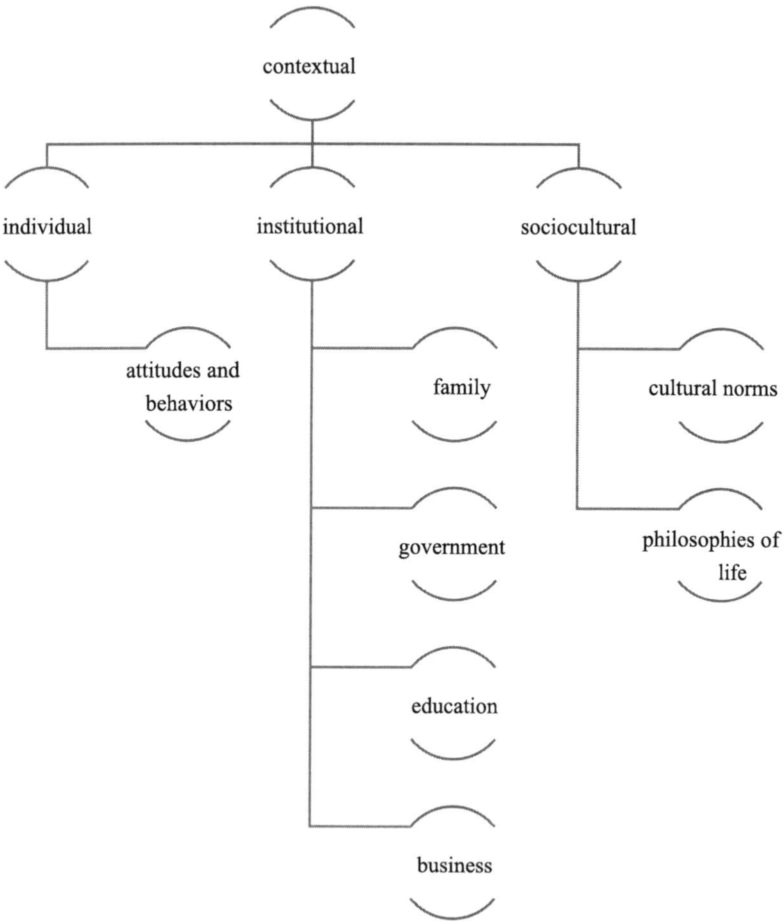

Consider the various systems of oppression that appear in "Bloodchild," *The Hunger Games*, *The Hunger Games: Catching Fire*, and *Dawn*.

- Be able to identify the systems of oppression in each.
- Be able to articulate how these systems operate.
- What happens when someone tries to escape or to question these systems?
- The "faces" of oppression include exploitation, marginalization, powerlessness, cultural imperialism, and violence. What do these words mean?

- How do these systems of oppression contribute to our discussion of consent?
- How do these systems of oppression lead us to define (and perhaps redefine) victim, villain, and victor?

APPENDIX 2:
Virtual Classroom Prep

The virtual classroom will revolve around the issue of consent.

1. Read one or more of the following short news articles:

   "Woman, 29, Chooses to Die Two Days after Husband's Birthday"

   Wade Goodwyn, "The Strange Case of Marlise Muñoz and John Peter Smith Hospital"

   Chris Hamby, "Government Set Up a Fake Facebook Page in This Woman's Name"

2. Create your own thread with a descriptive title that describes the nature of your post.
3. Discuss how the issue of consent informs the case or cases you read or watched. Keep in mind the questions implicit in Butler's *Dawn* and "Bloodchild": Who gets to have consent? When is consent not relevant? How do we define consent: forced consent, implied consent, uninformed consent, informed consent?
4. The Terrans and the Oankali hope to keep the best interests of the human beings at heart, but this pact is violated through genetic testing, rape, coercion, and misinformation. Is a guaranteed quality of life (or death) a good reason for giving up agency and one's right to accept or deny (that is, consent to) treatment? In what ways do these questions about consent in both Butler's works help us think about the news stories? Use textual examples from *Dawn* to support your claims.

Dawn Peer-Reviewed Article Response

1. Create your own thread. Title the thread Author's Last Name, Author's First Name, "Article Title."
2. At the beginning of the post, provide the citation of the article in MLA citation format.
3. Write an annotation of the article.
4. Indicate how the critical article helped you understand some part of *Dawn*.
5. Do you agree with the article's analysis of *Dawn*? Why or why not? Explain.

APPENDIX 3:
Fledgling Discussion Board

Refresh your memory of one of the following articles:

Jake New, "The 'Yes Means Yes' World"

Hanna Rosin, "When Men Are Raped"

Jen Mann, "Sorta Racist Lesbian Couple Sues Sperm Bank"

1. Create your own thread with a descriptive title that describes the nature of your post as it relates to the article of your choosing and *Fledgling*.

2. Discuss how race, consent, or sexuality informs the case or cases you chose to post on. Keep in mind the questions implicit in Butler's *Fledgling* (and in Butler's work in general):

> Who gets to have consent? When is consent not relevant? How do we define consent: forced consent, implied consent, uninformed consent, informed consent?
>
> Questions of race: racial miscegenation, rape, racial difference, racial tension.
>
> Hierarchies of oppression: structural, familial, social, other.

In what ways do these questions in *Fledgling* help us think about one of the preceding news stories? Use textual examples from *Fledgling* to support your claims.

3. Respond to four people who were not in your speed dialogue group and evaluate each person's claims. Do you agree or disagree with what was said? Why or why not? What did the person say that you had not considered (whether or not you agree)? How could the person have stated his or her point more strongly?

Butler as Feminist Philosopher: A Care-Ethics Approach to Teaching *Kindred* and *Dawn*

Rekik Scholler-Mekonnen

Like many of Octavia Butler's novels, *Kindred* and *Dawn* portray encounters riddled with conflict. While the contexts vary, the trope of painful and often violent encounter with the other—raced, gendered, or alien other—is central in both. In *Kindred*, Butler makes what Hortense Spillers describes as "the most daring of fictional moves" (5): the African American protagonist, Dana, is involuntarily and repeatedly taken from her California home in 1976 to her ancestors' plantation in nineteenth-century Maryland, where she interacts with Rufus—her white ancestor who "[draws her] to him somehow" (26)—as he grows into adulthood. Realizing that she is there to protect him and thereby secure the survival of her family, she submits to enduring the life of a slave. As a slave, she hopes to create better relations with Rufus. *Dawn* is Butler's equally daring vision of a human-alien encounter in the aftermath of a global nuclear war. The narrative probes the question of humanity's chance for survival with powerful, gene-trading aliens known as the Oankali. Selected by the aliens to be the progenitor of a new hybrid species, the black protagonist, Lilith, negotiates the conflicting needs of her fellow human beings, who must relinquish human ways and enter into cross-species symbiotic relations, and her new Oankali family. Dana and Lilith both resist oppositional confrontation and engage in a relational ethics of care.

It may at first seem surprising to reference care in the same breath as slavery and catastrophe. In such violent contexts, what insights does a care-focused examination of relations have to offer? As care ethicists have pointed out, relations of care, and indeed all relations, are inherently asymmetrical and thus prone to conflict. It would be inaccurate to view care as "anything like harmony and an absence of violence" (Held 138). A care perspective does not seek to elide conflict. It seeks, instead, to respond to people in specific situations while remaining alert to shifting power differentials. Butler's remark that science fiction gives her "freedom" to "extrapolate" ("Sci-Fi Visions" 4) suggests that the fantastic elements of time travel and postapocalyptic-alien imagination in *Dawn* are not incidental to the narrative but fundamental to her project of interrogating existing structures of relations. Readers are invited to partake of this freedom and reconsider human (and nonhuman) relationships that emerge in these unexpected encounters.

What follows is a proposal for teaching *Kindred* and *Dawn* through the lens of care ethics in order to develop a positive interpretation of unlikely partnerships. I strive to anticipate student responses and questions so that instructors can adapt this material as needed. The aim is to promote an understanding of care as not merely an attitude but also an empowering strategy for survival and social change. Helping students recognize and appreciate caring practices in extreme contexts is difficult, because the temptation is strong to read the conflicted encounters in Butler's texts in dualistic terms (master/slave, black/white, male/female, human/nonhuman). But a dualistic reading obscures Butler's other-oriented approach to relations. A care perspective highlights how the protagonists respond to rather than resist the other and thus moves beyond dichotomy.

In the English department curriculum, the novels could be taught on their own or form a subunit in a course devoted to feminist speculative fiction along with Butler's *Fledgling*, Sherley Anne Williams's *Dessa Rose*, and Jewelle Gomez's *The Gilda Stories*, to name a few examples of ethnic American women's fiction depicting unconventional caring relationships. Science fiction offers cross-curricular opportunities, so Butler's novels also can be included on the reading list of a philosophy course surveying traditional and feminist approaches to ethics.

The popularity of science fiction means that most students will be familiar with the alien-encounter trope and immediately recognize *Dawn* as an example of it. But pairing *Kindred* with *Dawn* requires some explanation, although the connection between slave narratives and science fiction is not so tenuous. As Gregory Hampton and Wanda Brooks point out, there is a long-standing link between "narratives of the alienated and/or marginalized 'other'" and science fiction, which expands notions of alienation beyond its conventional association with extraterrestrials, robots, and intergalactic travel (70). Once this link becomes clear, students should have little trouble extending the trope of alien encounter to raced and gendered others in *Kindred*. For further examples of writing in this tradition, I recommend selected readings from Sheree Thomas's groundbreaking anthology *Dark Matter: A Century of Speculative Fiction from the African Diaspora*.

An effective way to steer students' attention to issues of care is to lead with the following questions about the novels' opening scenes: Who are the characters? Under what circumstances do they encounter one another? How can we characterize their response? Certainly the "dizziness, nausea, and "blur[ring] and darken[ing]" that Dana experiences as she is pulled into the past (*Kindred* 13) invokes the trauma of the Middle Passage. Might it also anticipate a metaphorical crossing of boundaries? After the disorientation subsides, Dana finds herself on the banks of a river. She registers a child's screams, realizes it is drowning, pushes aside her many questions, and "react[s] to the child in trouble" (13). This action conveys caring values, but questions linger. Some students, tipped off by the book's cover illustration of a black woman or by a plot summary, may point out the incongruity of talking about care in the context of black women and white children, seeing in Dana the stereotypically self-sacrificing, nurturing mammy. Butler's fiction draws attention to women's historically marginalized roles as caregivers, but her women also "call to the future with incredible acts of compromise and imagination" (Hairston 297). As Andrea Hairston reflects, a man who sacrifices himself is heroic; why, then, is a woman who "accommodates the 'enemy'" a "suspect feminist" (298)? Because the text is unclear at first about racial identities, the reader is not sure about the accommodations Dana makes. Lilith, before her first interaction with the aliens, also shows a capacity to care. The Oankali observe her behavior with "a foreign child of her own species" (*Dawn* 60), presumably to determine her suitability as intermediary between human beings and aliens. Her attentiveness and her concern with "how to protect [Sharad]" (10) immediately distance her from her namesake, the biblical Lilith, whose "demonic" and vengeful nature tells a different story, one of fear and harm (Osherow 70). Her distress at Sharad's sudden disappearance and her subsequent inquires into his well-being reveal the depth of her care.

From the beginning, then, we discern a care-oriented approach to the other that echoes Sara Ruddick's concept of "maternal thinking," a practice that "begins with a double vision—seeing the fact of biological vulnerability as socially significant and as demanding care" (18). For Ruddick, mothering does not presume a biological relationship. In their new surroundings, Dana and Lilith are not biological mothers, yet they embody something akin to the "preservative love, nurturance, and training" that constitute maternal thinking (17). The awareness that Rufus will gain authority over the plantation and the fates of the slaves on it motivates Dana to act to ameliorate this possible future by "plant[ing] a few ideas in his mind" to "keep him from growing up into a red-haired version of his father" (*Kindred* 68, 81). Strengthening an earlier claim that she could not have "ignored any child in trouble" (29), she continues to influence Rufus, advising him to resist at least some of the ideological foundations of slavery (139) and succeeding sometimes in persuading him to "co-operate" and "make compromises" (121). "If history could be changed," she reasons, then her intervention "might be the thing to change it" (141). Such "disciplined reflection," consisting of "intellectual capacities," "judgments," "metaphysical attitudes," and "values" (Ruddick 24) and grounded, perhaps, in Dana's orphanhood, also characterizes Lilith's response to the other. Her self-conscious reflections on how to approach the Oankali (through imagination, critical questioning, and touch [*Dawn* 23, 25]) represent caring values, as do her empathy and ability to assume the perspective of another—with Sharad; with Nikanj, her alien mate whom she sees as "[j]ust a child" (72); with Kahguyaht, whose pain she understands when its child is injured; and with Jean, whose grief at losing her human mate makes her look "like a large child" (194). Given her sympathetic imagination and mode of deliberation, it is not surprising that the Oankali appoint her to select, train, and lead the first human beings in a cross-species partnership. Lilith seeks out "thoughtful people who would hear what she had to say and not do anything violent or stupid," "people who could give her ideas, push her mind in directions she might otherwise miss," and "whose arguments she could respect" (117).

At this point in the course, students read excerpts from Carol Gilligan's *In a Different Voice*, Virginia Held's *The Ethics of Care: Personal, Political, and*

Global, and Joan C. Tronto's *Moral Boundaries: A Political Argument for an Ethic of Care* to explore how care has been theorized. A foundational text in care ethics, Gilligan's book strategically uses fiction (Shakespeare, Chekhov, Ibsen, Joyce, Eliot)—as I do in this proposal—to contextualize care ethics. She takes issue with the prevailing model of moral reasoning that views people as autonomous, rational, and impartial agents guided by universal principles. She offers an alternative conception, one that sees "a world [composed] of relationships rather than of people standing alone, a world that coheres through human connection rather than through systems of rules" (29). She draws attention to the "different voice" of women who are motivated to preserve relationships rather than merely to resolve conflicts (2, 28).

According to Held, this focus on relationships constitutes one of five features of care ethics; the other four are the recognition of the dependent nature of life, an appreciation of "sympathy, empathy, sensitivity, and responsiveness," an insistence on the "moral significance of the 'private' domains of family and friendship," and a conception of relational rather than autonomous selves (10, 13, 14). Equipped with this theoretical background, students can articulate aspects of care in the early scenes of Butler's novels and see how these interactions prefigure caring relationships in the later, more conflicted encounters.

Is care gendered? Is it confined to the personal sphere? Tronto's broader definition of *care* as "everything we do to maintain, continue, and repair our 'world' so that we can live in it as well as possible" (103) directs attention to the Oankali, who, in their relations with virtually everything in their environment, are quintessential figures of care. They have a "strong, symbiotic relationship" with their ship, without which the ship "would die" and they "would be planet-bound" (*Dawn* 35). The "carnivorous plant[s]" on their ship serve as nourishing pods, taking care of others by providing sustenance and shelter (54). And, just as Lilith parents her brood of human beings, the Oankali become surrogate parents to all of them. Butler's portrayal of care is thus neither gender- nor species-specific. Care is "both a practice and a disposition" (Tronto 104), both social and moral, and applicable to all spheres of life.

What exactly makes carers attentive? Tronto's view of care highlights "conditions of vulnerability and inequality" (134). Students are now introduced to the concept of vulnerability, which has been theorized as a universal characteristic of life "arising from our embodiment" and "which carries with it the ever-present possibility of harm, injury, and misfortune" (Fineman 5). In *Precarious Life: The Powers of Mourning and Violence*, Judith Butler speaks of embodied vulnerability in similar terms: "The body implies mortality, vulnerability, agency: the skin and the flesh expose us to the gaze of others, but also to touch, . . ." (26). In *Kindred* and *Dawn*, the figure of the child—neglected, injured, powerless—epitomizes a vulnerability that demands sympathy. Dana likes Rufus almost from the start, finding his presence "comforting." The "possibility of meeting a white adult" (*Kindred* 33), by contrast, is frightening. She is dismayed by Tom

Weylin's abuse of his son and tries to shield Rufus from his father's wrath. When Rufus implores her to stay with him after a tree-climbing injury, she is reluctant to leave him with a father who behaves "as though he didn't care" (69): "I didn't want to go. I liked the boy, . . ." (66). In *Dawn*, the Oankali adeptly pair Lilith with Nikanj, a "subadult" (186); they are aware of her capacity to respond to childlike qualities, as illustrated by her behavior with Sharad, her incredulity at Kahguyaht's careless insinuation that she might hurt an Oankali child (50), her attachment to Nikanj (72), and her concern for Jean (194).

The proliferation of images of frailty and wounding throughout the texts reminds us of this "ever-present" vulnerability. We see it in the awakening of Lilith as she lies in a fetal position, "helpless, alone, and ignorant" (*Dawn* 5); in the recurring motif of the womb—the Oankali home world (37), the womb-like space of their ship (54), and Lilith's pregnant womb—which evokes the fragility of birth or rebirth; in the biological imperative that makes the Oankali permanently open, and thus also vulnerable, to others; and in the human dependency on the Oankali as a result of the global catastrophe. It is Dana's mutilated body, a site of the trauma of slavery—and also of care—with which the reader is first confronted in *Kindred*. The threat of punishment, rape, and death inflicted on black bodies hovers constantly. These images function cumulatively to disturb conceptions of subjects as invulnerable and self-possessed. In *Kindred*, this destabilization works on a textual level as well. Through the deliberate blurring of temporal, historical, and racial boundaries, the narrative refuses to adhere to simple binaries, thus collapsing the idea of "absolute sovereignty" (Duchamp 93) and the "cultural myth of alien encounter" (Parham 1318–19). The various iterations of vulnerability signify its sharedness, making it less a quality of otherness and more "an existential state that may belong to any one of us" (Shildrick 1).

If the body reminds us of vulnerability, how do we account for the refusal to acknowledge vulnerability? In *Dawn*, the tension between trying to maintain the illusion of autonomy and accepting its loss is dramatized in the conflict between Lilith and her followers, on the one hand, and the resisters, on the other. As a classroom activity, students can locate examples of these tensions and analyze how they are expressed. Some male resisters view the Oankali way of being, including sex, as a negative state: "[H]e had been humiliated and enslaved. . . . His humanity was profaned. His manhood was taken away" (192). Human-alien sex is equated with loss of self-control and marked as "deprivation" (Fineman 1). Noting how dependency is opposed to the masculine ideals of autonomy and humanity, invite students to consider how the invocation of the "monstrous other" (Shildrick 3) in racist or human-centric terms also signifies loss—loss of agency, independence, and humanity (*Dawn* 33, 57, 58, 159, 277)—and how dualistic thinking signals a revolt against vulnerability.

Lilith is initially complicit in this human revolt—she seeks security (5) and is "embarrassed" and "ashamed" by dependency (37, 39)—but her evolving ability to imagine a posthuman future that values relational identities clashes with the human tendency to cast vulnerability as a "negative attribute . . . largely projected onto the other and held at bay lest it undermine the security of closure and self-sufficiency" (Shildrick 1). The "intimate" and "vulnerable" act of care that Dana shows Nikanj when it is injured stigmatizes her as a "traitor" and "whore" (*Dawn* 232, 241). Her ostracism underscores the (human) failure to acknowledge vulnerability, a fact that has not escaped the Oankali, who chemically manipulate the newly awakened human beings into a state of dependency on Lilith in an effort to make them accept their "helpless[ness]" (152) as an inevitable aspect of life.

For Dana, accepting her corporeal vulnerability becomes a matter of urgency: if she insists on asserting her identity as a twentieth-century black woman instead of a slave on the plantation, she risks not just brutal punishment but her very life and that of her family. On her return from her first journey to the past, she remarks, "Maybe I'm just like a victim . . . who survives, but who doesn't feel safe anymore" (*Kindred* 17). The past threatens her sense of "comfort and security" (9) in the present; the present impinges materially on the past. Like Lilith, Dana must abandon the illusion of a sovereign self, free from the touch of the past, even if this makes her a "traitor" (223) in the eyes of the slave community. Her severed arm, interpreted predominantly as a symbol of disconnection, is a sign also of connection (with Rufus, with the past). Time travel thus literalizes interdependency and vulnerability.

What implications does acknowledging vulnerability have for care ethics? By now students can connect the protagonists' altered views of the human condition to their ability to care for the other. Acceptance of her "embeddedness in familiar, social, and historical contexts" (Held 46) allows Dana to disrupt expected racial and historical boundaries. Ashraf Rushdy describes this disruption as a break with ideologies of the black power movement, which judged black people "by the purity of their motives, the purity of their actions, even the purity of their descent" (100–01). Butler makes Dana "the agent responsible for a mulatta's birth" (Barr, *Lost* 100). Likewise, abiding hope in the possibility of flourishing through symbiotic relations of care is given shape in the hybrid child that Lilith carries in her womb. She too becomes an agent of change. With this understanding, students recognize care as much more than a way to survive. It is also a public act of resistance to oppressive structures and exclusionary discourses. By reconfiguring care as a form of resistance, Butler's texts invariably connect it to larger social and political structures.

Returning to the theme of conflict that pervades Butler's fiction, we note that the protagonists do not reject the impulse to care even as they remain alert to the reality of asymmetrical relationships. Unable to simply "turn off" her "conscience . . . and be a coward, safe and comfortable" (*Kindred* 106), Dana "[gambles] against history" (83). "I didn't want to care," she says (202), capturing the same ambivalence that Lilith feels: "We're all a little bit co-opted" (*Dawn* 240). The discussion ends where it began, with the recognition of care "not as a utopian device that will end all conflict" (Tronto 172) but as something requiring constant negotiation. As readers, we must be open to taking risks; we too must gamble against normative conceptions of a relationship. Adopting a care-ethics approach requires a painful rethinking of how we engage with others, but it also opens up spaces in which we can envision new structures of being in a more compassionate way.

The Allegory of Shori's Cave: Teaching *Fledgling* as the Science Fiction of Racism

Marleen S. Barr

I teach English at the City University of New York (CUNY), perhaps the most diverse university in the country. My classes contain immigrants from all over the world as well as black and Hispanic native-born New Yorkers. Reading science fiction can mitigate these students' feeling of estrangement from the American hegemony. Science fiction functioned in this manner for Octavia E. Butler: "[R]eading and writing science fiction actually enabled her [Butler] to transcend racism and sexism. Science fiction—by letting her imagine and create new worlds on the page—was a conduit for feelings of citizenship" ("Why"). Butler's *Fledgling*, in addition to imparting feelings of citizenship to Butler herself, functions as a transcendent conduit of inclusion for minority and immigrant students, a conduit that assuages cultural differences. Since Shori Matthews, the protagonist of *Fledgling*, is biologically different to the extent that she is akin neither to human beings nor to fantastic aliens, no student can feel more estranged than she does.

Students from both the south Bronx and South America have more in common with each other than they do with Shori. *Fledgling* is a stellar example of science fiction's unifying characteristics:

> Whether or not anyone looks or talks like you at school, on TV, or in the movies doesn't matter when you're dealing with time travel, extraterrestrials, or alternative universes. If we can assign more texts to students that ask them to let go of the everyday shorthand for finding themselves in a story, they often open themselves up to deeper and more surprising ways to relate to each other. ("Why")

Fledgling is the perfect text to generate solidarity in a diverse CUNY classroom. CUNY students, acknowledging their commonality when they encounter Shori's difference, are more apt to engage with each other outside the classroom. Alondra Nelson speaks to my CUNY teaching experience when she observes that teaching science fiction "creates the opportunity for dialogue that 'allows for generative re-imaginings of what students are doing outside the classroom.' . . . [She] observes that science fiction . . . fosters among students a compelling kind of intellectual re-mixing . . . that empowers them to connect their studies . . . with activism" ("Why"). Science fiction in general and *Fledgling* in particular can enable CUNY students to join together, step outside the classroom, and change the world.

Nalo Hopkinson connects Nelson's science fiction pedagogy approach to Butler's work and the black experience:

> Alondra said the thing about *Kindred* is that black people . . . know that at any moment, they can be snatched back to the past. They can be snatched back to the plantation and be living that nightmare again. . . . And so, science fiction fantasy can give you a way of coding that experience so that you have a little bundle of knowledge for what that might be like where before you had nothing. (Jenkins)

Fledgling, which describes how a lone other confronts a hostile present, provides a little bundle of knowledge that can help students cope with the age of Trump. In the words of Bill O' Brien, the senior adviser for program administration for the National Endowment for the Arts, "[S]cience fiction . . . invites marginalized people to . . . imagine themselves as participants and agents in changing the systems of culture, technology, and politics that govern their lives. To change the world, students have to believe that change is possible in the first place" ("Why"). Shori changed her world. Students can view her as a role model in these troubled times.

Fledgling, in the vein of Nelson's ideas about inclusive science fiction pedagogy, can be taught as a didactic treatise about the exploding of categorization. Sandra Y. Govan points out that *Fledgling* itself is a generic composite that wears "a number of masks—murder mystery, crime novel, coming-of-age, innocence-to-experience, initiation, quest tale, and outsider/survivor novel" (Govan, "*Fledgling*" 41). The Ina, aliens who are both vampires and beneficial to human beings, cannot survive without the blood of human symbiotes. Shori, part human and part Ina, is a complete contradiction in that she is benevolent toward human beings yet ingests human blood. Although in her early fifties, she looks like a ten-year-old child. Shori defies definition and acts as an exemplar of generic confusion. Readers cannot hate or fear her, because she is not a static target of hate or fear.

In this essay I show how to position *Fledgling* as a teaching tool to resee the knee-jerk, normalized, and patently untrue science fictional categories that form the foundations for racism.

The Color Continuum

The incessant ambiguity characterizing the science fictional elements in *Fledgling* directs students toward the scientific truth that there is no such thing as specifically black people or specifically white people, that human skin comes in various hues of brown. This lack of racial fixed definition is analogous to Adrienne Rich's notion of "the lesbian continuum," which includes "a range—through each woman's life and throughout history—of woman-identified experience, not simply the fact that a woman has had or consciously desired sexual experience with another woman" (239). Both Shori's sexuality and skin color are multifaceted: she is not only bispecies, the result of a genetic experiment—her "family had [success] with blending human and Ina DNA and having children who can stay awake through the day and not burn so easily in the sun" (*Fledgling* 153)—but also bisexual and biracial. She insists, "I had been about to protest that I was brown not black" (37). *Fledgling*, a science fiction vampire novel, is therefore about blood, yet scientifically blood is categorized only by blood type; it has nothing to do with skin color. Butler is making the point that using racial categories to deny people of darker brown skin access to equal citizenship and denying that all human beings originated in Africa are more removed from biological, anthropological fact than any science fiction. Shori, the biracial, bispecies protagonist, makes students step out of their usual automatic racial mythologizing.

The Allegory of Shori's Cave

Fledgling begins with the inability to see: "I [Shori] awoke to darkness" (7). She is in a cave, and the darkness is locational, not racial. Plato's allegory of the cave is a useful classroom companion for teaching Butler's novel. Comparing "the effect of education and the lack of it on our nature," it demonstrates how *Fledgling* works to correct the lack of education and remove the necessity of hate and fear. In Plato's allegory, chained prisoners must face a blank wall all their lives, watching and naming the shadows that are their only view of reality. Freed from the cave, they learn that the shadows are not reality.

Reading about what happens to Shori outside the cave, students learn that racist mythologies imprison us all in an unreality that results in the past chains of American slavery and the present cell bars restraining the predominantly dark-brown-skinned American jail population. *Fledgling* is didactic science fiction art that challenges the perpetuation of racial categories.

Butler's Category Busters

Butler repeatedly avoids fixed definitions to speak against mythological racist categories. No "tragically double-voiced" Eliza Doolittle (Z. Smith 3) or cowardly Nellie Forbush who initially equates biracial children with bug-eyed monsters (from the musical *South Pacific*), Shori is resplendently multivoiced and characterized by multifaceted racial, sexual, and species categories.

Wright Hamilton, her first symbiote, asks, "[W]hat are you?" (25), when he first encounters her. *What*, not *who*. He sees Shori as a thing to be generically categorized, not as a person. When he bluntly states, "[Y]ou're not human," she answers, "What would that mean?" (26). Students see that racism routinely relegates human beings to the category of nonhuman. What does it mean when a vampire is part alien and part human? To gain self-awareness, Shori reads vampire fiction, which she decides is "a huge amount of nonsense about vampires" (36). Feeding on a human being once and killing the person is absurd, she feels: "Who could need that much blood? Why kill a person who should willingly feed you again and again if you handled them carefully? No wonder vampires in folklore were feared, hated, and hunted." Garden-variety folklore vampires feed in an ecologically unsound manner, she believes. Yet she can be more vicious than a usual vampire: "I ate a man without recognizing him as a man. I had not yet read of a vampire doing that, but I had done it" (43). Shori deeply loves her human symbiotes yet, since she is part human, she can also be a cannibal. Her complexity underscores to students that all people are too complex to be reduced to a singular textual mythology.

Shori is on a quest to categorize herself. She says, "I have to know who I am . . . and what I am" (63), yet no category applies to her. Her father, Iosif, questions even the alienness of the Ina: "There's a recently developed belief among some of our younger people that the Ina landed here from another world thousands of years ago. I think it's nonsense, but who knows. . . . I think that we evolved right here on Earth alongside humanity as a cousin species like the chimpanzee" (73). That a character's origin is unknown can draw together students who come from many different places.

What Shori says of so many vampire stories—"Human beings made up these fantasy safeguards, little magic, like garlic, and crucifixes, that would somehow keep them safe from my kind—or from what they imagined my kind to be" (95)—applies to the myth of the drop of black blood: it is a fantasy safeguard that leads to the construction of the other, a false dichotomy between us and them. The black other is an imagined monster, a relegation of an all to a one. All white people are not Jeffrey Dahmer; all black people are not Willie Horton. We are taught to think in stereotypes. *Fledgling* helps students unlearn this thinking.

Butler uses humor to revise the syllabus of hatred. Shori's symbiote, Theodora, doesn't believe that Shori, an elfin black girl who does not look like a stereotypical vampire, is a vampire: "[A]ccording to what I've read, you're supposed to be a tall handsome fully grown white man" (97). Note that Butler does not look like a stereotypical science fiction writer, who in an earlier generation was a white male. Shori feels "that she [Theodora] was teaching me about herself every moment" (96). What she learns from Theodora might relate to Ursula K. Le Guin's mother, Theodora Kroeber, a writer and anthropologist who specialized in the retelling of traditional narratives. *Fledgling* retells a traditional vampire tale and mythological narratives that teach racism.

That Iosif's relatives "died during the twentieth century—most of them during World War II when a lot of European Ina were killed. . . . The Nazis got them" (136) suggests that Shori's identity may include Jewish ancestry. Butler is a black writer who does not limit her discussion of racism to blacks. Nor does she limit her discussion to human beings. She asserts that being taught to hate and fear is a lesson that should transcend race and species.

But Shori is targeted by "Ina racists" simply because she is black (153). Victor Colon, a human being, calls her "[d]irty little nigger bitch" (179) but then takes back his words: "I didn't mean to call you . . . what I called you. My sister, she married a Dominican guy. Her kids are darker than you, and they're my blood, too" (180 [the ellipsis is in the original text]). Students realize that in *Fledgling* the lack of categorization regarding blood has really nothing to do with vampires. Note that the Ina live in houses they share with their symbiotes.

That Katharine Silk, Shori's major Ina antagonist, declares that "Shori is not Ina" (310) resonates with the assertion that blacks are not human beings. It is as false as Russell Silk's insistence that the Ina and human beings are separate entities: "But we are not them! We are not them" (298). But we are what we eat, and the Ina eat human blood. Education about Shori's Ina heritage is at the heart of her future. "I have to re-educate myself. Right now, you [an Ina named Joel] probably know more about Ina history and about being Ina than I do. I have to learn" (293). We all have to learn.

Shori ultimately loses her mothers, sisters, fathers, and brothers—as well as her memory. She also loses herself. "The person I had been was gone." This bispecies vampire is, first and foremost, a person. Her self-actualization trajectory involves learning what her particular, unique personhood means. To learn about the Ina and her families, she must depend on her Ina teachers. "Joan [a member of the Ina Braithwaite family] says if you're [Shori] going to survive on your own, you'll need good teachers, and she's willing to be one of them" (316). We—the members of a family of English professors who teach *Fledgling* as a counternarrative to stories that teach hate and fear—are the colleagues of Joan Braithwaite.

Teaching *Parable of the Sower* through Afrofuturism

Isiah Lavender III

In my courses on African American literature and science fiction, I often teach Octavia E. Butler's *Parable of the Sower*, where the concept of Afrofuturism always proves useful in unlocking the various meanings of the text in relation to the past, present, and future of race and racism in the United States of America. A critical stance for reading science fiction produced by black writers, Afrofuturism blends myth and history with social science and technologies to produce alternative futures centered on black culture. Emerging from a consideration of the particular cultural relation between African Americans and Western technology, Afrofuturism sees in science fiction's motifs of abduction, displacement, and alienation fitting metaphors for black life. To be sure, Afrofuturism effectually draws attention to racial issues in science fiction because of its exploration of cultural memories like chattel slavery and the host of racial stereotypes concerning African Americans that emerged from the antebellum era. While these painful memories reverberate into the future, Afrofuturism grants us the opportunity to restructure our understanding of them in Butler's novel.

I hope to demonstrate to my Louisiana students who went through Hurricane Katrina exactly how *Parable of the Sower* and its sequel, *Parable of the Talents*, delve deeply into American cultural memory and how the social and political realities of a racist past continually haunt us. I declare that we must avoid future repetitions of this history and that Butler's message about literacy as the key to freedom prevails in both scientific and religious thinking, especially when our survival as a species is put into question. Dismantling the color line requires diversity and teamwork to find solutions to problems stemming from slavery. As the literary scholar Madhu Dubey puts it, "The process of finding unity in diversity is necessarily risky and difficult, requiring the ability to interpret unfamiliar cultural codes and the alert balancing of suspicion and trust typical of urban social interactions" (113). As an Afrofuturist text, *Parable of the Sower* demonstrates Butler's complex views of racial consciousness. My approach to the novel is by no means limited to Afrofuturism, but Afrofuturism lets students see black people at the center for once as emotional, spiritual, and technological beings in the body politic, even if that body is failing.

I normally teach Butler's novel as a near-future dystopian novel. In fact, students across the country are familiar with the dystopian idea because of the recent glut of young adult novels featuring human misery and oppression, such as Suzanne Collins's *The Hunger Games*. I immediately gain from teaching *Parable of the Sower* in this fashion an understanding of my students' preoccupation with imagining their own destruction. We can then investigate what generates the frequent end-of-the-world scenario, what happens to such a fictional society when it finds itself living in fear, and how people survive in these circumstances. But when I teach *Parable of the Sower* as an Afrofuturist work, my students see how the convergence of political, environmental, and economic crises causes social chaos and the quick return to racial (and other) binaries to cope with them. We explore how business, politics, and religion intensify the turmoil, because the people in each group think they have the answers. Through *Parable of the Sower*, Butler wrestles with the legacies of slavery—oppression, racism, prejudice, stereotypes, and violence—in the time after the civil rights moment and offers a radical solution to issues of the color line.

By considering the projective possibilities of science fiction, my students grasp parallels between the world of the text and the one in which we live. For example, Butler's protagonist, Lauren Olamina, tells us about a hurricane that kills seven hundred people, most of them poor, near the beginning of the novel. This event seems to prefigure what happened to the more than eighteen hundred people who lost their lives during Hurricane Katrina in 2005. Butler could not see the future but described a dominant and continuing pattern of neglect already in place when she wrote the novel, and she extrapolated a grossly inadequate government response to the natural disaster and the people it affected, particularly poor blacks. As my students think about many of the alarming details of this bleak novel, like declining public educational systems or escalating energy, food, and water prices, they realize that the world of *Parable* is not so very different from their own and that class divisions run along racial lines. They also recognize that people of color suffer the most. In this way, Afrofuturism helps students bind together the language of science fiction and black experiences of race to create and assess an awareness of historically grounded cultural projections.

Afrofuturist Theory

First, students must learn about Afrofuturism. They—and their teachers—must understand that Afrofuturism is both a genre in itself and a method of reading. This fusion of genre and method applies well to black science fiction—and to much more.

I begin by tracing the immediate history of this idea in scholarship while drawing out its deeper story during discussion of Butler's novel. As a critical ideology, Afrofuturism first materializes in the *South Atlantic Quarterly* (1993), where the culture critic Mark Dery interviews three prominent black thinkers—Samuel R. Delany, Tricia Rose, and Greg Tate. Dery offers a definition of this new term: "Speculative fiction that treats African-American themes and addresses African-American concerns in the context of twentieth century technoculture—and, more generally, African-American signification that appropriates images of technology and a prosthetically enhanced future" (736). His overemphasis on technology and artificial body parts causes confusion for students, because he does not make allowances for the supernatural beliefs of conquered peoples. This disdain for the supernatural does not permit a vital reclamation of the past that can transform how we think of the present and the future.

The theorizing of the black British scholar Kodwo Eshun comes closer to what Afrofuturism means as a praxis and extends Dery's original description. In describing black music as a sonic fiction, Eshun thinks of Afrofuturism as "a perpetual fight for human status, a yearning for human rights, a struggle for inclusion within the human species . . . any intimation of an AfroDiasporic futurism, of a 'webbed network'. . . which routes, reroutes and criss-crosses the Black Atlantic" (*More Brilliant* 6). The continual striving of black people for acknowledgment of a common human status across time and space creates a consciousness that links past, present, and future through creative production—mainly art, music, and literature. Eshun adds elsewhere, "Afrofuturism therefore stages a series of enigmatic returns to the constitutive trauma of slavery in the light of science fiction" ("Further Considerations" 299). He rightly indicates how chattel slavery still echoes into the future, continually shaping and shadowing race relations in which blacks are literalized as aliens. From this undead past, rather a past not yet dead, black people seek and find potential futures.

Alondra Nelson, a sociologist and early Afrofuturist scholar, explains this webbed network, this looped consciousness or chronotopal awareness, in words students will understand. She writes that "our imaginings of the future are always complicated extensions of the past" ("AfroFuturism" 35). She later challenges the raceless futures presented in and projected by science fiction when she edits a special issue of the journal *Social Text* (2002), where she and her contributors directly engage Afrofuturism as a critical paradigm. Afrofuturism, she believes, offers "unique analytical frameworks for interpreting black cultural production, as imagery of the near-future," where "other stories to tell about culture, technology and things to come" derive from black creators ("Introduction" 9). Therefore these scholars discuss, through Afrofuturism, emerging arts that appeared after the civil rights movement in an increasingly technological world.

Afrofuturism concerns much more than black technology usage—Dery's assertion—because it provides a future-oriented worldview that respects the past. Later Afrofuturist scholars emphasize this point. De Witt D. Kilgore posits how Afrofuturism protects "peoples of African descent, their ways and histories," while ensuring that they "will not disappear in any credible future" ("Afrofuturism" 569). Lisa Yaszek declares, "Afrofuturism is not just about reclaiming the history of the past, but about reclaiming the history of the future as well" (300). The past can be an inspirational source for present and future black people to imagine black identities and worlds differently. Afrofuturism affords new approaches to black cultural studies as well as science fiction scholarship. A black cultural lens changes science fiction as much as postcolonial, postmodern, and Marxist critical lenses do. But Afrofuturism becomes its own speculative genre; it is not a subset of science fiction, because it entails entire cultures.

Liberation politics coupled with critical race theory infuse the unconventional cultural matrix that is Afrofuturism to reimagine the meanings of blackness, in the sense of identity politics, across space and time with and without technology. The black writer and activist Ytasha L. Womack redefines *Afrofuturism* as "[b]oth an artistic aesthetic and a framework for critical theory [that] combines elements of science fiction, historical fiction, speculative fiction, fantasy, Afrocentricity, and magical realism with non-Western beliefs" (9). This more expansive definition puts black writers who do not use science and technology in ways that we typically recognize as such under Afrofuturism's umbrella, like Nnedi Okorafor, N. K. Jemisin, and Nalo Hopkinson. (Note that Butler's continuing legacy can be directly traced in each of these black women writers.) As both a body of work and a reading protocol, Afrofuturism is the everyday science fictional experiences of black people specific to black texts by black creators (writers, artists, musicians, filmmakers), and nothing else fits through this lens. Although I and others have called Afrofuturism an ideology, a theory, an analytical framework, and a genre, students may best understand it as a critical stance that presents a unique way of reading.

Parable of the Sower *as Afrofuturist Text*

Butler's novel offers hope for humanity, hope for future social changes despite the hell that the author subjects her characters to. We see how through community building—represented by the walled neighborhood of Robledo and its multiracial fusion of blacks, whites, Latinos, and Asians as well as Lauren's fledgling Earthseed group—people cope with mounting problems by working together. Butler's meticulous incorporation of diversity provides a positive message in her otherwise grim imagining of the future. Education, community, and adaptation, things that Butler stresses through Lauren, will ensure human survival. As she writes, "Embrace diversity. . . . Or be destroyed" (197). Through an Afrofuturistic lens, she boldly states that cultural change itself is a necessary mechanism for humanity's continued existence.

Butler sets the novel in a twenty-first-century Los Angeles, where a failing middle class attempts to hang on to the trappings of prosperity while the world falls apart around it. Lauren relates her intimate experiences of the crumbling world in a journal that she keeps over the course of four years—a hybrid of epistolary and bildungsroman forms. She is the drug-damaged daughter of a black Baptist minister professor, and a hyperempathy syndrome affects all her human interactions: she feels intensely the pain and pleasure of everyone around her. This illness, inherited through her mother, makes her compassionate toward others. She does not harm people unless she is determined to do it. She recounts beating up her younger brother, Keith, who tricked her into bleeding with fake blood, even though she "felt every blow that [she] struck," as if hitting herself (11). When she meets other sufferers of this illness, she concludes that it makes for good slaves, because they are easily controlled. But her hyperempathy prepares her to actively resist the total surround of hopelessness and apathy; it gives her the wisdom to lead people. Once out on the road, she becomes the leader of a "modern underground railroad," as slavery returns in manifold forms, particularly debt bondage (292).

Lauren comes to appreciate community even more—unity, self-government, and protection—when she begins to share her new faith, Earthseed. She and her followers educate themselves to better adapt to this chaotic world. "God is change" in Lauren's religion, and her flight north conveys this truth on the road after Robledo falls to the massed poor, drug addicts, and scavengers (3). She and her multiracial crew of survivors endure general mistrust, gang warfare, and an arson-induced wildfire, among other things, to establish the first Earthseed community, which Butler further develops in *Parable of the Talents*. Butler draws on American history and culture to demonstrate the consequences of perpetuating racial oppression, shows that we must take stock of our attitudes and assumptions from the past in order to not repeat them. In this respect, Earthseed and Lauren's personal journal represent an important and mindful metanarrative on slavery.

The theme of education unlocks Butler's novel for Afrofuturism. To tease out this theme, my students and I discuss the many interconnections between slavery and religion in *Parable of the Sower*. I mention how Lauren's harrowing story reminds me of slave narratives, particularly *Narrative of the Life of Frederick Douglass* (1845). Douglass stresses the importance of literacy after he learns that it is the key to freeing a slave's mind. He overhears his new master, Hugh Auld, say to his wife, "If you teach that nigger (speaking of myself) how to read, there would be no keeping him. It would forever unfit him to be a slave (48). Like Douglass, Lauren recognizes that reading is the key to freedom.

Halfway through the novel we learn that Zahra Moss, a member of Robledo who joins Lauren after its fall, cannot read. Her husband, Richard, denied her the opportunity to learn while living in the walled confines of the community, since she was his third and youngest wife and he felt that she "already knew enough to suit him" (186). We learn that another character, Natividad Douglas, does not know how to read. Her husband, Travis, can. He was surreptitiously taught by his mother, who worked as "a live-in cook" for a rich man who had a big library but did not want Travis near the books. Lauren immediately thinks, "Of course. Slaves did that two hundred years ago. They sneaked around and educated themselves as best they could, sometimes suffering whipping, sale, or mutilation for their efforts" (218). Without doubt, Butler references Douglass's *Narrative*, in which Douglass recollects the many dangers of learning to read and write, such as watching his Mistress Sophia, corrupted by slavery, rush him with "tiger-like fierceness . . . and snatch from [him] a newspaper" (52) or using a "board fence, brick wall, and pavement" as his "copy-book" or "writing in the spaces left in master Thomas's copy-book" (57). These small moments may seem innocuous, but slaves could be sold or even killed for attempting to gain the ability to read. Douglass and his enslaved friends write themselves free passes, get caught before the attempted escape, and barely manage to destroy the incriminating papers. Douglass and Butler are connected by the webbed network across history.

Butler presents a newfangled form of corporate sharecropping that reduces future American citizens to little more than slaves. Lauren's father decides to keep his family from joining the foreign-owned company town of Olivar. He notes how people "accept smaller salaries . . . in exchange for security, a guaranteed food supply, [and] jobs" despite exploitation (119). That labor laws have been weakened in this future makes it possible for debt slavery to return. People become liable for the tools, food, clothing, shelter, and other supplies they rent from the company and go into debt as company costs rise. The company makes them pay their balances off by working them harder and for company scrip instead of actual money. Her father declares, "This business sounds half antebellum revival and half science-fiction" (122). Later in the novel we learn from Emory Solis, a half-Japanese, half-black escaped slave, that she was made responsible for her deceased husband's debt and that the company took her two sons away and sold them. She ran north with her remaining child, a daughter. An Afrofuturistic lens foregrounds the traumatic history of slavery in America. Lauren accurately thinks of Emory as a runaway slave, because that is exactly what Emory becomes when she bolts to freedom. Lauren and the survivors she has gathered have little to hope for without Earthseed as America's slavery past becomes the future to them.

An Earthseed verse frames each chapter of the novel, much as spirituals do in W. E. B. Du Bois's classic *The Souls of Black Folk* (1903). Lauren uncovers her religious beliefs through her poetry. She recruits new believers from among her group by using Earthseed verses to teach reading and writing to those who cannot read or write, thus indoctrinating them into her way of thinking. For example, when her white friend and fellow survivor of Robledo, Harry Balter, asks her to share something about herself that he never knew, she carefully selects the verse "All that you touch / You Change" (195). When Travis and Natividad join the group, Harry says that her poetry "isn't bad" and that she should read it to them (212). Her view is challenged by Travis, who cannot envision God as entropy or change, but she counters with "[S]how me a more pervasive power than change" (219). She takes advantage of her literacy to grow her religion, proselytizing in the streets, inciting debate, converting people, and winning over Travis, then Zahra Moss, and then the others.

Like her father in his Baptist ministry, Lauren attracts people with her intensity, but not with emotion, repetition, and an invisible God. She thinks of Christianity as a lie but does not have the courage to tell her father while he is living that her God is not his God after her baptism early in the novel. Instead she preaches using logic, the inevitability of change, and a tangible heaven: "The Destiny of Earthseed" will "take root among the stars" (77). "God exists to be shaped" by Lauren and others as they adapt, change, and survive (25). Her God demands respect, not worship, as Earthseed followers act and respond to their environment in a direct and practical fashion. In Afrofuturist terms, Butler reminds us how religion in black America has served as the community's foundation, supporting its members, providing services, and focusing on important social issues, the issues mirrored in her dark vision of the future—crime, poverty, drug abuse, and the pronounced lack of equal opportunities and full citizenship for African Americans and other minorities. Lauren creates Earthseed and will use it to change the course of human history.

Butler demonstrates the courage needed to revisit slavery and look past its tragedy. She presents a dark vision of America that still resonates hope through black leadership. Such an impossible thought recognizes that in Afrofuturism we have a tool for questioning black forms of being, for exploring dark realities and their alternatives.

Teaching Butler's "Bloodchild" and the Tenets of Afrofuturism

Kristen Lillvis

This essay focuses on the pedagogical benefits of teaching Octavia E. Butler's short story "Bloodchild" in concert with Afrofuturist theory. Marc Dery coined the term *Afrofuturism* in 1993, almost two decades after Butler published her first novel, *Patternmaster*, yet theorists and fans alike position her as one of the practice's foundational authors. Her appointment as foremother to a movement that gained definition years after she began writing but began developing almost a century before her birth (with the 1859–62 serial publication of Martin R. Delany's *Blake; or, The Huts of America* [Womack 121]) denotes the temporal interplay at the heart of Afrofuturism.

In this essay, I propose that educators use "Bloodchild" to introduce the tenets of Afrofuturism—including its exploration of black pasts, presents, and futures—and then reciprocally use those tenets to illuminate significant themes and issues in Butler's story. While my students have discovered Afrofuturist attributes in *Kindred*, *Lilith's Brood*, *Fledgling*, and other book-length works, the compressed narratives of Butler's short fictions compel them to identify and interpret Afrofuturist concepts. "Bloodchild" in particular encourages discussions about historical and modern systems of oppression by being set in an alien future but replete with references to a familiar past as well as to the present.

Exploring "Bloodchild" and Afrofuturism together allows students and instructors to realize that stories set in unfamiliar places and times inspire conversation about contemporary hot-button issues but in ways that feel less threatening. Because the subjects of the story are presented as alien or other, students can discuss topics such as sexuality and substance abuse without taking a political stance that might make them (or others) uncomfortable.

Whether introducing "Bloodchild" in an African American literature, American literature, or speculative literature course, instructors should be prepared for students to express surprise and confusion when they are exposed to Butler's unfamiliar characters and setting. As the story opens, Gan, the first-person human or "Terran" narrator, recalls consuming "sterile eggs" with his family while lounging against the "long, velvet underside" of T'Gatoi, a female of the Tlic species ("Bloodchild" 3). The non-Western names and insect-like physiognomies featured in the story will puzzle students unfamiliar with science fiction genre conventions. Having Terran males made pregnant by aliens will shock them—a response that Butler no doubt anticipated, given her self-imposed challenge to reconcile her fear of the parasitic botfly while writing "a dramatic story of a man becoming pregnant as an act of love" (*"Bloodchild"* 30–31).

But instructors should embrace students' emotional responses to "Bloodchild" and utilize them to explore the novel's formal elements and the conventions of Afrofuturist literature. I open class discussion of the story by writing on the board or displaying on a screen two definitions of *Afrofuturism*: the original description from Dery and an updated version from Ytasha L. Womack. In "Black to the Future: Interviews with Samuel R. Delany, Greg Tate, and Tricia Rose," Dery introduces the term:

> Speculative fiction that treats African-American themes and addresses African-American concerns in the context of twentieth-century technoculture—and, more generally, African-American signification that appropriates images of technology and a prosthetically enhanced future—might, for want of a better term, be called "Afro-futurism."
>
> ([*Flame Wars*] 180)

Drawing on Dery's definition, Womack asserts in *Afrofuturism: The World of Black Sci-Fi and Fantasy Culture*, the first book-length investigation of the topic, that "Afrofuturism combines elements of science fiction, historical fiction, speculative fiction, fantasy, Afrocentricity, and magical realism with non-Western beliefs" (9). I ask for student volunteers to read each definition aloud, and then we work as a class to determine their overlapping words and concepts. Students note that both Dery and Womack use the term "speculative fiction" but otherwise rely on different phrases to express similar ideas; for example, Dery mentions "African-American themes" and "concerns" while Womack talks about "Afrocentricity" and "non-Western beliefs." Students also note that while Dery focuses on the future, Womack mentions the past ("historical fiction"). This structured examination of the definitions helps students begin to understand Butler's "Bloodchild" as an Afrofuturist text. But only by analyzing the definitions and the story together do students fully grasp either.

My students enter their coinvestigation of Afrofuturist theory and Butler's "Bloodchild" by sharing what they feel most familiar with: their initial emotional responses to the story. I ask them to use their responses to "Bloodchild" to explain, in their own words, what each element of Womack's definition of Afrofuturism might mean. I focus on her explanation of Afrofuturism rather than Dery's because, again, I want students to begin in a place of familiarity, and she mentions genres that they have likely encountered in readings from our class or their other courses.

We start with the earliest element of Afrofuturism that Womack names, science fiction. Students use their reading of "Bloodchild," particularly those elements they were surprised or disgusted by, to identify such science fiction tropes as interspecies relationships, interstellar travel, superhuman powers, and alien invasion. When students channel their responses in this way, their emotions become a part of the critical discussion rather than an obstacle to their understanding of the theory. Moreover, contextualizing characters and plot points from Butler's story in terms of science fiction tropes leads students to analyze the significance of Butler's adherence to and departure from genre conventions. Instructors may consider detailing her biography, including her interactions with the science fiction writers Harlan Ellison and Samuel R. Delany, or introducing more focused examinations of her innovative revisions of classic principles, such as Amanda Thibodeau's exploration of Butler's queered aliens or Marty Fink's study of Butler's reimagined vampires.

As students use Butler's short story to illuminate the next component of Afrofuturism—historical fiction—they continue sharing their preliminary responses and probing the deeper meanings of the text. They begin to appreciate Afrofuturism's liminality: by contemplating how the science fictional elements they named relate to American and other histories, they blur the boundaries between genres (science fiction and history) and time periods (the future and the past). For example, they often suggest that the Tlic-Terran interspecies relationships in "Bloodchild" mirror the master-slave interracial power dynamics of antebellum America. Briefly introducing the class to the neo–slave narrative, a subgenre of historical fiction, allows students to move beyond this generalized reading of "Bloodchild" and to discover specific connections between the future-located Terrans and historically situated human beings. Neo–slave narratives, according to Valerie Smith, "approach the institution of slavery from a myriad [of] perspectives and embrace a variety of styles of writing: from realist novels grounded in historical research to speculative fiction, postmodern experiments, satire, and works that combine these diverse modes" (168). Armed with this definition, students get more specific with their analyses, joining scholars such as Brigitte Scheer-Schäzler, Elyce Rae Helford, and Jane Donawerth in identifying T'Gatoi's interactions with Gan as a type of "sexual exploitation" reminiscent of the slave master's control over the enslaved (Scheer-Schäzler 320).

However, students' consideration of "Bloodchild" as not only a work of science fiction and historical fiction but also an example of speculative fiction and fantasy—the next two components of Afrofuturism, as defined by Womack—complicates the reading of the story as a neo–slave narrative. To help students track the speculative and fantastic elements of the text, instructors could highlight Butler's assertion in her afterword to "Bloodchild" that the story focuses not on slavery but on love, maturation, pregnancy, parasitism, and compromise (30–32). Many scholars consider *speculative fiction* an umbrella term that encompasses genres such as science fiction, fantasy, horror, and dystopian fiction, but for Lauren J. Lacey it is a "fantastic" genre—hence my grouping of speculative fiction and fantasy together here—in that it "redefine[s] the relationship between the past and the present so that the past becomes a site of possibility rather than a closed story" (19). Thus situated, "Bloodchild" reveals to students alternative endings (or, to use Lacey's language, sites of possibility) to familiar stories. Perhaps T'Gatoi's relationship with Gan results in feelings of maternal love rather than oppression (Bollinger; Lillvis). Or perhaps a scientific approach to Tlic-Terran pairings could be used, such as Maria Aline Ferreira's evolutionary assessment of parasitism in Butler's texts.

Investigating the variety of interpretations available to readers of "Bloodchild" prepares students for a discussion of the final elements of Womack's definition: Afrocentricity, magical realism, and non-Western beliefs. I ask students to discuss Afrocentricity and non-Western beliefs together, since the Terrans of the story do not explicitly belong to any particular race or nationality, yet their worldview—when juxtaposed with Tlic ways of life—can be understood as analogous to Afrocentrism and other non-Western philosophies, especially as they function in the context of an opposing and dominant system.

I aid students in applying Afrocentric and non-Western worldviews to "Bloodchild" by bringing Sun Ra into the conversation. Sun Ra, a jazz musician, filmmaker, and poet, joins Butler as an anachronistic founder of Afrofuturism. In the film *Space Is the Place*, he recruits African Americans to join him in populating a new planet. In one scene, he visits a youth center in Oakland, California, where black teenagers question his outfit and his claim to be from outer space, asking one another and themselves, "Is he for real?" Sun Ra answers:

> I'm not real. I'm just like you. You don't exist in this society. If you did, your people wouldn't be seeking equal rights. You're not real. If you were, you'd have some status among the nations of the world. So we're both myths. I do not come to you as a reality; I come to you as the myth because that's what black people are: myths.

He is telling the African American youths that non-Afrocentric, white, Western worldviews erase them—a message not lost on student audiences today, regardless of their racial makeup. Twenty-first-century students chuckle at Sun Ra's fantastic ideas and futuristic costuming as well as at the 1970s fashions and turns of phrase featured in the clip, but they join the film's black teens in taking seriously Sun Ra's solemn account of the difference between Afrocentric and white, Western perspectives of African Americans. With these divergent attitudes toward a subjugated group in mind, they can compare Tlic and Terran ways of being in "Bloodchild" in a way that allows for deeper analysis of the story's characters. For example, Butler's Qui, like Sun Ra, locates himself as a myth in the Terran world, telling his brother that Terran "animals" do not enjoy the rights or freedoms held by the Tlic ("Bloodchild" 21). Discussing Afrocentrism and non-Western belief systems puts in a larger cultural and theoretical context his desire that his species and subjectivity be valued by the dominant system.

Finally, students consider the magical realist elements of Butler's story in order to cement its position in the genre of Afrofuturist literature. I often discuss works such as Gabriel García Márquez's *One Hundred Years of Solitude* and Toni Morrison's *Beloved* when introducing magical realism so that students will recognize that the tone of a text often renders fantastical creatures or events ordinary. Students acknowledge that although the appearance of a Tlic female in a Terran household strikes them as frightening or disgusting, Butler's protagonist regards T'Gatoi's presence as an everyday occurrence. Students speak freely about the magical realist elements of the text: Gan's affinity for T'Gatoi, his consumption of sterile Tlic eggs, the presence of Terrans on a Tlic "Preserve," and the Tlic implantation of Terran males for reproductive purposes ("Bloodchild" 5, 21). The conversation situates "Bloodchild" in the field of magical realism and Afrofuturism but, in time, also draws ties between the story and issues common in our world, including substance use, internment, mass incarceration, sexual abuse, and discrimination.

Studying Butler's engagement with multiple genres in "Bloodchild" reveals the relation between past and present systems of oppression as well as historical, contemporary, and futuristic strategies for emancipation. As students come to understand both "Bloodchild" and Afrofuturism, they join the instructor in pointing out other books, television shows, films, and songs by African Americans that make connections to important and difficult subjects across time. During this exercise, I encourage students to circle back to Dery's definition of Afrofuturism and consider texts that focus on advanced technologies and appraise how even those texts represent multiple temporalities. This lesson fits well in a larger unit that examines technology-heavy Afrofuturist works such as Walter Mosley's short story cycle *Futureland*, Nalo Hopkinson's novel *Midnight Robber*, and Janelle Monáe's short film and music video "Many Moons." If time permits, students may also explore in more detail the ways in which "Bloodchild," as a work of Afrofuturist literature, incorporates non-Western religious, political, and philosophical belief systems into its plot. They may study Gan's role as a storyteller—an important position in cultures of the African diaspora—by investigating how education and other factors shape his tale as well as his narrative strategy. Students discover through these investigations that Butler, like her characters and her fellow Afrofuturist writers, has "other stories to tell about culture, technology, and things to come" (Dery [*Flame Wars*] 182). Studying these stories alongside Afrofuturism allows us, her audience, to consider more fully how we might respond and reply.

Teaching Afrofuturistic Thought Leadership in Butler's Fiction

Tarshia L. Stanley

"A choice to change the world"

—Spelman College tag line

This essay discusses the strategies I used to introduce students to the concept of Afrofuturism as embodied by the black speculative fiction writer Octavia E. Butler, and it argues for the usefulness of Afrofuturistic thought processes when we contemplate what it means to be a leader in this society. The idea of leadership is a particularly important conversation at Spelman College, an institution whose tag line expresses the commitment to produce women who serve as leaders and agents of change. The black female protagonists in *Wild Seed*, *Mind of My Mind*, and *Survivor* were my primary means of exploring Butler's practice of Afrofuturism and showing how Afrofuturism might serve those in search of progressive models of leadership in their family, community, and culture. The course content and format allowed experimentation with multimodal writing: among the assignments were humanities poster presentations, critical and creative essays, and freewriting responses formulated for the Octavia E. Butler Literary Society blog (oebsociety.wordpress.com).

Butler's Daughters: Imagining Leadership in Black Speculative Fiction was taught for the first time in the spring of 2014 at Spelman College, one of only two women's institutions in the country that are also designated a historically black college or university. Among the challenges for me was overcoming a history of black women's literature that had been defined mostly by the social protest model. For many of my students, black women's fiction worthy of critique did not involve vampires or aliens. These same students were perfectly comfortable in a class that featured Bram Stoker's *Dracula* or Mary Shelley's *Frankenstein*, but most felt that literature written by black women was too serious to be framed in a speculative world. I introduced the syllabus and asked if they liked to read speculative fiction. It was an opportunity to introduce this umbrella term as denoting science fiction, fantasy, horror, and magical realism. The students seemed skeptical, but as we began to build a list of their childhood reading and mentioned the likes of Virginia Hamilton, Garth Nix, and Suzanne Collins, they became more open to the idea. There was still in them an underlying sense that black women's literature was for studying and not for experiencing the kind of reading pleasure that speculative fiction had given them.

Only one of those first students knew Butler's name in that she remembered that her mother had a collection of Butler's work. There was one male student in that class, taking advantage of the Atlanta University cross-registration policy; he had joined because he loved video games and comic books and thought my course description sounded interesting. The rest, having seen a digital trailer that I'd created to advertise my class, came to investigate. Since none of the students had encountered Afrofuturism as a term or a mode of literary inquiry, it helped solidify their decision to stay in the class when I revealed that I'd be team teaching with an actual writer of speculative fiction.

It was important to begin discussions of black speculative fiction with W. E. B. Du Bois's short story "The Comet," found in Sheree R. Thomas's *Dark Matter: A Century of Speculative Fiction from the African Diaspora*. It was exciting to watch students discover a new way to read this work by Du Bois. He became for them not only one of the leaders of the struggle for civil rights in the twentieth century but also an Afrofuturist writing himself and his people into yet another space that had traditionally been denied them.

We looked at the Spelman College mission statement:

> Spelman College, a historically Black college and a global leader in the education of women of African descent, is dedicated to academic excellence in the liberal arts and sciences and the intellectual, creative, ethical, and leadership development of its students. Spelman empowers the whole person to engage the many cultures of the world and inspires a commitment to positive social change.

We then looked at the "Spelman College Visual Identity Guidelines," including numbers 2, 3, and 4 of the "Brand Promises":

> Spelman College has a legacy of empowering women to succeed and to lead.
>
> Spelman College empowers Black women to be leaders by inspiring them to recognize their purpose and realize their potential.
>
> Spelman College prepares forward-thinking, socially conscious women to change the world in meaningful ways.

Inherent in these statements is the fact that the college belongs to a cohort of institutions whose founding purpose was to enable people of color to overcome their legacy of slavery and oppression. Students who choose a historically black college or university are in many ways joining a movement and committing to a cause. For Spelman College students, that cause involves accepting the role of leadership. One must then ask what is meant by *leadership* for the college, the community, and ultimately the student.

I used excerpts from *Charisma and the Fictions of Black Leadership*, by Erica R. Edwards, to highlight the traditional-historical depictions of leadership that Spelman students would need to consider and hopefully challenge.

For many of the students, Edward's characterization of black leadership as synonymous with charisma and a Y chromosome rang true. Having grown up with out-of-context sound bites and low-resolution images of Martin Luther King, Jr., and Malcolm X as the quintessential examples of political, religious, and philosophical leadership and some fleeting but sonorous models of hip-hop activist leadership, many students had been left with limiting notions of what it means for women of color to lead.

While their first classes introduced them to Anna Julia Cooper's liberation scholarship and to Fanny Lou Hamer's and Ella Baker's activism during the civil rights movement, their contemporary understanding of leadership was often narrowly focused on corporate and nonprofit models. Leadership for many of them meant being one of the first black women directors, presidents, or CEOs, or it meant founding a nonprofit. My goal became to help them challenge these ideas and to create their own definitions using Butler's work and Afrofuturist thought as models of inquiry. They were asked to first think about what being a leader meant to them and then to investigate whether traditional and contemporary delineations of leadership could be reimagined in ways that might fit them.

I introduced Afrofuturism as a theoretical movement, a cultural lens, a way of reading, and a framework that could be applied to culture—technology, art, film, music, and literature. I said that it was a concept in flux as it grew and expanded to accommodate the various needs of cultural critique. I said that we would be thinking of Butler as an Afrofuturist because in her speculative fiction she created black female protagonists who operated beyond traditional definitions of leadership. The term *Afrofuturism* as proffered by Mark Dery and further developed by Alondra Nelson (and the Afrofuturism electronic discussion group), and Kodwo Eshun in the 1990s, invites a reimagining of what have been Eurocentric and male-dominated speculative texts through a black cultural lens. Eshun's characterization of Afrofuturism as "a program for recovering the histories of counter-futures created in a century hostile to Afrodiasporic projection" and as "a tool kit developed for and by Afrodiasporic intellectuals" is particularly useful for my students' understanding ("Further Considerations" 301).

Thinking through Butler's protagonists and their performance of leadership encourages students to do the work of an Afrofuturist themselves. As they reimagine leadership as female and having many different expressions, they too engage in the Afrofuturist practice of futurescaping. They examine Butler's process of creating protagonists and narratives to incorporate images of leadership that a Western patriarchal lens has ignored, dismissed, or erased. They think about whether characters' blackness, femaleness, or otherness made them leaders for their times. Seeing leadership through Butler's prism as an Afrofuturist empowers them to expand definitions of leadership and practices of community beyond the dynamic, the masculine, or the corporate.

In Butler's worlds the protagonists, who are almost exclusively young women of African descent, face incredible social, economic, cultural, and environmental challenges. Their response is to assess creatively, engage strategically, and draw their strength from their particular identities. Anyanwu, Mary, and Alanna are women who lead their communities not from positions of isolation or power but while in the midst of relationships with lovers, family members, friends, and enemies. Butler presents these roles as enriching rather than diminishing their ability to lead.

Lauren Olamina in *Parable of the Sower*, at age sixteen, must think of ways for herself and her community to survive in their dystopian society. Both cursed and blessed with hyperempathy, she is an ideal case study for the young, black, female leader, because her disability becomes a valuable asset as she leads a group of survivors to build a new community. Because her own well-being is so connected to that of the people around her, her worldview considers both how one person's actions affect the group and how the group's actions affect one person. She develops a new philosophy of life—a new religion—to help herself and her followers not only cope with their circumstance but also act to survive and thrive in it.

But *Parable of the Sower* comes at the end of the course. I want students to begin with the concepts of speculative fiction and Afrofuturism and work with them through some of Butler's least taught texts. We begin with several short stories, including "Bloodchild," "Speech Sounds," and "The Book of Martha." We read *Wild Seed*, *Kindred*, and excerpts from *Mind of My Mind* and the out-of-print novel *Survivor*. Anyanwu, Ayanna, Dana, Martha, Mary, Valerie, and even Gan become case studies for us. We examine the narratives and their literary devices as well as the circumstances of leadership. We look at each of the dystopian societies in which these people have been placed and ponder their strengths for leading their communities.

In *Wild Seed* students are fascinated with Anyanwu as a shapeshifter, and we have great fun determining which Hollywood actor could best portray her in a film. The novel spans 150 years of her life and delineates her relationship with the evil disembodied spirit Doro. Doro's quest to breed a race of children who will not die echoes her need for lasting companionship. Throughout the novel their love-hate relationship is also a competition between two immortals. Anyanwu's needs manifest in her role as mother, while Doro is the killer-conqueror. He cuts down any one of his children who doesn't obey. It is the tension between Anyanwu and Doro that is important for students to study. She is impossibly strong, always vibrant, and perpetually healthy, yet he is able to trap her into breeding with him and for him by threatening her children. His power over her is that threat. Students question whether black motherhood is a strength or weakness and whether there is a way to release it from that binary.

It takes more than a century for Anyanwu and Doro to reach a tenuous compromise. She decides to commit suicide; he pleads with her not to leave him. She agrees but only if he stops killing the offspring whom he cannot control or use. He accepts this compromise because of his need for her. Students see that compromise is an important strategy in this woman's leadership.

According to traditional and patriarchal interpretations, compromise is a concession, a loss, but students celebrate Anyanwu's ability to gain her life and the lives of her present and future children as a victory. They also see her continued relationship with Doro as a benefit: Anyanwu needs Doro as much as Doro needs her. Central to her development as a leader is her role as a mother and community member. Students consider that human connections are integral to their construction of themselves as leaders and consider problematic the traditional depictions of leaders as loners making decisions from places of superiority and distance rather than as an integral part of a whole.

Mary, a descendant of Anyanwu, is the central character in *Mind of My Mind.* This novel follows the story line in *Wild Seed* even though Butler wrote it as the first in the Patternist series. Mary is the culmination of Doro and Anyanwu's breeding program. Doro has been searching for offspring who live forever. The result is a daughter powerful enough to defeat him. Before her final battle with Doro, Mary's journey into adulthood and the full manifestation of her mind-control abilities are difficult and dangerous. Her ability to hear and control the thoughts of others has driven her relatives with lesser forms of this power insane. It is her realization that her power derives in part from the minds of the others in her family—the minds are the pattern—that enables her to defeat Doro. Mary is the evolution and future text of Doro and Anyanwu, but the change she brings is so great that it overwhelms those who are unwilling to embrace it.

Herein lies another consideration for students grappling with defining their own leadership potential. *Mind of My Mind*, written sixteen years before *Parable of the Sower*, anticipates Lauren's dilemma. Much of her frustration lies in the fact that her father, and the other adults in her community, refuses to acknowledge the grave circumstances in which he lives. He is so angry when he learns that she has been formulating a plan of escape and survival should their community fail that he punishes her. Doro and Anyanwu must die so that the new society Mary is forming can be born. Mary comes to terms with the cost of leadership when she is forced to sacrifice a number of her relatives as she drains their life force to kill Doro. Students confront the knowledge that dramatic change and acute loss are inevitably costs of leadership.

Perhaps Butler's least known protagonist is Alanna Verrick. Written in 1978 as the third entry in the Patternist series, *Survivor* features the one heroine whom Butler did not like. I chose to teach it because there is much in Alanna's role as a leader that resembles the roles of Butler's other heroines. *Survivor* is the story of the human beings who flee Earth to preserve humanity after it has been devastated by Claryarks disease. The Patternists use the mind-control abilities they inherited from their foremother Mary to enslave many of the non-telepathic human beings and to battle the Clayarks, the human beings mutated by an alien virus. Alanna survives as a wild human being after the death of her parents and is adopted by a missionary and his wife. She eventually leaves Earth, along with her adopted parents and their missionary group, to settle a new planet where the group can carry out their spiritual mandate to multiply and preserve humanity in its original form.

Once the human beings land on the new planet, they are caught between two factions of Kohn humanoids. The Garkohn seemingly choose to befriend the offworlders as they help them build a settlement and otherwise adapt to the planet. The Tehkohn, seeing Alanna's group as intruders, raid the human camp and take prisoners, Alanna among them. She is the only one of the kidnapped to survive, because she has learned the intricacies of Tehkohn society and the truth about the Garkohn: the Garkohn addicted the human beings to a local drug and convinced them that the Tehkohn were their enemies. They hope to use human technology to become dominant over the Tehkohn. She is the only one who cares enough about each of the groups to broker peace and expose the Garkohns' plan.

Alanna's role in the novel ranges from abandoned to adopted and from captive to intermediary. Her prowess and purpose, like those of both Anyanwu and Mary, are shaped by her identity. It is precisely because Alanna has to survive on her own as a wild human being after the death of her parents that she can negotiate captivity and then peace talks. Her African and Asian blood sets her apart from the rest of the white missionaries (even on another planet) and enables her to understand the Tehkohn and their own hierarchical culture.

Returning to the human encampment, she must convince the human beings of the truth of their circumstances. This is made all the more difficult because not only does she respect the Tehkohn but also she has fallen in love with their leader and borne him a child. Her position is as precarious as that of an antebellum slave as she walks the line between hero and whore, traitor and savior. My students are able to assess Butler's parallels to European colonization and transatlantic slavery and allow the parallels to become extrapolations as they read their own future texts out of Alanna's dilemma. Her abilities to survive, access, accommodate, and negotiate are at the forefront of an exercise in leadership as preservation and adaptation.

As my students consider Butler's fictional daughters, they come to understand Butler as an Afrofuturist and read leadership in the same vein. They acknowledge that speculative fiction in general enables them to approach familiar topics in new ways. When they write their creative essay for the course, they conceptualize a black female whose leadership is necessary in her speculative world.

The first time the course was taught, my coteacher, the speculative fiction author Tananarive Due, spent a significant amount of time with the students on world building and character formation. She placed them in conversation with artists and musicians who were also practitioners and theorists of Afrofuturism. At the college's student research day, students shared their critical work or produced a conference poster. Some did a comprehensive presentation on a real-world leader whose oeuvre spoke to the major themes in Butler's work. Some picked their best journal or freewriting assignments for inclusion on the Octavia E. Butler Literary Society Web site.

My course was focused on African American women and concepts of leadership, but its strategies are useful in many other settings. Other college mission statements might not be as focused on leadership as Spelman's, but most schools hope to make leaders of their students. Examining Butler's work can open up conversations about leadership particularly in our current socioeconomic and political climate.

I believe that my students leave the course with an understanding of Afrofuturistic thought practice that—at the very least—informs their reading of black speculative fiction. They also become interested in the way the Afrofuturist aesthetic operates across art, music, film, and other cultural practices. They most certainly leave looking for expanded definitions of leadership that are not mired solely in past expectations but that inform both present and future interpretations.

NOTES ON CONTRIBUTORS

Amy Absher is the author of *The Black Musician and the White City: Race and Music in Chicago, 1900–67* (2014). Her essay in this volume profiles her class Django Chained. She would like to express her gratitude to the students for contributing to this essay and for making her six years as a SAGES fellow at Case Western Reserve University intellectually riveting.

Laura Apol, associate professor at Michigan State University, has published widely on historical children's and young adult literature, children's literature and literary theory, and the pedagogy of children's literature. Her poetry has appeared in literary journals and anthologies, and she is the author of four collections of poems.

Marleen S. Barr teaches English at the City University of New York. She is the author of *Alien to Femininity: Speculative Fiction and Feminist Theory* (1987), *Lost in Space: Probing Feminist Science Fiction and Beyond* (1993), *Feminist Fabulation: Space/Postmodern Fiction* (1992), and *Genre Fission: A New Discourse Practice for Cultural Studies* (1992); a short fiction anthology, *When Trump Changed: The Feminist Science Fiction Justice League Quashes the Orange Outrage Pussy Grabber* (2018); and the novels *Oy Pioneer!* (2003) and *Oy Feminist Planets: A Fake Memoir* (2015).

Susan M. Bernardo, professor of English at Wagner College, teaches courses in science fiction, Victorian literature, and fairy tales. She is the editor of *Environments in Science Fiction: Essays on Alternative Spaces* (2014) and the author of a chapter on *Batman Returns, Corpse Bride*, and *Sleepy Hollow* in *Tim Burton: Essays on the Films*, edited by Johnson Cheu (2016).

Laurel Bollinger is professor of English and director of English Graduate Studies at the University of Alabama, Huntsville, where she teaches modernist American literature and science fiction. She has published on James, Faulkner, Porter, Twain, and Frost as well as on science fiction writers, including Jack London, Richard Matheson, Greg Bear, and Octavia Butler.

Edmond Y. Chang is assistant professor of English at Ohio University. He is the author of "Teaching Harry Potter: Pedagogy as Play, Performance, and Textual Poaching," in *Reading Harry Potter*; "Love Is in the Air: Queer (Im)Possibility and Straightwashing in *FrontierVille* and *World of Warcraft*," in *QED*; and "Queergaming," in *Queer Game Studies*.

Claire P. Curtis is professor of political science at the College of Charleston. She is the author of *Postapocalyptic Fiction and the Social Contract* (2010), "Post-apocalyptic Fiction as a Space for Civic Love" (*English Studies in Africa*, 2015), and "Utopian Possibilities: Disability, Norms, and Eugenics in Octavia Butler's *Xenogenesis*" (*Journal of Literacy and Cultural Disability Studies*, 2015) and the coeditor of a special issue of *Utopian Studies* dedicated to Octavia Butler (2008).

Ximena Gallardo C. is professor of English at LaGuardia Community College. She has been a *Wikipedia* editor since 2012 and a Wiki Education instructor since 2014.

Among her current *Wikipedia* projects are the LaGuardia WikiProject Octavia E. Butler and the LaGuardia and Wagner Archives Koch Scholars initiative.

Deborah Wood Holton is associate professor at DePaul University's School for New Learning, where she teaches courses in oral interpretation, African American culture, history and literature, and creativity. She received a National Endowment for the Humanities Summer Institute Fellowship on the Black Aesthetic (2014) and is the recipient of DePaul's 2018 Excellence in Teaching award.

Lauren J. Lacey is associate professor of English and director of Women's and Gender Studies at Edgewood College, where she regularly teaches courses in contemporary literatures, feminist theory, and speculative fiction. She is author of *The Past That Might Have Been, the Future That May Come: Women Writing Fantastic Fiction, 1960s to the Present* (2014).

Isiah Lavender III, Sterling-Goodmann Professor of English at the University of Georgia, researches and teaches courses in African American literature and science fiction. He is the author of *Race in American Science Fiction* (2011) and the editor of *Black and Brown Planets: The Politics of Race in Science Fiction* (2014) and of *Dis-Orienting Planets: Racial Representations of Asia in Science Fiction* (2017).

Kristen Lillvis is associate professor of English at Marshall University. She is the author of *Posthuman Blackness and the Black Female Imagination* (2017) and the coeditor of *Community Boundaries and Border Crossings: Critical Essays on Ethnic Women Writers* (2016). Her current project examines diverse identities in electronic literature.

Ann Matsuuchi is an instructional technology librarian and professor at LaGuardia Community College, CUNY. She has been involved with *Wikipedia* educational projects such as one centered on the history of HIV/AIDS in New York City with the LaGuardia and Wagner Archives. Her other published essays center on the work of the writer Samuel R. Delany.

Beth A. McCoy is distinguished teaching professor of English at the State University of New York, Geneseo. Her most recent essay, "The Archive of the Archive of the Archive: The FEMA Signs of Post-Katrina New Orleans and the Vévé of Vodoun" appears in *The Year's Work in the Oddball Archive* (2016).

Shreyashi Mukherjee is assistant professor of English at Assam University, Diphu Campus, which she joined after completing her doctoral project on transnationalism, postcolonial identity, and representation in Palestinian, Irish, and African American literature. She is currently working on a comparative project examining authorial identity with respect to the social function of literature and theories of spatiality.

Matthew Mullins, assistant professor of English and the history of ideas at Southeastern Baptist Theological Seminary, is the author of *Postmodernism in Pieces* (2016). His articles and reviews have appeared in *Callaloo, Arizona Quarterly, SubStance, Los Angeles Review of Books, The Comparatist,* and other venues. His research and teaching focus on contemporary fiction, critical race theory, and literary history.

Aparajita Nanda, recipient of a visiting associate professorship to the University of California, Berkeley, now teaches there and at Santa Clara University. She is the editor of *Ethnic Literatures and Transnationalism* (2014) and *Black California: A Literary*

Anthology (2011) and the coeditor of *The Strangled Cry* (2013). She has published a number of book chapters, and her articles appear in *Callaloo*, *Ariel*, and *Oxford African American Studies*.

Kendra R. Parker, assistant professor of English at Georgia Southern University, is the author of "Unchaining Selves: Contemporary Slavery and Healthcare Freedom in Tananarive Due's *Blood Colony*" (2015) and *She Bites Back: Black Female Vampires in African American Women's Novels, 1977–2011* (2018).

John Paul Riquelme, professor of English at Boston University and cochair of the Modernism Seminar at the Mahindra Humanities Center, has published books and essays on modernist writers, on the gothic, and on literary theory. He has edited *Dracula* (2016) and is currently writing a study of Oscar Wilde's place in literary modernism.

Bevin Roue is assistant clinical professor in the Department of Educational Foundations, Leadership, and Technology at Auburn University. His research explores how reader engagement with speculative literature influences innovative thinking, critical consciousness, and social justice education.

Sami Schalk is assistant professor of gender and women's studies at the University of Wisconsin, Madison. Her research focuses on disability, race, and gender in contemporary American literature and culture. She is the author of *Bodyminds Reimagined: (Dis)ability, Race, and Gender in Black Women's Speculative Fiction* (2018).

Rekik Scholler-Mekonnen is an independent scholar living in Switzerland. Her areas of interest are science fiction and fantasy, Afrofuturism, posthumanism, utopian and dystopian studies, postcolonial literature, African women's writing, and feminist ethics.

Tarshia L. Stanley, dean of the School of Humanities, Arts, and Sciences at St. Catherine University, teaches courses in visual imagery, is the author of articles critiquing black women's iconography in African American, African, and Caribbean cinema and American popular culture, and is the editor of *The Encyclopedia of Hip Hop Literature* (2008).

SURVEY PARTICIPANTS

Maria Hamilton Abegunde, *Indiana University, Bloomington*
Harold Abramowitz, *Charles R. Drew University of Medicine and Science*
Amy Absher, *Case Western Reserve University*
Amy Branam Armiento, *Frostburg State University*
Monifa Love Asante, *Bowie State University*
Raffaella Baccolini, *University of Bologna*
Moya Bailey, *Northeastern University*
Florian Bast, *Leipzig University*
Laurel Bollinger, *University of Alabama, Huntsville*
Alissa Bourbonnais, *University of Washington*
Kate Boyd, *University of Washington*
Tonya S. Braddox, *Michigan State University*
Jenn Brandt, *High Point University*
Joshua Burnett, *Florida State University*
Robert Butler, *Canisius College*
Gerry Canavan, *Marquette University*
Brooke Carlson, *Chaminade University*
Laura Carroll, *La Trobe University*
Edmond Y. Chang, *Drew University*
Seo-Young Chu, *Queens College*
Lauren Coodley, *Napa College*
Shelby L. Crosby, *University of Memphis*
Claire P. Curtis, *College of Charleston*
Melanie Dawson, *College of William and Mary*
Louisa MacKay Demerjian, *Quincy College*
Alexander R. DeRosa, *Boston College*
Lisa DiBartolomeo, *West Virginia University*
Anne Donadey, *San Diego State University*
James Donelan, *University of California, Santa Barbara*
Tracy Egbert, *Bangor University*
Shari Evans, *University of Massachusetts, Dartmouth*
Ramona Fernandez, *Michigan State University*
Ryan Fong, *Kalamazoo College*
Conseula Francis, *College of Charleston*
Ximena Gallardo C., *LaGuardia Community College*
John Garrison, *Carroll University*
Susan A. George, *University of California, Merced*
Richard Grinnell, *Marist College*
Alfred Guy, *Yale University*
Roxanne Harde, *University of Alberta, Augustana Faculty*
Sarah Hentges, *University of Maine, Augusta*
Heather Humann, *University of Alabama*
Jeffry J. Iovannone, *State University of New York, Fredonia*

Ayana A. H. Jamieson, *State University of New York, Empire State College*
Anne Mai Yee Jansen, *University of North Carolina, Asheville*
Melissa Shields Jenkins, *Wake Forest University*
A-Yemisi Jimoh, *University of Massachusetts, Amherst*
Alicia Kent, *University of Michigan, Flint*
Arthur Samuel Kimball, *University of North Florida*
Lauren J. Lacey, *Edgewood College*
Erin Gentry Lamb, *Hiram College*
Isiah Lavender III, *Louisiana State University*
Janina Levin, *Holy Family University*
Leslie W. Lewis, *Ithaca College*
Kristen Lillvis, *Marshall University*
William Malcuit, *University of Wisconsin, Washington County*
Devona Mallory, *Albany State University*
Kya Mangrum, *University of Michigan, Ann Arbor*
Rhon Manigault-Bryant, *Williams College*
Ann Matsuuchi, *LaGuardia Community College*
Beth A. McCoy, *State University of New York, Geneseo*
Kitty Millet, *San Francisco State University*
Chandra Mountain, *Oakwood University*
Shreyashi Mukherjee, *Duquesne University*
Matthew Mullins, *Southeastern Baptist Theological Seminary*
Olivia Murphy, *Murdoch University*
Aparajita Nanda, *University of California, Berkeley*
Pramod K. Nayar, *University of Hyderabad*
Adele Newson-Horst, *Morgan State University*
Wendy C. Nielsen, *Montclair State University*
Stephen Park, *University of Texas, Brownsville*
Kendra R. Parker, *Georgia Southern University*
Diana R. Paulin, *Trinity College*
John Pennington, *St. Norbert College*
Jenne Powers, *Wheelock College*
Wanda Raiford, *Florida International University*
Leslie Rapparlie, *Rutgers University*
Robin Anne Reid, *Texas A&M University, Commerce*
Meghan K. Riley, *University of Waterloo*
John Paul Riquelme, *Boston University*
Beth Buhot Runquist, *Butler County Community College*
Joy Sanchez-Taylor, *University of South Florida*
Sami Schalk, *State University of New York, Albany*
Rekik Scholler-Mekonnen, *University of Fribourg*
Stella Setka, *Loyola Marymount University*
Ashley Shannon, *Grand Valley State University*
Evie Shockley, *Rutgers University*
Barbara A. Silliman, *Providence College*
Barbara Simerka, *Queens College*
Stephanie A. Smith, *University of Florida*
Nicole L. Sparling, *Central Michigan University*

Walter Squire, *Marshall University*
Karen Steigman, *Otterbein University*
Hilary Strang, *University of Chicago*
Darko Suvin, *McGill University*
Shirley Toland-Dix, *UNCF / Mellon Programs*
Rachel Trousdale, *Northeastern University*
Jennifer Wagner-Lawlor, *Penn State University*
Linda Weinhouse, *Community College of Baltimore County*
Briana Whiteside, *Southern Illinois University, Edwardsville*
Roland L. Williams, Jr., *Temple University*
Vincent Williams, *Drexel University*
Jewon Woo, *Lorain County Community College*
Yung-Hsing Wu, *University of Louisiana, Lafayette*

WORKS CITED

Ackerley, C. J., and S. E. Gontarski, editors. *The Grove Companion to Samuel Beckett*. Grove Press, 2004.

Adnan, Etel. *Sitt Marie Rose*. Translated by Georgina Kleege, Post-Apollo Press, 1982.

Akomfrah, John, director. *The Last Angel of History*. 1996.

Alaimo, Stacy. "'Skin Dreaming': The Bodily Transgressions of Fielding Burke, Octavia Butler, and Linda Hogan." *Ecofeminist Literary Criticism: Theory, Interpretation, Pedagogy*, edited by Greta C. Gaard and Patrick D. Murphy, U of Illinois P, 1998, pp. 123–38.

Aliens. Directed by James Cameron, widescreen edition, Twentieth-Century Fox Home Entertainment, 2004.

All about Competency Based Education: New Learning Model Offers Credit for Existing Knowledge and Skills. Council for Adult and Experiential Learning, doingwhatmatters.cccco.edu/portals/6/docs/AllAboutCompetencyBasedEducation.pdf.

Allen, Brenda J. "Working Assumptions for Class Interaction." *Difference Matters*, www.differencematters.info/uploads/pdf/allen-crit-pedag-mumby-rdr.pdf.

Angelou, Maya. *A Song Flung Up to Heaven*. Random House, 2002.

"Assessing Learning." *School for New Learning*, 31 May 2016, snl.depaul.edu/faculty-and-staff/faculty-resources/course-development/Pages/assess-learning.aspx.

Athey, Stephanie. "Reproductive Health, Race, and Technology: Political Fictions and Black Feminist Critiques, 1970s–1990s." *Sage Race Relations Abstracts*, vol. 22, no. 1, Feb. 1997, pp. 3–27.

Baccolini, Raffaella. "Gender and Genre in the Feminist Critical Dystopias of Katharine Burdekin, Margaret Atwood, and Octavia Butler." *Future Females, the Next Generation: New Voices and Velocities in Feminist Science Fiction Criticism*, edited by Marleen S. Barr, Rowman and Littlefield, 2000, pp. 13–34.

Badr, Liana. *The Eye of the Mirror*. Translated by Samira Kawar, Garnet, 2008.

Baldwin, James. "Here Be Dragons." *Challenging Male Supremacy Project*, challengingmalesupremacy.org/wp-content/uploads/2015/04/Here-be-Dragons-James-Baldwin.pdf.

Bales, Kevin. *Disposable People: New Slavery in the Global Economy*. U of California P, 2000.

Barr, Marleen S., editor. *Afro-Future Females: Black Writers Chart Science Fiction's Newest New-Wave Trajectory*. Ohio State UP, 2008.

———, editor. *Future Females: A Critical Anthology*. Popular Press, 1981.

———. *Lost in Space: Probing Feminist Science Fiction and Beyond*. U of North Carolina P, 1993.

Beckett, Samuel. *Endgame: A Play in One Act*. Grove Press, 1958.

Bhabha, Homi K. *The Location of Culture*. Routledge, 1994.

Bishop, Elizabeth. *The Complete Poems*. Farrar, Straus and Giroux, 2011.

———. "The Fish." Bishop, *Complete Poems*, pp. 43–44.

———. "Santarém." Bishop, *Complete Poems*, pp. 207–09.

Bogdan, Robert. "The Social Construction of Freaks." *Freakery: Cultural Spectacles of the Extraordinary Body*, edited by Rosemarie Garland-Thomson, New York UP, 1996, pp. 23–37.

Bollinger, Laurel. "Placental Economy: Octavia Butler, Luce Irigaray, and Speculative Subjectivity." *Taylor and Francis Online*, 30 Nov. 2007, doi.org/10.1080/10436920701708044.

"Books of the Year (Part 2)." *Guardian*, 26 Nov. 2005, www.theguardian.com/books/2005/nov/27/bestbooksoftheyear.bestbooks.

Brown, Wendy. *States of Injury: Power and Freedom in Late Modernity*. Princeton UP, 1995.

Butler, Judith. *Precarious Life: The Powers of Mourning and Violence*. Verso, 2004.

Butler, Octavia E. "Bloodchild." O. Butler, *"Bloodchild,"* pp. 3–29.

———. *"Bloodchild" and Other Stories*. 2nd ed., Seven Stories Press, 2005.

———. "The Book of Martha." O. Butler, *"Bloodchild,"* pp. 187–213.

———. *Clay's Ark*. O. Butler, *Seed*, pp. 453–624.

———. "A Conversation with Octavia E. Butler." O. Butler, *Parable of the Sower*, pp. 333–41.

———. *Dawn*. *Lilith's Brood*, Grand Central Publishing, 2000, pp. 5–248.

———. "Devil Girl from Mars: Why I Write Science Fiction." Media in Transition project, MIT, 19 Feb. 1998. Transcript of speech, 4 Oct. 1998.

———. *Fledgling*. Grand Central Publishing, 2007.

———. "Going to See the Woman: A Visit with Octavia E. Butler." Interview by Sandra Y. Govan. *Obsidian III*, vol. 6, no. 2, Fall-Winter 2005 and vol. 7, no. 1, Spring-Summer 2006, pp. 14–39.

———. Interview. By Charlie Rose, *Charlie Rose*, 1 June 2000, charlierose.com/videos/28978. Transcript.

———. "An Interview with Octavia Butler." Interview by Randall Kenan. Francis, pp. 27–37.

———. "Interview with Octavia Butler." Interview by Larry McCaffery and Jim McMenamin. Francis, pp. 10–26.

———. "An Interview with Octavia E. Butler." Interview by Charles H. Rowell. *Callaloo*, vol. 20, no. 1, 1997, pp. 47–66.

———. "Interview with Octavia Butler: Black Women and Science Fiction Genre." Interview by Frances M. Beal. *Black Scholar*, vol. 17, no. 2, 1986, pp. 14–18.

———. *Kindred*. Beacon Press, 2003.

———. "The Monophobic Response." Thomas, *Dark Matter*, pp. 415–16.

———. *Parable of the Sower*. Grand Central Publishing, 2000.

———. *Parable of the Talents*. Warner Books, 1998.

———. "Positive Obsession." O. Butler, *"Bloodchild,"* pp. 125–36.

———. "'Radio Imagination': Octavia Butler on the Poetics of Narrative Embodiment." Interview by Marilyn Mehaffy and AnaLouise Keating. Francis, pp. 98–122.

———. "Sci-Fi Visions: An Interview with Octavia Butler." Interview by Rosalie G. Harrison. Francis, pp. 3–9.

———. *Seed to Harvest.* Grand Central Publishing, 2007.

———. "Speech Sounds." O. Butler, *"Bloodchild,"* pp. 87–110.

———. *Wild Seed.* O. Butler, *Seed,* pp. 5–253.

Calvin, Ruth. "An Octavia E. Butler Bibliography, 1976–2008." *Utopian Studies,* vol. 19, no. 3, 2008, pp. 485–516.

Canavan, Gerry. *Octavia E. Butler.* U of Illinois P, 2016. Modern Masters of Science Fiction Series.

Carrington, André M. *Speculative Blackness: The Future of Race in Science Fiction.* U of Minnesota P, 2016.

Carroll, Lewis. *Through the Looking-Glass. Project Gutenburg,* 6 Oct. 2016, www.gutenberg.org/files/12/12-h/12-h.htm.

Collins, Suzanne. *The Hunger Games.* Scholastic, 2008.

"Competencies and Criteria." *School for New Learning,* 31 May 2016, snl.depaul.edu/student-resources/undergraduate-resources/Documents/UGradForms/competencies_and_criteria.pdf.

Crossley, Robert. *Critical Essay. Beacon Press,* www.beacon.org/Assets/PDFs/Kindredrg.pdf. On O. Butler's *Kindred.*

Csicsery-Ronay, Istvan. "Science Fiction and Empire." *Science Fiction Studies,* vol. 30, no. 2, 2003, pp. 231–45.

Cummings, Robert E. *Lazy Virtues: Teaching Writing in the Age of Wikipedia.* Vanderbilt UP, 2009.

Davin, Anna. "Imperialism and Motherhood." *Tensions of Empire: Colonial Cultures in a Bourgeois World,* edited by Frederick Cooper and Ann Laura Stoler, U of California P, 1997, pp. 87–151.

"Definition of Affirmative Consent." *The State University of New York,* system.suny.edu/sexual-violence-prevention-workgroup/policies/affirmative-consent/.

Delany, Martin R. *Blake; or, The Huts of America.* Beacon, 1970.

Dery, Mark. "Black to the Future: Interviews with Samuel R. Delany, Greg Tate, and Tricia Rose." *Flame Wars: The Discourse of Cyberculture,* edited by Dery, Duke UP, 1994, pp. 179–222.

———. "Black to the Future: Interviews with Samuel R. Delany, Greg Tate, and Tricia Rose." *South Atlantic Quarterly,* vol. 92, no. 4, 1993, pp. 735–78.

Dick, Philip K. *Do Androids Dream of Electric Sheep?* 1965. Del Rey, 1996.

Donawerth, Jane. *Frankenstein's Daughters: Women Writing Science Fiction.* Syracuse UP, 1997.

Douglass, Frederick. *Narrative of the Life of Frederick Douglass.* 1845. Signet Classics, 2005.

Dubey, Madhu. "Folk and Urban Communities in African-American Women's Fiction: Octavia Butler's *Parable of the Sower.*" *Studies in American Fiction,* vol. 27, no. 1, 1999, pp. 103–28.

Du Bois, W. E. B. "The Comet." Darkwater: *Voices from within the Veil, Project Gutenberg,* 28 Feb. 2005, www.gutenberg.org/files/15210/15210-h/15210-h.htm.

———. *The Souls of Black Folk*. 1903. Signet Classics, 1995.

Duchamp, L. Timmel. "'Sun Woman' or 'Wild Seed'? How a Young Feminist Writer Found Alternatives to White Bourgeois Narrative Models in the Early Novels of Octavia Butler." Holden and Shawl, pp. 82–94.

Duffaud, Briege. *A Wreath upon the Dead*. Poolbeg, 1993.

Dyer, Richard. *The Matter of Images: Essays on Representations*. 1993. Routledge, 2013.

Edwards, Erica R. *Charisma and the Fictions of Black Leadership*. U of Minnesota P, 2012.

Eliot, T. S. *The Waste Land*. *Bartleby.com*, www.bartleby.com/201/1.html.

Ellison, Ralph. *The Invisible Man*. Random House, 1982.

Eshun, Kodwo. "Further Considerations on Afrofuturism." *CR: The New Centennial Review*, vol. 3, no. 2, 2003, pp. 287–302.

———. *More Brilliant than the Sun: Adventures in Sonic Fiction*. Quartet, 1998.

Ethnic Notions. Directed by Marlon Riggs, narrated by Esther Rolle, California Newsreel, 1986. DVD.

Evans, Shari. "From 'Hierarchical Behavior' to Strategic Amnesia: Structures of Memory and Forgetting in Octavia Butler's *Fledgling*." Holden and Shawl, pp. 237–62.

Ferreira, Maria Aline. "Symbiotic Bodies and Evolutionary Tropes in the Work of Octavia Butler." *Science Fiction Studies*, vol. 37, no. 3, 2010, pp. 401–15.

Fineman, Martha Albertson. "The Vulnerable Subject: Anchoring Equality in the Human Condition." *Yale Journal of Law and Feminism*, vol. 20, no. 1, 2008, pp. 1–21.

Fink, Marty. "AIDS Vampires: Reimaginging Illness in Octavia Butler's *Fledgling*." *Science Fiction Studies*, vol. 37, no. 3, 2010, pp. 416–32.

Forster, E. M. *A Passage to India*. Harcourt, 1984.

Foster, Thomas. "We Get to Live, and So Do They: Octavia Butler's Contact Zones." Holden and Shawl, pp. 140–67.

Francis, Conseula, editor. *Conversations with Octavia Butler*. UP of Mississippi, 2010.

García Márquez, Gabriel. *One Hundred Years of Solitude*. Translated by Gregory Rabassa, Harper, 2006.

Gardner, John. *The Art of Fiction: Notes on Craft for Young Writers*. Random, 1985.

Gilligan, Carol. *In a Different Voice: Psychological Theory and Women's Development*. Harvard UP, 1982.

Glotfelty, Cheryll. "Introduction: Literary Studies in an Age of Environmental Crisis." *The Ecocriticism Reader: Landmarks in Literary Ecology*, edited by Glotfelty and Harold Fromm, U of Georgia P, 1996, pp. xv–xxxvii.

Gomez, Jewelle. *The Gilda Stories*. Firebrand Books, 1991.

Goodwyn, Wade. "The Strange Case of Marlise Muñoz and John Peter Smith Hospital." *NPR*, 28 Jan. 2014, www.npr.org/sections/health-shots/2014/01/28/267759687/the-strange-case-of-marlise-munoz-and-john-peter-smith-hospital.

Goss, Theodora, and John Paul Riquelme. "From Superhuman to Posthuman: The Gothic Technological Imaginary in Mary Shelley's *Frankenstein* and Octavia Butler's *Xenogenesis*." *Modern Fiction Studies*, vol. 53, no. 3, 2007, pp. 434–59.

Govan, Sandra Y. "*Fledgling*." *Obsidian III: Literature in the African Diaspora*, vol. 6, no. 2, Fall-Winter and 2005 and vol. 7, no. 1, Spring-Summer 2006, pp. 40–43. Review of *Fledgling*, by Octavia E. Butler.

———. "Speculative Fiction." *The Oxford Companion to African American Literature*, edited by William L. Andrews et al., Oxford UP, 1997, pp. 683–87.

Gross, Mathew Barrett, and Mel Gilles. *The Last Myth: What the Rise of Apocalyptic Thinking Tells Us about America*. Prometheus, 2012.

Gutiérrez, Elena R. *Fertile Matters: The Politics of Mexican-Origin Women's Reproduction*. U of Texas P, 2009.

Hairston, Andrea. "Octavia Butler—Praise Song to a Prophetic Artist." *Daughters of Earth: Feminist Science Fiction in the Twentieth Century*, edited by Justine Larbalestier, Wesleyan UP, 2006, pp. 287–304.

Hamby, Chris. "Government Set Up a Fake Facebook Page in This Woman's Name." *BuzzFeed*, 6 Oct. 2014, www.buzzfeed.com/chrishamby/government-says-federal-agents-can-impersonate-woman-online?utm_term=.auz0wqdy4M#.rr6kA9wb2W.

Hampton, Gregory J. *Changing Bodies in the Fiction of Octavia Butler: Slaves, Aliens, and Vampires*. Lexington Books, 2010.

Hampton, Gregory Jerome, and Wanda M. Brooks. "Octavia Butler and Virginia Hamilton." *The English Journal*, vol. 92, no. 6, 2003, pp. 70–74.

Haraway, Donna. "A Cyborg Manifesto: Science, Technology, and Socialist Feminism in the Late Twentieth Century." *Simians, Cyborgs, and Women: The Reinvention of Nature*, Routledge, 1991, pp. 149–83.

Hardiman, Rita, et al. "Conceptual Foundations." *Readings for Diversity and Social Justice*, edited by Maurianne Adams et al., 3rd ed., Routledge, 2013, pp. 26–35.

Hartman, Saidiya. *Scenes of Subjection: Terror, Slavery, and Self-Making in Nineteenth-Century America*. Oxford UP, 1997.

Heaney, Seamus. "Alphabets." *Genius*, genius.com/Seamus-heaney-alphabets-annotated.

Heinlein, Robert. "On the Writing of Speculative Fiction." 1947. *mab333*, mab333.weebly.com/uploads/3/2/3/1/32314601/writing_sf_-_01_on_the_writing_of_speculative_ficiton.pdf.

Held, Virginia. *The Ethics of Care: Personal, Political, and Global*. Oxford UP, 2006.

Helford, Elyce Rae. "'Would You Really Rather Die Than Bear My Young?': The Construction of Gender, Race, and Species in Octavia E. Butler's 'Bloodchild.'" *African American Review*, vol. 28, no. 2, 1994, pp. 259–71.

Herbert, Frank. *Dune*. Ace Books, 1990.

Hobbes, Thomas. *Leviathan*. 1668. Hackett Publishing, 1994.

Holden, Rebecca J., and Nisi Shawl, editors. *Strange Matings: Science Fiction, Feminism, African American Voices, and Octavia E. Butler*. Aqueduct Press, 2013.

hooks, bell. "Representing Whiteness in the Black Imagination." *Cultural Studies*, edited by Lawrence Grossberg et al., Routledge, 1992, pp. 338–46.

Hopkinson, Nalo. *Midnight Robber*. Warner, 2000.

The Hunger Games. Directed by Gary Ross, Lionsgate, 2012. DVD.

The Hunger Games: Catching Fire. Directed by Francis Lawrence, Lionsgate, 2013. DVD.

Hurston, Zora Neale. *Their Eyes Were Watching God*. Harper Perennial, 2006.

Hyde, Megan, and Sue Shon. *Xenology: Drawing in Response to Octavia Butler's* Dawn. Simpson Center for the Humanities, 2014.

Imarisha, Walidah, and Adrienne Maree Brown, editors. *Octavia's Brood: Science Fiction Stories from Social Justice Movements*. AK Press, 2015.

Jackson, Sandra, and Julie E. Moody-Freeman, editors. *The Black Imagination: Science Fiction, Futurism, and the Speculative*. Peter Lang, 2011.

Jacobs, Harriet. *Incidents in the Life of a Slave Girl*. *Documenting the American South*, 26 Aug. 2003, docsouth.unc.edu/fpn/jacobs/jacobs.html.

Jacobs, Naomi. "Posthuman Bodies and Agency in Octavia Butler's *Xenogenesis*." *Dark Horizons: Science Fiction and the Dystopian Imagination*, edited by Raffaella Baccolini and Tom Moylan, Routledge, 2003, pp. 91–111.

Jenkins, Henry. "Science Fiction and the Civic Imagination: Whose Future Does Science Fiction Foretell? (Part 2)." *Confessions of an Aca-Fan*, 19 May 2017, henryjenkins.org/blog/2017/05/science-fiction-and-the-civic-imagination-whose-future-does-science-fiction-foretell-part-one.html.

Jesser, Nancy. "Blood, Genes, and Gender in Octavia Butler's *Kindred* and *Dawn*." *Liverpool University Press Online*, doi.org/10.3828/extr.2002.43.1.05.

Joyce, James. *A Portrait of the Artist as a Young Man*. *Project Gutenberg*, 5 Dec. 2017, www.gutenberg.org/files/4217/4217-h/4217-h.htm.

Keating, AnaLouise. "Interrogating 'Whiteness,' (De)Constructing 'Race.'" *College English*, vol. 57, no. 8, 1995, pp. 901–18.

———. "Investigating 'Whiteness,' Eavesdropping on 'Race.'" *JAC*, vol. 20, no. 2, 2000, pp. 426–33.

Kilgore, De Witt Douglas. "Afrofuturism." *The Oxford Handbook of Science Fiction*, edited by Rob Latham, Oxford UP, 2014, pp. 561–72.

———. *Astrofuturism: Science, Race, and Visions of Utopia*. U of Pennsylvania P, 2003.

———. "Beyond the History We Know: Nnedi Okorafor-Mbachu, Nisi Shawl, and Jane Tangh Rethink Science Fiction Tradition." Barr, *Afro-Future Females*, pp. 119–29.

Kingsley, Charles. *His Letters, and Memories of His Life: Edited by His Wife*. *Internet Archive*, 16 July 2016, archive.org/details/charleskingsleyh01king_0.

Kolb, David A. "Characteristics of the Basic Learening Styles." *Experiential Learning: Experience as the Source of Learning and Development*, Prentice Hall, 1984, pp. 76–98.

Lacey, Lauren J. *The Past That Might Have Been, the Future That May Come: Women Writing Fantastic Fiction, 1960s to the Present*. McFarland, 2014. Critical Explorations in Science Fiction and Fantasy.

Lavender, Isiah, III. *Race in American Science Fiction*. Indiana UP, 2011.

Lawrence, D. H. "Adolf." *The Complete Short Stories*, 2nd ed., Blackthorn Press, 2014, pp. 298–301.

Lea, Susan J., et al. "Higher Education Students' Attitudes to Student-Centered Learning: Beyond 'Educational Bulimia'?" *Studies in Higher Education*, vol. 28, no. 3, 2003, pp. 321–34.

Levecq, Christine. "Power and Repetition: Philosophies of (Literary) History in Octavia E. Butler's *Kindred*." *Contemporary Literature*, vol. 41, no. 3, 2000, pp. 525–53.

Lillvis, Kristen. "Mama's Baby, Papa's Slavery? The Problem and Promise of Mothering in Octavia E. Butler's 'Bloodchild.'" *MELUS*, vol. 39, no. 4, 2014, pp. 7–22.

"Linking Learning and Work to Help Adults Succeed." *Council for Adult and Experiential Learning*, 29 Oct. 2018, www.cael.org.

Locke, John. *Second Treatise of Government*. Hackett Publishing, 1980.

Mann, Jen. "Sorta Racist Lesbian Couple Sues Sperm Bank." *People I Want to Punch in the Throat*, www.peopleiwanttopunchinthethroat.com/2014/10/sorta-racist-lesbian-couple-sues-sperm.html.

Marotta, Melanie. "Liberation through Acceptance of Nature and Technology in Octavia Butler's *Parable of the Sower*." *Theory in Action*, vol. 3, no. 1, Jan. 2010, pp. 38–50.

Mayer, Sylvia. "Genre and Environmentalism: Octavia Butler's *Parable of the Sower*, Speculative Fiction, and the African American Slave Narrative." *Restoring the Connection to the Natural World: Essays on the African American Environmental Imagination*, edited by Mayer, LIT Verlag, 2003, pp. 175–96.

McDowell, Deborah E. Introduction. *Of One Blood; or, The Hidden Self*, by Pauline Hopkins, Washington Square Press, 2004, pp. i–xx.

McElroy, Ruth. "Whose Body, Whose Nation? Surrogate Motherhood and Its Representation." *European Journal of Cultural Studies*, vol. 5, no. 3, 2002, pp. 325–42.

Miévelle, China. "Cognition as Ideology: A Dialectic of SF Theory." *Red Planets: Marxism and Science Fiction*, edited by Mark Bould and Miéville, Wesleyan UP, 2009.

Miller, Jim. "Post-apocalyptic Hoping: Octavia Butler's Dystopian/Utopian Vision." *Science Fiction Studies*, vol. 25, no. 2, July 1998, pp. 336–60. *JSTOR*, www.jstor.org/stable/4240705.

Mills, Charles "Racial Liberalism." *PMLA*, vol. 123, no. 5, 2008, pp. 1380–97.

Monáe, Janelle. "Many Moons." *YouTube*, 1 Oct. 2008, www.youtube.com/watch?v=Yy-ugv9kxG0.

Morris, Susana M. "Black Girls Are from the Future: Afrofuturist Feminism in Octavia E. Butler's *Fledgling*." *WSQ: Women's Studies Quarterly*, vol. 40, nos. 3–4, 2012, pp. 148–68.

Morrison, Toni. *Beloved*. Plume-Penguin, 1998.

———. *Sula*. Penguin Books, 1982.

Mosley, Walter. *Futureland*. Warner, 2001.

Mulan. Directed by Barry Cook and Tony Bancroft, Walt Disney Home Video, 1998. DVD.

Nagda, Biren (Ratnesh) A., and Patricia Gurin. "The Practice of Intergroup Dialogue." *Dialogue across Difference: Practice, Theory, and Research on Intergroup*

Dialogue, edited by Nagda, Gurin, and Ximena Zúñiga, Russell Sage Foundation, 2013, pp. 32–73.

Nagda, Biren (Ratnesh) A., et al. "Evaluating Intergroup Dialogue: Engaging Diversity for Personal and Social Responsibility." *Diversity and Democracy*, vol. 12, no. 1, Winter 2009, pp. 4–6.

Nanda, Aparajita. "Power, Politics, and Domestic Desire in Octavia Butler's *Lilith's Brood*." *Callaloo*, vol. 26, no. 3, Summer 2013, pp. 773–88.

Nasrin, Taslima. *Shame*. Prometheus, 1997.

Nayar, Pramod K. "A New Biological Citizenship: Posthumanism in Octavia Butler's *Fledgling*." *MFS: Modern Fiction Studies*, vol. 58, no. 4, 2012, pp. 796–817.

Nelson, Alondra. "AfroFuturism: Past-Future Visions." *Color Lines*, Spring 2000, pp. 34–37.

———. "Introduction: Future Texts." *Social Text*, vol. 20, no. 2, 2002, pp. 1–15.

New, Jake. "The 'Yes Means Yes' World." *Inside Higher Ed*, 17 Oct. 2014, www.insidehighered.com/news/2014/10/17/colleges-across-country-adopting-affirmative-consent-sexual-assault-policies.

Newsom, Jennifer Siebel. *MissRepresentation*. *YouTube*, 11 Dec. 2011, www.youtube.com/watch?v=d77mMXahsME&vl=en. TEDx lecture.

Nussbaum, Martha. *Frontiers of Justice: Disability, Nationality, Species Membership*. Belknap–Harvard UP, 2007.

Oakeshott, Michael. *On Human Conduct*. Oxford UP, 1975.

Omi, Michael, and Howard Winant. *Racial Formation in the United States: From the 1960s to the 1980s*. Routledge and Kegan Paul, 1986.

O'Neill, Geraldine, and Tim McMahon. "Student-Centered Learning: What Does It Mean for Students and Lecturers?" *Emerging Issues in the Practice of University Learning and Teaching*, edited by O'Neill et al. *AISHE Readings*, 16 Jan. 2016, www.aishe.org/readings/2005-1/.

Orwell, George. "Shooting an Elephant." *eBooks @Adelaide*, 17 Dec. 2014, ebooks.adelaide.edu.au/o/orwell/george/o79s/.

Osherow, Michele. "The Dawn of a New Lilith: Revisionary Mythmaking in Women's Science Fiction." *NWSA Journal*, vol. 12, no. 1, 2000, pp. 68–83. *JSTOR*, www.jstor.org/stable/4316709?seq=1#page_scan_tab_contents.

Outterson, Sarah. "Diversity, Change, Violence: Octavia Butler's Pedagogical Philosophy." *Utopian Studies*, vol. 19, no. 3, 2008, pp. 433–56.

Oziewicz, Marek. "Speculative Fiction." *Oxford Research Encyclopedia of Literature*, March 2017, doi:10.1093/acrefore/9780190201098.013.78.

Parham, Marisa. "Saying 'YES': Textual Traumas in Octavia Butler's *Kindred*." *Callaloo*, vol. 32, no. 4, 2009, pp. 1315–31. *Project MUSE*, 11 Nov. 2013, muse.jhu.edu/article/367934/summary.

Paul, Marilyn. *An Oasis in Time: How a Day of Rest Can Save Your Life*. Rodale, 2017.

Peet, Melissa. "The Integrative Knowledge Portfolio Process: A Program Guide for Educating Reflective Practitioners and Lifelong Learners (out of Print)." *Mededportal Publications*, doi:10.15766/mep_2374-8265.7892.

"Philosophy of Education." *Hope College*, 16 Jan. 2016, www.hope.edu/academic/gened/purposes/philosophy.htm.

Pickens, Theri. "'You're Supposed to Be a Tall, Handsome, Fully Grown White Man': Theorizing Race, Gender, and Disability in Octavia Butler's *Fledgling*." *Journal of Literary and Cultural Disability Studies*, vol. 8, no. 1, 2014, pp. 33–48.

Plato. *The Republic*. Translated by Benjamin Jowett, *The Internet Classics Archive*, classics.mit.edu/Plato/republic.html.

Potts, Stephen W., and Octavia Butler. "'We Keep Playing the Same Record': A Conversation with Octavia E. Butler." *Science Fiction Studies*, vol. 23, no. 3, Nov. 1996, pp. 331–38.

Pratt, Mary Louise. "Arts of the Contact Zone." *Profession*, 1991, pp. 33–40.

Price, Margaret. "The Bodymind Problem and the Possibilities of Pain." *Hypatia*, vol. 30, no. 1, 2015, pp. 268–84.

Pritam, Amrita. *The Skeleton and That Man*. Translated by Khushwant Singh, Sterling, 1987.

Rich, Adrienne. "Compulsory Heterosexuality and Lesbian Existence." *The Lesbian and Gay Studies Reader*, edited by Henry Abelove et al., Routledge, 2012, pp. 227–54.

Ridley, Matt. *Genome: The Autobiography of a Species in Twenty-Three Chapters*. HarperCollins, 1999.

———. *The Red Queen: Sex and the Evolution of Human Nature*. HarperCollins, 2003.

Rieder, John. *Colonialism and the Emergence of Science Fiction*. Wesleyan UP, 2008.

Rivlin, Gary. "Everybody's Mayor." *Chicago Reader*, 19 Mar. 1992, www.chicagoreader.com/chicago/everybodys-mayor/Content?oid=879359.

Roberts, Dorothy. *Killing the Black Body: Race, Reproduction, and the Meaning of Liberty*. Pantheon, 1997.

Rosin, Hanna. "When Men Are Raped." *Slate*, 29 Apr. 2014, www.slate.com/articles/double_x/doublex/2014/04/male_rape_in_america_a_new_study_reveals_that_men_are_sexually_assaulted.html.

Rousseau, Jean-Jacques. *Discourse on the Origin of Inequality*. Translated by Donald A. Cress, Hackett Publishing, 1992.

Roth, Amy, et al. "Assigning Wikipedia Editing: Triangulation toward Understanding University Student Engagement." *First Monday*, 3 June 2013, firstmonday.org/ojs/index.php/fm/article/view/4340/3687.

Ruddick, Sara. *Maternal Thinking: Towards a Politics of Peace*. Women's Press, 1990.

Ruffin, Kimberly J. "Parable of a Twenty-First-Century Religion: Octavia Butler's Afrofuturistic Bridge between Science and Religion." *Obsidian III*, vol. 6, no. 2, Fall-Winter 2005 and vol. 7, no. 1, Spring-Summer 2006, pp. 87–104.

Rushdy, Ashraf H. A. *Remembering Generations: Race and Family in Contemporary African American Fiction*. U of North Carolina P, 2001.

Ryan, Pat. "School for New Learning: Purpose and Philosophy." *School for New Learning*, 1 June 2016, snl.depaul.edu/student-resources/undergraduate-resources/Documents/UGradForms/Chap10.pdf.

Said, Edward. *Orientalism*. Routledge / Kegan Paul, 1978.

Sandoval, Chela. "U.S. Third World Feminism: The Theory and Method of Oppositional Consciousness in the Postmodern World." *Genders*, vol. 10, 1991, pp. 1–24.

Scheer-Schäzler, Brigitte. "Loving Insects Can Be Dangerous: Assessing the Cost of Life in Octavia E. Butler's Novella 'Bloodchild.'" *Biotechnological and Medical Themes in Science Fiction*, edited by Domna Pastourmatzi, University Studio Press, 2002, pp. 314–22.

Schuyler, George S. *Black No More*. Penguin Books, 2018.

Senna, Danzy. *Caucasia*. Riverhead, 1998.

"SFWA Announces Honorees of the 2012 Solstice Awards." *SFWA: Science Fiction and Fantasy Writers of America*, 2012, www.sfwa.org/2012/03/sfwa-announces-honorees-of-the-2012-solstice-awards/.

Shamsie, Kamila. *Burnt Shadows*. Bloomsbury, 2009.

Shaviro, Steven. "Exceeding the Human: Power and Vulnerability in Octavia Butler's Fiction." Holden and Shawl, pp. 221–32.

Shildrick, Margrit. *Embodying the Monster: Encounters with the Vulnerable Self*. Sage, 2002.

Siebers, Tobin. *Disability Theory*. U of Michigan P, 2008.

Smith, Valerie. "Neo-Slave Narratives." *The Cambridge Companion to the African American Slave Narrative*, edited by Audrey Fisch, Cambridge UP, 2007, pp. 168–86.

Smith, Zadie. "Speaking in Tongues." *Double Operative*, doubleoperative.files.wordpress.com/2009/12/zadiesmith2c_22speakingintongues_22.pdf.

"Spelman College Mission Statement." *About Us*, www.spelman.edu/about-us.

"Spelman College Visual Identity Guidelines." *About Us*, www.spelman.edu/about-us/administration/communications/visual-identity-guidelines.

Spillers, Hortense. "Imaginative Encounters." Barr, *Afro-Future Females*, pp. 3–5.

Stewart, Jocelyn Y. "Octavia Butler, 58; Author Opened the Galaxies of Science Fiction to Blacks." *Los Angeles Times*, 28 Feb. 2006, articles.latimes.com/2006/feb/28/local/me-butler28.

Stoker, Bram. *Dracula*. *Project Gutenburg*, 16 Aug. 2013, www.gutenberg.org/files/345/345-h/345-h.htm.

Stoler, Ann Laura. *Carnal Knowledge and Imperial Power: Race and the Intimate in Colonial Rule*. U of California P, 2002.

Stone, Douglas, et al. *Difficult Conversations: How to Discuss What Matters Most*. Penguin, 2010.

Sun Ra. *Space Is the Place*. Plexifilm, 2003.

Suvin, Darko. *Metamorphoses of Science Fiction: On the Poetics and History of a Literary Genre*. Yale UP, 1979.

———. "On the Poetics of the Science Fiction Genre." *College English*, vol. 34, no. 3, 1972, pp. 372–82.

Swanwick, Michael. "Slow Life." *Science Fiction: Stories and Contexts*, edited by Heather Masri, Bedford–St. Martin's, 2009, pp. 161–79.

Thaler, Ingrid. *Black Atlantic Speculative Fictions: Octavia E. Butler, Jewelle Gomez, and Nalo Hopkinson*. Routledge, 2010.

Thibodeau, Amanda. "Alien Bodies and a Queer Future: Sexual Revision in Octavia Butler's 'Bloodchild' and James Tiptree, Jr.'s 'With Delicate Mad Hands.'" *Science Fiction Studies*, vol. 39, no. 2, 2012, pp. 262–82.

Thomas, Sheree R., editor. *Dark Matter: A Century of Speculative Fiction from the African Diaspora*. Warner Books, 2000.

———. "Dark Matter II: Call for Submissions." *Artthrob*, 10 Mar. 2000, artthrob.co.za/00oct/exchange.html.

Tronto, Joan C. *Moral Boundaries. A Political Argument for an Ethic of Care*. Routledge, 2009.

Van Meter, Peggy, and Joanna Garner. "The Promise and Practice of Learner-Generated Drawing: Literature Review and Synthesis." *Educational Psychology Review*, vol. 17, no. 4, Dec. 2005, pp. 285–325.

Vint, Sherryl. "Speciesism and Species Being in *Do Androids Dream of Electric Sheep?*" *Mosaic*, vol. 40, no. 1, Mar. 2007, pp. 111–26.

Washington, Harriet. *Medical Apartheid: The Dark History of Medical Experimentation on Black Americans from Colonial Times to the Present*. Anchor Press, 2008.

Wendell, Susan. *The Rejected Body: Feminist Philosophical Reflections on Disability*. Routledge, 1996.

White, Deborah Gray. *Ar'n't I a Woman? Female Slaves in the Plantation South*. 1985. Norton, 1999.

"Why Science Fiction Matters." *Vox*, 16 Nov. 2014, www.vox.com/2014/11/16/7223107/science-fiction-matters.

"Wikifying Science Fiction's 'Grand Dame.'" *News from WikiEd*, 25 May 2016, wikiedu.org/blog/2015/10/22/wikipedia-students-octavia-butler/.

Wilderson, Frank B., III. *Red, White, and Black: Cinema and the Structure of U.S. Antagonisms*. Duke UP, 2010.

"*Wild Seed* (novel)." *Wikipedia*, 16 May 2016, en.wikipedia.org/wiki/Wild_Seed_(novel).

Williams, Sherley Anne. *Dessa Rose*. Harper Perennial, 1999.

Wolfe, Cary. *What Is Posthumanism?* U of Minnesota P, 2009.

Womack, Ytasha L. *Afrofuturism: The World of Black Sci-Fi and Fantasy Culture*. Lawrence Hill, 2013.

"Woman, 29, Chooses to Die Two Days after Husband's Birthday." *WNEP*, 7 Oct. 2014, wnep.com/2014/10/07/woman-29-chooses-to-die-two-days-after-husbands-birthday/.

Wood, Roy, Jr., performer. *Another White Oscars. The Daily Show with Trevor Noah*, 14 Jan. 2016, www.cc.com/video-clips/s3luw4/the-daily-show-with-trevor-noah-another-white-oscars.

Woolf, Virginia. "The Death of the Moth." *"The Death of the Moth" and Other Essays. eBooks @Adelaide*, 14 Sept. 2015, ebooks.adelaide.edu.au/w/woolf/virginia/w91d/chapter1.html.

———. *A Room of One's Own*. Harcourt, 1989.

Yaszek, Lisa. "An Afrofuturist Reading of Ralph Ellison's *Invisible Man*." *Rethinking History*, vol. 9, nos. 2–3, 2005, pp. 297–313.

Yeats, William Butler. "Crazy Jane Talks with the Bishop." *Representative Poetry Online*, rpo.library.utoronto.ca/poems/crazy-jane-talks-bishop.

———. "Leda and the Swan." *Collected Poems of W. B. Yeats*, 1 Sept. 1998, www.csun.edu/~hceng029/yeats/yeatspoems/LedaAndTheSwan.

Zúñiga, Ximena, and Biren (Ratnesh) A. Nagda. "Classroom and Workshop Exercises: C1: Identity Group Exercise." *Multicultural Teaching in the University*, edited by David Schoem et al., Praeger, 1993, p. 323.

Zúñiga, Ximena, et al. *Intergroup Dialogue in Higher Education: Meaningful Learning about Social Justice. Wiley InterScience*, doi:10.1002/aehe.3204.